SOLITARY IN THE RANKS

AIRCRAFTMAN SHAW (T. E. LAWRENCE)

From the original drawing by Augustus John
in the Ashmolean Museum, Oxford

SOLITARY
IN THE RANKS

Lawrence of Arabia
as Airman and Private Soldier

H. Montgomery Hyde

Constable London

First published in Great Britain 1977
by Constable and Company Ltd
10 Orange Street, London WC2H 7EG
Paperback edition 1987
Copyright © 1977 by Harford Productions Ltd
All rights reserved

ISBN 0 09 468070 1

Set in Monotype Fournier 12pt
Printed in Great Britain by
St Edmundsbury Press Ltd
Bury St Edmunds, Suffolk

For Clare and Squeak
to whom Tes
meant so much

I have become curiously at home
in the ranks, and wouldn't leave
them for anything, so long as I
am fit.

T. E. Lawrence to Sir Hugh Trenchard
27 December 1928

Contents

Illustrations

Acknowledgements

My prime sense of gratitude for their ready help and co-operation in various ways I must express to the trustees of the T. E. Lawrence literary estate, particularly to Professor A. W. Lawrence, T. E. Lawrence's surviving brother and his principal trustee and literary executor, for permission to quote freely from T. E. Lawrence's writings and letters, published and unpublished; likewise to Lawrence's English publishers, Jonathan Cape Ltd and Basil Blackwell Ltd, and to Lawrence's official biographer and editor of *T. E. Lawrence Studies*, Mr J. M. Wilson. Similarly my gratitude is expressed to Viscount Trenchard for allowing me unrestricted access to his father's correspondence with T. E. Lawrence, and also for introducing this book to the general public in a Foreword in which he has recalled his boyhood recollections of Lawrence, or rather Aircraftman Ross and Private (later Aircraftman) Shaw as he was successively called in the armed forces in which he served in the lowest rank for almost the whole of the last thirteen years of his life.

I am also most grateful to Professor Lawrence for allowing me to see the material relating to his brother at present under restriction in the Bodleian Library, Oxford. Contrary to the opinion held in certain quarters, there is nothing whatever of a scandalous or scabrous nature in this material. Most of it consists of typed manuscripts of original letters which are now in other collections, such as that of the Humanities Research Center in the University of Texas. I hope that it may eventually be found possible to lift the embargo, which is otherwise due to last until the year 2000, after Mr J. M. Wilson has completed his official biography and it is ready for publication. Incidentally Mr Wilson has been good enough to read the draft of the present book and I have benefited considerably from his constructive criticism and his unrivalled knowledge of T. E. Lawrence's life.

I have also received valuable help and advice from Group Captain E. B. Haslam, head of the Air Historical Branch of the Ministry of Defence, where Lawrence's personal files have been retained with other details of his service in the Royal Air Force such as the interesting recollections recorded by Air Commodore F. J. Manning of the last months of Aircraftman Shaw's service in Bridlington.

Mrs Clare Sydney Smith, widow of Lawrence's commanding officer at Mount Batten, Plymouth, who has herself written an excellent and very moving account of Lawrence at this period in her book *The Golden Reign*, has supplemented her memories of him in several conversations I have had with her. My thanks are also due to her for putting her collections of photographs at my disposal and for allowing me to make a selection from them for reproduction here.

Besides the Bodleian Library, other institutions from which I have received assistance are All Souls College and the Ashmolean Museum in Oxford, the British Library and the Imperial War Museum in London, the National Trust in Dorset as custodians of Clouds Hill, and the Society of Authors as administrators of the Bernard Shaw literary estate; also the Royal Air Force College at Cranwell and the R.A.F. station at Uxbridge, and the officers and staffs of these institutions, notably Group Captain K. Hebborn and Mrs J. M. King, Director of Studies and Librarian respectively at Cranwell, and Group Captain J. M. Lewendon and Wing Commander W. A. Wilkinson at Uxbridge.

Others to whom I am indebted for their help are Mrs Thais Atkins, Mr M. V. Carey (solicitor to the Lawrence Trust), Mr Brian Carter, Mr A. E. Chambers, Dr Martin Gilbert, Mr Philip Knightley, Air Commodore F. J. Manning, Mr Paul J. Marriott, Air Vice-Marshal John Marson, Mr D. S. Porter, Dr D. A. Rees, Mr Colin Simpson, Mr George Sims and Professor and Mrs Stanley Weintraub. I must also thank Mrs Barbara Lawrence for the friendly hospitality which she and her husband Professor Arnold Lawrence extended to my wife and myself in their Yorkshire home while this book was being written.

I gratefully acknowledge permission to reproduce the illustrations from the sources in the list given in the following pages. If I have inadvertently omitted any acknowledgement in respect of any permission involving copyright I offer my sincere apologies to those concerned.

Finally, as ever, my wife's willing help in the preparation of this book has been invaluable, and I cannot thank her enough for her contribution to the finished product.

H.M.H.

August 1977

Foreword

by

The Rt. Hon. Viscount Trenchard, M.C.

As I was born in 1923 my own recollections of a noisy motor-bike and an obviously welcome visitor are really too vague to be worth very much. However, as I grew up I heard and gradually attended more carefully to my father talking with many people about Colonel T. E. Lawrence. Then, more so even than now, he was inevitably a 'conversation piece'. I heard of their first meeting at the Cairo conference, of Lawrence agreeing when my father told Gertrude Bell that the Air Force would land and give the inhabitants of a dissident village Eno's fruit salts rather than bomb it. Lawrence in his quiet, distinctive voice said, 'I agree with Sir Hugh.'

While there was clearly much mutual respect, there was also sympathy, and the phrase most often used by my father, with much feeling in the tone, was 'Poor Lawrence'. He recognised his brilliance, appreciated his unorthodoxy which was not so far removed from his own approach, understood the turmoil of his spirit and character, knew of the unreliability that it produced, but, as I have said on more than one occasion, I never knew my father be intolerant of human failings. His firm philosophy was always to raise standards by emphasising the best and the positive, and deliberately not mentioning or emphasising the undesirable and the negative.

The correspondence between them makes clear that my father's purpose in enlisting him in the Air Force was rehabilitation, and the hope, if that process was successful, that this genius could make a bigger contribution, either to the Air Force or to the country, in one form or another.

I think my father understood Lawrence pretty well. He clearly guessed the content of *The Mint* before he had ever read it. Maurice Baring has written of my father that he had 'never known

such intuition in man or woman'. I can support that assessment
having lived with the embarrassment of a father who knew what
you were thinking without your saying it, and, worse still, knew
what you were going to think next week!

My mother, who combined enormous energy, absolute deter-
mination, and as much self-denial as any human being I have
encountered, found Lawrence a most attractive visitor – interesting, even fascinating. She had very high and very strict standards,
so that this reaction in retrospect is, I think, very interesting.

I write this Foreword very willingly because Harford Montgomery Hyde has, as I know my father would have wished,
brought out the strength of the plus points of this eccentric and
courageous genius.

In a letter to T. E. Lawrence's youngest brother and literary
executor, Professor A. W. Lawrence, on the subject of Richard
Aldington's widely publicised 'debunking' biography, which had
recently been published, my father wrote on 15 February 1955,
less than a year before he died: 'Aldington will be forgotten and
your brother remembered in years to come – that is a certainty.'

[1]

The Background

On the 11th March 1935, Aircraftman T. E. Shaw, in which name and rank the legendary figure known as Lawrence of Arabia had served twelve years in the ranks of the Royal Air Force and the Royal Tank Corps, was discharged on completing the full term of his engagement. He had recently been posted to the marine aircraft establishment at Bridlington on the Yorkshire coast. When he learned the news of his impending departure he wrote to the then Chief of the Air Staff, Air Chief Marshal Sir Edward Ellington.

Bridlington
Yorks
25.2.35

Dear Sir Edward,

Not many airmen, fortunately, write to their Chief of Staff upon discharge; but I was admitted by the first C.A.S. so hesitantly that perhaps it is in order for me to thank his successor for the forbearance which has let me complete the twelve years.

I've been at home in the ranks, and well and happy: consequently I leave with a sense of obligation, though always I have tried in return to do everything that the rules – or my chiefs – would allow.

So if you still keep that old file about me, will you please close it with this note which says how sadly I am going? The R.A.F. has been more than my profession.

Yours sincerely,
T E SHAW

This letter was accordingly placed in Lawrence's personal file, or rather Shaw's, since he had changed his name to Shaw some years previously. But it was not the last entry in the official file. This was the laconic statement added when the news reached the Air Ministry less than three months later that Shaw had been killed in a motor-cycle accident: 'There is little that can be said of a period devoted to self-effacement.' The period included a spell of more than two years between 12 March 1923 and 18 August 1925 when Lawrence was a private soldier in the Royal Tank Corps.[1]

Generally speaking Lawrence's biographers have tended to deal briefly with his time as an airman and a private soldier and have concentrated upon his earlier exploits as the desert hero who successfully united the Bedouin Arabs against the Turks, an achievement which gained for him high decorations from the British and French Governments which he refused, and the popular title of Lawrence of Arabia which he tacitly accepted. Yet the later years during which he served in the ranks, though less physically adventurous, were equally rich in record and achievement and no less exciting in their way, since they afforded him an opportunity for literary work in his leisure time and they opened up a new and rewarding range of friendships, notably that with the playwright George Bernard Shaw and his wife, a friendship which was to jeopardise the anonymity he sought as an airman in the ranks of the R.A.F.

Lawrence arrived back in England in October 1918, barely thirty years old, a full Colonel, with a C.B., D.S.O. and a recommendation for the V.C. Somewhat surprisingly, on the face of it, Lawrence actually asked for the 'odd pip', as he called promotion to full Colonel. After his spectacular entry into Damascus at the head of the Arab troops ahead of General Allenby and the British forces, he went to G.H.Q. at Taranto where he made his request. He explained that he wanted to return to England which he had not seen for four years and that the promotion would entitle him to a berth on the staff train through Italy. 'So they told me to put it up – special, temporary and acting. I called it "Taranto rank".'[2]

On 30 October, a few days after his arrival in England, King George V sent for Colonel Lawrence so that he could be formally invested with the military decorations which he had been awarded during the Arab campaign and which had already been officially gazetted. To the King's intense astonishment, Lawrence begged to be allowed to forgo all the honours, including the promotion in the Order of the Bath which the King proposed so that he could receive the royal accolade and be dubbed 'Sir Thomas'. But Lawrence again respectfully declined on the ground that, as he told his biographer Robert Graves:

> The part he had played in the Arab Revolt was dishonourable to himself and to his country and government. He had, by order, fed the Arabs with false hopes and would now be obliged if he might be quietly relieved of the obligation to accept honours for succeeding in his fraud. He said respectfully as a subject, but firmly as an individual, that he intended to fight by straight means or crooked until His Majesty's ministers had conceded to the Arabs a fair settlement of their claims.

At first the King misunderstood the purport of Lawrence's request and his refusal of a K.C.B., and thought he was aiming higher, so he offered him the Order of Merit. When Lawrence refused even that, the King sighed resignedly and said: 'Well, there's one vacant: I suppose it will have to go to Foch.' Lawrence made no reply but was amused at the irony of the French Marshal and former Generalissimo of the Allied Forces being given the O.M. which he had refused.[3]

Lawrence recalled the occasion vividly when talking to Graves a year or two later. The interview, he said, began with the King warming his coat tails in front of the fire in his room in Buckingham Palace, the ultra-Conservative *Morning Post* in his hands, and complaining: 'This is a bad time for kings. Five new Republics yesterday!' 'Courage, sir,' replied Lawrence. 'We have just made three new kingdoms in the east.' Before he left the royal presence, Lawrence gave the King the gold-plated rifle which had belonged to Enver Pasha, the leader of the Young Turks and at one time the absolute ruler of the country. It had afterwards been used by Faisal and each owner had 'notched it for victims'. Lawrence added that he once had a shot at the famous Mustafa Kemal, generally acknowledged as the founder of modern Turkey, but only hit a staff officer beside him. The King was delighted by his unconventional subject.[4]

Having done what he could for the Arab cause at the Peace Conference, where his appearance wearing a native headdress caused something of a sensation, Lawrence was appointed to a research fellowship at All Souls College, Oxford, where he settled down to writing his account of the Arab campaign under the title of *The Seven Pillars of Wisdom*. The fellowship was worth £200 a year and intended to run for seven years. However, Lawrence only drew it for three years and declined to receive any further payment after his work had been completed and published in a very small limited edition by the *Oxford Times* in 1922. Meanwhile he had been called in by Mr Winston Churchill, then Colonial Secretary, as political adviser to the newly formed Middle Eastern Department in the office.

Shortly after taking up this appointment he was sent back to Arabia as official British plenipotentiary to treat with King Hussein of the Hejaz, with credentials signed and sealed on behalf of the British sovereign, despite his renunciation of his honours, describing him as: 'Our trusty and well-beloved Thomas Edward Lawrence Esquire, Lieutenant-Colonel in our Army, Companion of Our Most Honourable Order of the Bath, Companion of Our Distinguished Service Order . . . ' While he was at the Colonial Office Lawrence also had the satisfaction of seeing his old friend and ally the Emir Faisal made King of Iraq and Faisal's elder brother Abdullah ruler of Trans-Jordan. Thereupon he relinquished both his Colonial Office post and his All Souls Fellowship to join the ranks of the R.A.F. as an aircraftman.

This he did in August 1922, bringing with him to the R.A.F. depot to which he was posted the document appointing him as plenipotentiary to the King of the Hejaz, which he had carefully preserved, although his object in joining the ranks of the Service was to hide his identity in a completely new milieu. A short while before this, the newly enlisted airman had refused an offer from Churchill to become High Commissioner in Cairo, a job worth £20,000 a year, with 'much entertaining, a large house, a silk hat, dignity', as he told Charlotte Shaw. 'Do you see me so ?'[5]

You may think that I should have kept on at All Souls and left the R.A.F. alone: but the company of airmen was more congenial to me. (I'm not a scholar in manner or taste and All Souls is a very comfortable and a very tiny club), and I'm better off in the ranks on £1 a week than I was in All Souls on £4 a week. It is all a question of standards.[6]

In another letter to Mrs Shaw written in the same year, 1927, by which time the fact that Lawrence was serving in the ranks of the R.A.F. had become common knowledge, Lawrence justified his decision in the following terms.

It's because I've chosen the R.A.F. that people make a fuss of my abdication of Arab affairs. If I'd accepted a Governorship – of Cyprus, or Jamaica, or Borneo, they would have taken for granted my leaving the Arab sphere. And that sense of proportion seems to be all wrong. It's as good to serve in the R.A.F. as it is to govern Ceylon: I'd say that it was much better. You may condemn all service life, by holding a pacifist view: and if so you will regard all soldiers and sailors and airmen as more or less brute beasts: but I have no such views – indeed few views of any sort: and no feeling that one sort or class or profession is better or worse than another.[7]

Lawrence's original meeting with Bernard and Charlotte Shaw, which took place one week-end in March 1922, was accidental. Charlotte had recently presented a portrait of her husband to the Fitzwilliam Museum in Cambridge, and the curator Sir Sydney Cockerell came to the Shaws' London flat in Adelphi Terrace to collect it. 'He induced a man who was lunching with him to come and help in the porterage, assuring him that I should not be at home,' Shaw afterwards told the Prime Minister Stanley Baldwin. 'To my astonishment, I recognised in this shy bird Luruns Bey [*sic*]. We hit it off fairly well; and he presently sent me a history of the Arabian campaign he had written.'[8]

Lawrence's correspondence, which began with a letter from him dated 17 August 1922 reminding Shaw of their meeting with Cockerell several months previously, was to continue until

Lawrence's death. In his first letter he explained why he 'wanted any decent person still more a person like yourself to read it'.

> Well, it's because it is history, and I'm ashamed for ever if I am the sole chronicler of an event, and fail to chronicle it: and yet unless what I've written can be made better I'll burn it. My own disgust with it is so great that I no longer believe it worth trying to improve (or possible to improve). If you read it or part of it and came to the same conclusion, you would give me courage to strike the match: whereas now I distrust my own judgement, and it seems cruel to destroy a thing on which I have worked my hardest for three years.[9]

Shaw received this letter at the Fabian Summer School at Godalming where he was lecturing, and as he was going on to the Labour Research Department's Summer School in Yorkshire he explained that, as he was travelling light and had hardly the chance of reading a paper, much less a work of 300,000 words, he asked Lawrence to let the reading stand over to the middle of September when he expected to join his wife at their country house at Ayot St Lawrence in Hertfordshire. 'There is not the smallest doubt (within human limits) that any publisher would jump at your book on Arabia; and there is no doubt at all that the book, having forced itself from you, will be published with whatever imperfections its mortal lot may involve. May I suggest it to Constable's? You may as well make up your own mind about it.'[10]

'I'm sorry, but I don't want to publish it,' Lawrence replied, thanking Shaw for his kindness. 'It's good of you to think of Constable's. They would be willing to publish part of it. I don't think it is good enough to bother about doing that: and to publish it all would be impossible. As you are going to try to read it I'll leave that to your later judgement: – but you will be of my mind. If you aren't, I won't be of yours.'[11]

Shaw had evidently addressed Lawrence on the envelope as Colonel T. E. Lawrence, C.B., D.S.O., but if Shaw wanted to get it 'just right', its recipient asked that in future the military title should be dropped, 'since that's a sign that you know me', and furthermore the Press used it. Nor should his name be followed by any alphabetical additions. 'My illustrious name has no letters after it,' he added. 'They offered me some, but I knew that I was just going to behave badly according to their lights, and so said "no". *Who's Who* next year will not have me in it, so I'd suggest your putting off its purchase for six months.'[12]*

On the other hand, he authorised two biographies of himself, both by English authors, to appear during his lifetime and he made extensive corrections and additions to both. In the event, the first, which was by his friend Robert Graves and appeared in 1927 under the title *Lawrence and the Arabs*, did not really satisfy him as much as the second, by Basil Liddell Hart, was to do on its appearance seven years later. 'The truth is so much less flattering than the rumour,' he wrote to another friend Edward Garnett when Graves's work first came out. 'And he follows the old fault of regarding my war trouble as the biggest part of the show. Whereas my effort of construction with Winston after the War was a harder and better effort. And in the distant future if the distant [publishers] F[aber & Faber] deign to consider my insignificance, I shall be appraised rather as a man of letters than as a man of action. You know my opinion well enough to acquit me of conceit in saying this: you know I think myself a contemptible writer, a bag of tricks. Best-selling tricks, I grant: but tricks that no man with his one eye on truth would have time for.'[13] With Liddell Hart, who had been a professional soldier before becoming military correspondent for the London *Daily Telegraph*, he could talk as one professional to another. 'I like your little book – wherever it does not repeat a told tale', he wrote to him on reading the first draft.

* In fact, his name did appear in the 1923 edition of *Who's Who* where he was described as 'Research Fellow of All Souls College, Oxford'. It originally appeared in the 1919 edition, the particulars, including his decorations, having been supplied to the publishers by Lionel Curtis, who had promoted his election to the Research Fellowship. In later editions, after he had changed his name to Shaw, he continued to be described as Research Fellow and his military record as an officer was given but his decorations were omitted. His publications were also listed.

Do make it clear that generalship, at least in my case, came of understanding, of hard study and brain-work and concentration. Had it come easy to me I should not have done it so well.

If your book could persuade some of our new soldiers to read and mark and learn things outside drill manuals and tactical diagrams, it would do a good work. I feel a fundamental crippling incuriousness about our officers. Too much body and too little head . . .

So please, if you see me that way and agree with me, do use me as a text to preach for more study of books and history, a greater seriousness in military art. With 2,000 years of examples behind us we have no excuse, when fighting, for not fighting well.[14]

However, the individual who did more to spread the Lawrence legend was an American named Lowell Thomas, when he delivered a series of highly successful lectures in the winter of 1919–20 entitled *With Allenby in Palestine* (later altered to *With Allenby in Palestine and Lawrence in Arabia*), illustrated by photographs with the emphasis on Lawrence and later worked up into a popular but thoroughly inaccurate book entitled *With Lawrence in Arabia*, which preceded Graves's biography by two years. Indeed Lawrence is said to have seen the illustrated lantern lecture himself no less than five times, although on one of these occasions he told Thomas: 'Thank God the lights were out', and on another occasion when he was recognised by the lecturer's wife he is said to have blushed crimson, laughed in confusion and hurried away with a stammered word of apology.

Lowell Thomas had left his teaching post at Princeton with the object of rousing American civilian morale in the war effort. Finding from his point of view the Western Front unproductive, he made his way early in 1918 to Jerusalem, where with an introduction from General Allenby he reached Aqaba. Helped by a skilled cameraman he had taken along with him, he was now able to collect a mass of pictures, although he did not get much information from Lawrence himself, whom he only met twice. 'I don't bear him any grudge', Lawrence wrote afterwards to an English officer who had commanded an armoured-car company in the Hejaz. 'He had invented some phantom thing, a sort of matinée idol in fancy dress, that does silly things and is dubbed romantic. Boy scouts and servants love it: and it's so far off the truth that I can go peacefully in its shadow without being seen.'[15] And, later still, when Liddell Hart's book was being made ready for the press, he told Major Wren Howard, the director of Jonathan Cape who published it: 'Few people, I fancy, could know there was a "life" of them on the stocks and not agree to read it first, for probable errors of fact to correct. Had I read Lowell Thomas, how much trouble I would have been saved!'[16]

T. E. Lawrence had already changed his name to Shaw by the time Thomas's book appeared in 1925, a fact which gradually became known and was indirectly responsible for another myth about its subject. Thomas claimed that Lawrence was closely related to the brothers Henry and John Lawrence of Indian Mutiny fame, and the fact that this claim was demonstrably absurd may well have encouraged inquiries into Lawrence's family background. At all events the rumour spread that Aircraftman Shaw was the illegitimate son of Bernard Shaw with whom he was known to be on intimate terms. It is true that T. E. Lawrence was illegitimate – in fact doubly illegitimate, since his mother had also been born out of wedlock. But his father was not Bernard Shaw. Nor indeed was his father's real surname Lawrence, a name he had assumed for particular personal reasons. It was Chapman.*

2

The Chapmans were an old Anglo-Irish landowning family originating in Leicestershire where Lawrence's ancestor John

---

* It is widely thought that Richard Aldington was the first to publish the fact of Lawrence's illegitimate birth in his 'debunking' biography *Lawrence of Arabia* (1955) and he was much criticised for making the disclosure. In fact it had already been made without arousing comment by Thomas Jones, the former Assistant Secretary of the Cabinet, in his *A Diary with Letters* (1954): see particularly Jones's description (on pp. 173–4) of meeting Lawrence's mother and her elder son at a lunch at Lady Astor's at Cliveden in 1936 and his conversation with Mrs Lawrence on the subject of her family.

Chapman, through the influence of his first cousin the Elizabethan Sir Walter Raleigh, received a grant of land in County Kerry in Ireland. After his kinsman's fall from royal favour, financial troubles obliged John Chapman to sell the property to the Earl of Cork. John had a brother William who went to Ireland with him, and William's son Benjamin, who was a captain of a cavalry regiment in Cromwell's army, obtained a large estate which included Killua Castle at Clonmellon in County Westmeath, which had formerly been a preceptory of the Knights Hospitallers when it was known as St Lucy's. Benjamin's great-grandson, also called Benjamin, represented County Westmeath in the old Irish House of Commons and in 1782 was created a baronet as a reward for his parliamentary service, no doubt in supporting the government by his votes in the House. The Westmeath property also included a place called South Hill, near the village of Delvin and the early Christian monastic foundation of Kells, which was settled on one of Benjamin's nephews called William, who was a Deputy Lieutenant of the county and also served as High Sheriff. The 'big house' at South Hill was a handsome Georgian building to which a new front had been added later in the eighteenth century with a strikingly beautiful fanlight window above the door.* William's son Thomas Robert Tighe Chapman, born in 1846 and brought up in the South Hill house, where he continued to live after his marriage, was Lawrence's father. He eventually succeeded to the baronetcy in 1914 but never claimed the title since by that date he had changed his name to Lawrence, for reasons which are presently explained.[17]

Although he seldom spoke or wrote about his family, T. E. Lawrence was proud of the connection with the great Elizabethan poet and pioneer of the New World. He once confessed to Charlotte Shaw that he would like to buy a few acres in Ireland: 'to keep some of Walter Raleigh's gift in the family of which I have the honour of being the not least active member.'[18] But he was careful not to claim Raleigh as a direct forbear. 'Raleigh isn't an ancestor, only the son of one. My father, middle-aged,

* The mansion is now occupied by a Belgian order of nuns, the Sisters of Charity of Jesus and Mary.

was his walking image. I'm not like that side of the family though.'[19] To Mrs Shaw he described his ancestry as a 'matter of fact', one which compelled him to carry his impulses into action.[20]

In 1873, Thomas Chapman married Edith, only surviving daughter of George Rochfort Boyd, who had inherited the considerable Rochfort fortune from his mother Jane, last Countess of Belvidere, in which Edith shared, to the benefit of the South Hill property. Edith, who lived long enough to claim to be styled Lady Chapman, bore her husband four daughters between 1874 and 1881. She was not popular in the neighbourhood, where she was irreverently known as 'the vinegar queen'. She was also given to attending prayer meetings and other good works and she thought her husband drank too much, with the result that he was obliged to hide the liquor from his wife's prying eyes.

About 1882 a girl in her twenties named Sarah Madden arrived at South Hill from Scotland as governess and companion to the four Chapman daughters, being known as Miss Lawrence for some reason. Exactly how she came to be engaged in this capacity has not been clearly established. According to one account, she was brought over by the Chapman estate agent Andrew Balfour who was presumably a Scot and knew of Sarah who was then living in the Isle of Skye, although she was not Scottish herself. In fact, she came from Sunderland in County Durham where she was born in 1861 and where her father John Junner, of Norwegian extraction, worked in the local shipyards as a journeyman. Her mother Elizabeth, whose maiden name was also Junner, may have been a relative, but Elizabeth was almost certainly John's mistress, since T. E. Lawrence once told Liddell Hart that his mother was illegitimate like himself.

At South Hill Miss Madden, or Lawrence, was much more than a governess and a companion to the Chapman children. She proved herself so capable and was so efficient and energetic that she was soon running the household. The girls liked her, their mother approved of her religious devotion and dislike of alcohol, while their father felt strongly drawn towards her physically. He was already bored with his wife, and one visitor to the house noted that his dour expression would change to one of gaiety whenever the attractive governess came into the room. Soon he was in love with her and his feelings evoked a sympathetic response from Sarah. Some time late in 1884 or early in 1885 Sarah agreed with Thomas to leave South Hill, telling Mrs Chapman that her mother needed her at home. Apparently they parted quite amicably, since Mrs Chapman gave her a locket containing pictures of the children when she said good-bye. But instead of returning to Scotland, Sarah went to a house in Dublin, 33 York Street, off fashionable St Stephen's Green in the middle of the town, which Tom Chapman had rented and in which he now established her as his mistress. Since Tom Chapman went to Dublin regularly on estate business – South Hill was only a few miles from Athboy railway station which served the capital with a good train service – his absences did not arouse his wife's suspicions despite the fact that they increased in frequency. Mrs Chapman on the other hand seldom visited the capital, which she regarded as a place of evil and sin. It was at the house in York Street that their first child Montague Robert ('Bob') was born on 27 December 1885.* Discovery of their guilty secret soon followed. By pure chance the Chapman butler at South Hill was in a Dublin grocery store when Sarah was ordering some provisions and he overheard her giving her name to the grocer as 'Mrs Thomas Chapman'. He followed her back to the house in York Street and then reported his discovery to the real Mrs Chapman and also to Tom's father, who still lived at South Hill. The upshot of the family row which ensued was that Tom agreed to leave Ireland with Sarah and their child in return for a small financial allowance so long as they did not return to Ireland. In the result they crossed the Irish Sea to Holyhead and eventually settled in North Wales, to be precise the village of Tremadoc in Carnarvonshire. Here, six months later, in a house called Gorphwysfa, their second son Thomas Edward was born, according to his mother, in 'the small hours' of 16 August 1888, although the birth was registered by the father, who gave his name as Thomas Lawrence and his occupation as 'Gentleman', as having taken place on the

* On the child's birth certificate the mother's name was registered as Sarah Chapman 'formerly Laurence' [*sic*], which supports the view that while she was employed as governess to the Chapman daughters she was known as Miss Lawrence.

15th.* It was a whim on the part of his father, as T. E. Lawrence once told Mrs Bernard Shaw, which made him adopt the name by which Sarah had been known in the Chapman family in Ireland. Always called Ned at home, T. E. Lawrence, so his mother tells us, was 'a big, strong active child; constantly on the move. He could pull himself over the nursery gate before he could walk.' After thirteen months Tremadoc was felt to be too damp and so they moved to Kirkcudbright where, according to his mother, Ned learned the alphabet without a single lesson merely through listening to his elder brother being taught. When he was about five he could read the *Standard* newspaper upside down, and in later life he told his brother Bob that he could always read the newspaper of the man opposite him in the train.[21] William George ('Will'), the third son, was born in Kirkcudbright in 1889. But the family did not remain in one place for very long and there were many moves, to Dinard on the Brittany coast, then to the Isle of Wight and the New Forest, and to St Helier in Jersey, where Frank Helier, the fourth son, was born in 1893. All these places, it will be noted, were on or near the sea, since Thomas and the family all liked sailing. However in 1896, mainly for educational reasons, they eventually settled in a house at 2 Polstead Road, Oxford, where the fifth and youngest son Arnold Walter ('Arnie') was born four years later. Although all this time Sarah and Thomas Lawrence were living as man and wife, she never referred to him as 'my husband', but always as 'the boys' father' or 'Tom' or as 'Mr Lawrence'.

All five boys were sent to Oxford High School. It was when he was there that, according to his mother, Ned first became interested in archaeology through seeing some old tiles in a pit which was being excavated by workmen and which he asked them to keep for him. He took them to the Ashmolean Museum, where they were regarded as an interesting find.[22]

It is worth noting here that none of the four Chapman daughters ever got married. The two survivors lived on at South Hill after their mother's death, and the present writer remembers them as

---

* The mother's name is given as Lawrence formerly Maden [*sic*], but in her third son's certificate it appears as Junner, her father's name and her real maiden name.

a boy in Ireland close on fifty years ago, when these two elderly maiden ladies openly acknowledged the legendary Lawrence of Arabia as their half-brother.

T. E. Lawrence was always reticent about his family antecedents. When Lionel Curtis was preparing his entry in *Who's Who*, Lawrence told him: 'Write anything you please so long as you don't give away . . . my original family.'[23] He told Robert Graves that his father was: 'Anglo-Irish with a quarter Dutch', while his mother was: 'Anglo-Scotch with a dash of Scandinavian'. He volunteered little else apart from the connection with Raleigh and that the Chapmans never intermarried with the native Irish, always with the English or Scots. He told Liddell Hart that his father had no interest in land but rather in field sports and was a particularly fine snipe and pheasant shot. Later he took up golf but 'never read a book until late in life'.[24]

Perhaps the most revealing disclosures about his parents were made to Charlotte Shaw in one of the letters he wrote to her while serving as an aircraftman in the R.A.F. station in Karachi in 1927.

Mother is rather wonderful: but very exciting. She is so set, so assured in mind. I think she 'set' many years ago before I was born. . . . She was wholly wrapped up in my father, whom she had carried away jealously from his former life and country, against great odds: and whom she kept as her trophy of power. Also she was a fanatical housewife, who would rather do her own housework than not, to the total neglect of herself. . . .

My father was on the large scale, tolerant, experienced, grand, rash, humoursome, skilled to speak, and naturally lord-like. He had been 35 years in the larger life, and a spendthrift, a sportsman, and a hard rider and drinker. My mother, brought up as a child of sin in the Island of Skye, by a Bible-thinking Presbyterian, then a nursemaid, then 'guilty' (in her own judgement) of taking my father from his wife . . . To justify herself she remodelled my father, making him a teetotaler, a domestic man, a careful spender of pence. They had us five children, and never more than £400 a year: and such pride against gain, and such pride in saving, as you cannot imagine. Father had to keep with Mother, to drop all his old life, and all his friends.

She by dint of will raised herself to be his companion: social things meant much to him: but they never went calling, or on visits together. They thought always that they were living in sin and that we should one day find out. Whereas I knew it before I was ten, and they never told me: till after my father's death something I said showed Mother that I knew, and didn't care a straw.

One of the real reasons (there are three or four) why I am in the service is so that I may live by myself. She has given me a terror of families and inquisitions. And yet you'll understand she is my mother, and an extraordinary person. Knowledge of her will prevent my ever making any woman a mother, and the cause of children. I think she suspects this: but she does not know that the inner conflict, which makes me a standing civil war, is the inevitable issue of the discordant natures of herself and my father, and the inflammation of strength and weakness which followed the uprooting of their lives and principles. They should not have borne children.[25]

Sarah Lawrence's strict Sabbatarian upbringing in the Hebrides implanted in her strong religious beliefs, which unlike her second son she never abandoned. On the contrary, after her husband's death she went out to China as a Christian missionary, being joined by Bob, the eldest, who had survived the Great War in which he served in France with the Royal Army Medical Corps. Will and Frank were both killed in action, and her new vocation separated her from her two other sons, as Ned explained to Charlotte Shaw.

And now two of my brothers are dead, and Arnie (the youngest) and I have left her, and avoid her as our first rule of existence: while my eldest brother is hardly her peer or natural companion. It is a dreadful position for her, and yet I see no alternative. While she remains herself and I remain myself it must happen. In all her letters she tells me she is old and lonely, and loves only us; and she begs us to love her back again, and points us to Christ, in whom, she says, is the only true happiness and truth. Not that she finds happiness herself.[26]

In the tribute which she wrote to the memory of her second son after his death, she recorded with pride that while they were living in Oxford before the war Ned was for many years a constant worshipper at St Aldate's Church and taught in the Sunday School there twice every Sunday, and that he had 'the great privilege' of Canon Christopher's gospel teaching at St Aldate's.[27] But neither his mother's nor the Canon's religious influence had any lasting effect. Not long before his death, Liddell Hart asked him if he had any views on religion.

T.E. replied that, although he had been brought up in conventional religion, he had discarded it, and did not notice its loss. Theological speculation and meditation were good as an intellectual exercise, but one could not get anywhere by such abstractions. He felt that thought was as material as everything else, within our human limitations. One couldn't conceive thought as apart from our material being.[28]

That a curious love–hate relationship existed between T. E. Lawrence and his mother is evident from this correspondence. When the missionaries were compelled to leave China on account of the political troubles there in the time of the 'War Lords', Sarah Lawrence came back to England and settled for a time in a private hotel in Bayswater and Lawrence asked Charlotte Shaw to see her, although he warned her that it was 'to take a risk'.

I wonder how you will like her. She is monumental, really, and so unlike you. Probably she is exactly like me; otherwise we wouldn't so hanker after one another, whenever we are wise enough to keep apart. Her letters are things I dread, and she always asks for more of mine. . . .
A very dominant person: only old now [she was 67] and, so my brother says, very much less than she has been. She has so lived in her children, and in my father, that she cannot relieve herself upon herself, and from herself at all. And it isn't right to cry out to your children for love. They are prevented, by the walls of time and function, from loving their parents.[29]

'No trust ever existed between my mother and myself,'

Lawrence confessed to Charlotte Shaw in another letter. 'Each of us jealously guarded his or her own individuality, whenever we came together. I always felt that she was laying siege to me, and would conquer, if I left a chink unguarded.'[30] Sarah Lawrence was certainly a strict disciplinarian in the home if her youngest son Arnold is to be believed; Ned was often the recipient of severe beatings for naughtiness such as refusing to learn the piano. She would whip him on the bare bottom, but we are not told with what – probably the tawse, a favourite instrument of punishment in schools and homes in Scotland in those days, consisting of a leather strap or thong, divided at the end into narrow strips, which could be very painful if applied with vigour, which Sarah was apparently in the habit of doing. 'I never had to do it to Bob, once to Frank and frequently to T.E.,' she once told Arnold, who also experienced it on one occasion. Such Puritan severity was distasteful to Tom Lawrence, who was 'too gentle, too imaginative', according to Arnold ' – couldn't bring himself to' beat any of his sons. Sarah Lawrence's whippings also seem to have had the purpose of breaking Ned's will – but if that is so, they were not successful in achieving their object. On one occasion, when he was at school he is said to have been caught in the act of mutual masturbation with another boy, and nearly expelled. 'The mother nearly went mad and belted the daylight out of him.'[31] Whether these childhood beatings which he suffered at his mother's hands can be linked in any way to his experiences in later life and the masochistic interest in flagellation which he was to develop is a matter of speculation for students of psychopathology in the context of T. E. Lawrence's persona, and one on which the reader must be left to form his or her own conclusions.

In 1906, when he was about seventeen and still at school in Oxford, Ned Lawrence enlisted in the Royal Artillery as a private. He was drafted to Cornwall and eventually bought out of the army by his father. 'This is hush-hush. I should not have told you. I ran away from home and served for six months,' he admitted to his biographer Liddell Hart, who had asked him how he got on under discipline. 'No trouble with discipline, I have always been easy,' he replied; 'but the other fellows fought all Friday and Saturday nights and frightened me with their roughness. I'd rather keep this out of print, please: the whole episode. It is negligible militarily, like my subsequent O.T.C. training.'[32]

The cause of his flight is not known, but it seems to have resulted from some domestic discord, and to prevent any recurrence his father built him a small two-roomed bungalow at the bottom of the garden at 2 Polstead Road where he could work undisturbed.

The eldest brother Bob, it should be noted, has painted a rather different picture of the boys' home life with their parents. 'We had a very happy childhood, which was never marred by a single quarrel between any of us', Bob was to write after Ned's death. 'Our parents were constantly with us, to our great delight and profit, for they shared in our progress, made the home the place of peace it was, planned the future and our education, and were the greatest influences in our lives.'[33]

Tom Lawrence died on 8 April 1919 and with him the Chapman baronetcy to which he had succeeded but which he had never claimed. He left Sarah the whole of his fortune which amounted to some £17,800, a sum rather less than he had inherited from an aunt who had died eight years previously.* Sarah apparently divided the money between her children, as Ned got about £4000 from her at this time. She survived her husband by forty years and lived to be ninety-eight, dying in November 1959.

The Argentinian writer Victoria Ocampo, who translated Lawrence's account of his experience as an airman, *The Mint*, into Spanish and got to know her in 1946, has written an interesting description of her in old age.

When I went to see her she was living modestly, with her eldest son Bob. At this first interview she kindled such sympathy (no doubt because of her love for Ned) and such respect (which she was herself sufficient to inspire) that I never came to England afterwards without paying her a visit. At the end she lived in a boarding house at Boars Hill near Oxford. She had broken a leg and as often happens with old people the

---

* She was his father's sister Caroline, who had married her cousin Sir Montagu Chapman, the 5th Baronet.

bones would not join. This must have given her a great deal of pain, but in the Lawrence fashion she appeared not to notice it.

The boarding house of two storeys has a narrow staircase such as you often find in old houses in England. She explained that it was very convenient for when she needed Bob, who slept in the room directly underneath hers, she had only to knock on the floor with her stick. Bob ran up at once if he was there. Such was what Mrs Lawrence understood by the word 'convenient'. Her broken leg, grown stiff, kept her almost immobile. The last time that I went to see her was in the middle of winter. One fire lit in the living room, in the only fireplace (very convenient also no doubt), took the chill off that room. It was really cold in Mrs Lawrence's bedroom and the cheek on which I placed my farewell kiss was cold too. . . .

I know by hearsay that Mr Lawrence was a very remarkable man. But I suspect that without the Mrs Lawrence I knew at Boars Hill there would have been no Lawrence of Arabia. There was a vitality and integrity in that woman which were astonishing. And a strength greater than oak. She must have lived in an inner hell during her youth. It must have been like a foretaste on earth of what according to her moral and religious code, was awaiting her in the next world. When I talked to her at Boars Hill these storms were over. Living almost in poverty – I repeat poverty – with no wealth but her memories, she had found peace, won by paying the price.[34]

One should not forget Sarah Lawrence's tribute to Ned after his death: 'He was a most loving son and brother, kind and unselfish, always doing kind deeds in a quiet way; everything that was beautiful in nature or art appealed to him. *Sans peur et sans reproche*.'[35]

3

The accident of his Welsh birth facilitated T. E. Lawrence's entry to Jesus College, which had a long-standing connection with the principality and contained more Welsh undergraduates than any other Oxford college, and he was thus able to gain a close exhibition there. His academic career, characterised by a deep and abiding interest in literature, archaeology and architecture, particularly medieval, prompted him to choose as a thesis, then accepted in part for a degree in history, on the subject of: 'The influence of the Crusades on European Military Architecture to the end of the Twelfth Century.'* He collected material for the thesis by visiting almost all the important castles in England and Wales, France, Syria, Northern Palestine, and the southern fringe of Turkey. The visits were made over three years by bicycle in England and Wales and on foot travelling light during the hottest part of the summer in the Middle East. Thus he first made acquaintance with the Moslem people and picked up some knowledge of Arabic.

In 1910 he got a first class in modern history and was awarded a senior demyship at Magdalen College tenable for four years. The award was made at the instance of D. G. Hogarth, the distinguished archaeologist and fellow of the college, who was Keeper of the Ashmolean Museum and had spotted Lawrence's talent. The two men were to become lifelong friends, and in 1911 Hogarth sent Lawrence on the British Museum expedition which was excavating the ancient Hittite city of Carchemish and at the same time secretly reporting to British Foreign Office intelligence on the progress of the consturction of the Berlin to Basra railway by the Germans which was designed to cross the Euphrates near the archaeological site. Then, after an interval in Egypt, he returned in the following year as principal assistant to the expedition's leader C. L. Woolley, with whom he collaborated in writing the official report of the excavations, published by the museum in 1914. 'It was the best life I ever lived', he wrote afterwards; having improved his knowledge of Arabic he acquired the habit of eating Arab food and wearing Arab dress.[36] During the first three months of 1914 he and Woolley carried out an archaeological survey of the Negev desert and the country south of Beersheeba for the Palestine Exploration Fund, which published their report in the following year under the title *The Wilderness of Zin*.

---

* The thesis was published in 1936 as *Crusader Castles*.

It was during his undergraduate years that Lawrence became friendly with a girl two years his senior called Janet Laurie. Her family had got to know the Lawrences when they were both living in the New Forest before moving to Oxford. Sarah Lawrence wanted her to marry Bob, but he appeared to her 'so terribly good', and once reproved her for using the accepted abbreviation for a public house. ('Pub is not a nice word.') In fact she preferred Will who was the tallest of the Lawrence brothers and in her eyes the most 'dashing'. Thus she was completely taken by surprise when one night after dinner at the Lawrences' house Ned suddenly proposed to her without kissing her or indulging in any other expression of feeling. Her reaction was to dismiss the unexpected proposal with a laugh. 'Oh, I see,' he said, 'all right,' looking hurt. The subject does not seem to have been mentioned between them again.

Janet always hoped to marry Will in spite of Mrs Lawrence's opposition, as she still wanted her for Bob. So the position dragged on until 1915 when the romance was ended by Will getting killed in the war. Four years later Janet married an artist named Guthrie Hallsmith. Since her father was dead, she asked T. E. Lawrence to give her away. At first he agreed, but shortly before the wedding he cried off on the pretext that he was too short and would look silly walking down the aisle with her. However, they remained friends, and he stood as godfather to Janet Hallsmith's first child. There is no doubt that Lawrence was deeply in love with her and the wound which her rejection of him caused took a long time to heal. 'You know Ned Lawrence adored you,' a mutual friend, the Rev. E. F. Hall, once told her. She replied that indeed she had known this but that she could not seriously consider him as a suitor.[37]

Janet's rejection of him as a husband may have played some part in his preference for the life of an archaeologist, an all-male society with 'digs' on the sites and meals cooked over a camp fire and sleeping in a tent. But there is no evidence that he hated women or was asexual, much less homosexual, as one biographer, Richard Aldington, has suggested. On the contrary he had many women friends whose company he enjoyed as they did his, such as Gertrude Bell, Charlotte Shaw, Florence Hardy, and Lady

Astor, as well as Clare Sydney Smith, the wife of one of his commanding officers, who was to write a book about him.* 'I try to talk to a woman as I would talk to another man,' he told Robert Graves; 'and if she does not return the compliment I leave her.' In particular his fellow archaeologist Gertrude Bell, who first met him in Carchemish in 1911, admired him immensely and gratefully accepted his professional expertise. 'Beloved boy' she called him, and 'wonderful person' he called her, though he thought that perhaps she was 'born too gifted'. But throughout the time he was 'digging' on archaeological sites and later when he was an Arab guerilla leader, a soldier, a government political adviser and finally after he joined the ranks of the R.A.F., he never felt impelled to take a woman either as wife or mistress for the reason that he had expressed in the letter to Charlotte Shaw already quoted. He was determined never to make any woman a mother, recalling as he did his experiences with his own mother. Thus, according to his brother Arnold, he was to remain a virgin until his death.

In another letter to Charlotte Shaw he wrote:

The motive which brings the sexes together is 99 per cent sexual pleasure, and only 1 per cent the desire of children, in men, so far as I can learn. As I told you, I haven't ever been carried away in that sense, so that I'm a bad subject to treat of it. Perhaps the possibility of a child relieves sometimes what otherwise must seem an unbearable humiliation to the woman: – for I presume it's unbearable.[38]

Robert Graves has suggested that his experience at Deraa rendered him impotent. There is no evidence of this, any more than that he was a homosexual, although his 'debunking' biographer Richard Aldington would have liked to believe that he was. 'Many of Lawrence's friends were homosexual, but not all', Aldington wrote to Alan Bird when he was working on his biography. 'Whatever his *practice*, of which one can naturally

* *The Golden Reign. The story of my friendship with 'Lawrence of Arabia'* (1940).

know nothing except by his own confession which doesn't exist, his *sympathy* was entirely with homos and against heteros. He had woman friends as homos often do, knowing better than a man the little attentions that please women, but sex relations with a woman caused him unfeigned horror and disgust.'[39]

While leading the Arab revolt against the Turks, Lawrence suffered a deeply mortifying and traumatic experience when he was captured in November 1917 at a place called Deraa on the railway between Damascus and Amman. Accounts of exactly what happened are conflicting; even the various versions given by Lawrence himself differ in important particulars. In the report which he subsequently wrote for G.H.Q. Cairo, Lawrence stated that he was identified by Hajim Bey, the Turkish governor, 'an ardent paederast', who 'took a fancy to me. So he kept me under guard till night and then tried to have me. I was unwilling and prevailed after some difficulty.'[40] In the fuller, shocking version in *The Seven Pillars*, he was then handed over to the Bey's guards who flogged him senseless, having previously buggered him in turn. He was then brought back to the Bey who rejected him 'as a thing too torn and bloody for his bed'. After that, apparently on the Bey's orders, he was taken to the hospital where his wounds were washed and bandaged by an Armenian dresser and then allowed to escape. According to Lawrence, the Bey was 'so ashamed of the muddle he had made that he hushed the whole thing up and never reported my capture and escape'. On the other hand Lawrence told Richard Meinertzhagen, with whom he served in the Middle East, that he had been 'sodomised' by the governor as well as his servants, but felt that he could not publish the account of the incident because it was too degrading and had 'penetrated his innermost nature'.[41] Meinertzhagen at first accepted the story as true but doubted its veracity after Lawrence's death. What is one to believe?

Lawrence wrote and rewrote the account of the Deraa incident nine times, he told Charlotte Shaw, while he told Edward Garnett in 1922 that he was really ashamed to include it in *The Seven Pillars*. 'I have put it into print very reluctantly, last of all the pages I sent to the press. For weeks I wanted to burn it in the manuscript: because I could not tell the story face to face with anyone, and I think I'll feel sorry when I next meet you that you know it. The sort of man I have always mixed with doesn't so give himself away.' However, in both the original Oxford edition in 1922 and in chapter LXXII of the subscribers' edition of 1926 (chapter LXXX as republished in the commercial edition of 1935) Lawrence states categorically that he resisted the Bey's advances, although he admits that the guards did 'play unspeakably with me', and one of them 'rode me astride'. On the other hand, he concludes the controversial chapter in *The Seven Pillars* with a reference to: 'how in Deraa that night the citadel of my integrity had been irrevocably lost', and the memory of it would remain with him as the nightmare it evidently was. The subject naturally cropped up in his correspondence about the book with the Shaws. 'You instance my night in Deraa', he wrote to Charlotte in 1924 when he was serving as a private soldier in the Royal Tank Corps.

> Well, I'm always afraid of being hurt: and to me, while I live, the force of that night will lie in the agony which broke me, and made me surrender. I'ts the individual view. You can't share it.
>
> About that night. I shouldn't tell you, because decent men don't talk about such things. I wanted to put it plain in the book, wrestled for days with my self-respect ... which wouldn't, hasn't let me. For fear of being hurt, or rather to earn five minutes respite from a pain which drove me mad, I gave away the only possession we are born into the world with – our bodily integrity. It's an unforgiveable matter, an irrevocable position: and it's that which has made me forswear decent living, and the exercise of my not contemptible wits and talents.
>
> You may call this morbid: but I think of the offence, and the intensity of my brooding over it for these years. It will hang about me while I live, and afterwards if our personality survives. Consider wandering among the decent ghosts hereafter crying 'Unclean, Unclean!'[42]

Lawrence's guilt complex was to last with him through the

years and it was to manifest itself in various self-imposed acts of penance. One of these, in part at least, was to join the ranks of the R.A.F. He told Robert Graves that it was a course he had decided on in 1919 and even before the Armistice, when he was still in Damascus he had suggested it to Air Marshal Sir Geoffrey Salmond, who then had the Middle East command of the force. But, he added, 'not till Winston had given the Arabs a fair deal was I able to please myself. That accounted for the delay till 1922.' He also begged Graves to make clear, when he came to write about him, the difference between the airman's view of himself and his view of the soldier. 'He is brought up to despise the Army. "Soldier" is our chief insult and word of derision. Soldiers are machines or part of machines. Airmen use machines and own them. Airmen (even the little ones) are men devoted to the conquest of an element. Whereas soldiers!'[43]

Yet complex as Lawrence's character was, and although many found it difficult to understand and were inclined to write him off as a showman with a gift for 'backing into the limelight', there was one thing which set him apart from his fellows whether as an Arab leader or a lowly aircraftman, and it accounted for the remarkable ascendancy, physical, intellectual and moral, which he was capable of exercising. He expressed it most aptly in *The Seven Pillars* when he contrasted the fact that among the British forces work suffered from the creation of a bar between the leaders and the men, with the custom among the Bedouins.

Among the Arabs there were no distinctions, traditional or natural, except the unconscious power given by a famous sheik by virtue of his accomplishment; and they taught me that no man could be their leader except he ate the ranks' food, wore their clothes, lived level with them, and yet appeared better in himself.[44]

In his new milieu Lawrence was to continue the habit of 'living level' with his service comrades, and yet appearing 'better in himself'.

Uxbridge and Farnborough

I

T. E. Lawrence's interest in the air and aviation dated from the days of the Royal Flying Corps in which his brother Will served until he was shot down and killed in November 1915. His own war experience in the Middle East impressed him with the use of aircraft, both as supporting ground forces and later for policing large areas from the air and thus releasing military units for other less extended and less costly operations. He learned to fly in the later stages of the war and often took over the controls in the air; but although he claimed to have flown 2000 hours, he apparently made no attempt to qualify as a pilot and get his 'wings'. He told Liddell Hart that he only once made a landing, an occasion on which he ripped off the machine's under-carriage. However, he added, he was in seven crashes in each of which the aircraft had to be written off, in the course of which he broke his collar bone, wrist, and several ribs, one of which penetrated a lung where it remained, thus rendering one lung useless with a tendency to cough up blood after any strenuous physical exercise.[1] His ambition to serve in the R.A.F. dates from the spring of 1919 when he spent three months with the crews of a squadron of Handley-Page 0/400 twin-engined aircraft which flew from France during the Peace Conference to Cairo with numerous stops on the way for repairs. By all accounts it was an exciting flight. The machine in which Lawrence was flying crashed at Rome killing the two pilots, but Lawrence escaped with a cracked shoulder and some other minor injuries. 'After the accident at Rome, we greatly admired his pluck in deciding to fly on with us,' the squadron commander later recalled; 'especially as he was incapacitated by his arm, and we had the Mediterranean to cross – the first time for a squadron not fitted for landing on water.' During the crossing, when all signs of land and shipping had disappeared, Lawrence pushed a note into the commander's hand which read: 'Won't it be fun if we come down?' 'I didn't think so,' the commander commented dryly. Lawrence recalled a similar incident on the same flight many years later to the pilot concerned.

> I'll never forget seeing your bus going down towards the Albanian coast, with one prop hardly turning, and groaning to myself 'There's another one gone.'
> That flight put the complete wind up me. We have better buses now.[2]

In Cairo, Colonel Lawrence, as he then was, encountered the Arabist St John Philby, who was also due to be demobilised. After recounting his experiences of the flight to Philby, who imagined that he must by now be fed up with flying, Lawrence insisted that this was by no means the case. In fact he was 'thinking of joining the Air Force', he told Philby. 'They will always want people who can fly,' he added. 'If they demobilise you too, you do the same. They may make *you* a sergeant!'[3]

Lawrence was still as keen on the Air Force two years later when he joined the Colonial Office at Churchill's express invitation and attended the Cairo Conference which the Minister had convened in March 1921 to endorse the policy of air control in the Middle East. Colonel Lawrence attended along with Air Marshal Sir Hugh Trenchard, the Chief of the Air Staff; Sir Percy Cox, the British High Commissioner in Baghdad, and Gertrude Bell, who had become Oriental Secretary in the Commission and who like Lawrence commanded great influence in the Arab world. The new policy, somewhat contemptuously described by Sir Henry Wilson, the Chief of the Imperial General Staff, as one of 'Hot air, aeroplanes and Arabs', was Trenchard's brain child, and warmly supported by Lawrence and Gertrude Bell against the views of Sir Percy Cox and the other delegates. It would help Britain as much as the Arabs, Trenchard argued, since it would be able to supply and reinforce itself in days rather than weeks, and as a peace-keeping force would enable Iraq and Jordan to grow and prosper. 'Sir Hugh is right and the rest of you are wrong,'

Lawrence told Cox and the others with quiet emphasis, thereby earning Trenchard's lasting gratitude when the policy was confirmed. In particular Lawrence was struck by Trenchard's declared aim of blazing an air trail above the desert from Cairo to Baghdad and Amman.

One night, after a lengthy conversation over dinner in Churchill's suite in the Semiramis Hotel, Lawrence casually remarked to Trenchard: 'I'd like to join this air force of yours some day.'

'And I'd be glad to have you.'

'Even as an ordinary ranker?'

'No certainly not,' the C.A.S. rejoined firmly. 'As an officer or nothing.'[4]

Churchill was not at all keen to part with Lawrence so long as there was any prospect of trouble remaining in the Middle East, particularly as regards the stability of Trans-Jordan, where Emir Abdullah was having trouble with the French, who demanded that certain Arab nationalists should be turned over to them. Later in 1921, at Churchill's request, Lawrence spent two months in Amman as official British representative, so arranging matters with the various parties concerned that Trans-Jordan should be freed from the control of the British High Commissioner of Palestine and should become an independent state with Abdullah as King, supported by Britain, which is what eventually happened. Lawrence thereupon handed over to St John Philby and returned to England, where he found his political master at the Colonial Office more reconciled than he had previously been to the idea of his resignation, but still reluctant to let him go.

Early in January 1922, Lawrence wrote to Trenchard.[5] He began with a point they had previously discussed about improvements to the standard service dress for airmen in the Middle East. He went on:

You know I am trying to leave Winston on March the first. Then I want about two months to myself, and then I'd like to join the R.A.F. – in the ranks, of course.

I can't do this without your help. I'm 33 and not skilled in the senses you want. Probably I couldn't pass your medical.

It's odd being too old for the job I want when hitherto I've always been too young for the job I did. However my health is good: I'm always in physical and mental training, and I don't personally believe that I'd be below the average of your recruits in either respect. If you think so that will end it.

You'll wonder what I'm at. The matter is that since I was 16 I've been writing: never satisfying myself technically but steadily getting better. My last book on Arabia is nearly good. I see the sort of subject I need in the beginning of your Force ... and the best place to see a thing from is the ground. It wouldn't 'write' from the officer level.

I haven't told anyone, till I know your opinion: and probably not then, for the newspapers used to run after me and I like being private. People wouldn't understand.

It's an odd request this, hardly proper perhaps, but it may be one of the exceptions you make sometimes. It is asking you to use your influence to get me past the recruiting officer!

Apologies for making it: if you say no I'll be more amused than hurt.

'The greatest employments are open to you if you are to pursue your new career in the Colonial Service,' Churchill told Lawrence at this time.

But Lawrence smiled what Churchill called his bland, beaming, cryptic smile, and said: 'In a very few months my work here will be finished. The job is done, and it will last.'

'But what about you?' queried Churchill.

'All you will see of me is a small cloud of dust on the horizon.'[6]

Trenchard replied to Lawrence's letter in his characteristically brusque style.

> Air Ministry,
> Kingsway, W.C.2.
> 11th January, 1922

My dear Lawrence,

I have your letter.

To take the public part first, about the clothing, I have dealt with that, and will try and get it going shortly. Thank you for the idea, which is certainly good.

With regard to your personal point, I understand it fully, and you too, I think. I am prepared to do all you ask me, if you will tell me for how long you want to join, but I am afraid I could not do it without mentioning it to Winston and my own Secretary of State, and then, whether it could be kept secret I do not know.

Why I feel I could not do it, without mentioning it, is first of all I should have to override the Recruiting Office, which I could do, but then it would be no good my saying I did not know you were joining, and I feel that it would be letting my two bosses in for me to let you do this without their knowing it.

What country do you want to serve in, and how? I would make things as easy as anything.

Let me know if I may mention this to my two Secretaries of State.

Yours

H. Trenchard[7]

In fact, it was not until the beginning of July 1922 that Churchill finally agreed to release Lawrence, having done his best to persuade him to stay on with attractive offers of high office in the service, in the shape of colonial governorships, all of which Lawrence turned down. Thus it was with sadness that Churchill saw the 'small cloud of dust' vanishing on the horizon. 'Your help in all matters and guidance in many has been invaluable to me and to your colleagues', Churchill wrote to him at this time. 'I should have been glad if you would have stayed with us longer.'[8] As for Lawrence he afterwards described Churchill to Charlotte Shaw, to whom Churchill was anathema politically, as 'my most considerate chief' and one 'for whom I have personal affection as well as admiration . . . '

He has so much zest, so much will, so much courage: and he enjoys his successes, and his food, and his drink, and his experiences, and his painting, and his writing. In many ways he is an example to everybody of a man who lives at full throttle . . .

It is quite true that the R.A.F. is my own fault: it is my deliberate and very happy choice. I should not leave it to become Prime Minister. And it is quite true that Winston would have given me Egypt, if I had been willing, early in 1922.[9]

In informing Trenchard of his impending release, Lawrence added that he had not told Churchill what he was going to do, since Sir Eric Geddes's economy committee was pruning the services and this might make it impossible for Trenchard to arrange for his recruitment. 'If there is still a chance of it may I come and see you?' he asked. Trenchard immediately replied by inviting Lawrence to spend the night at his house at Barnet in Hertfordshire, where they could talk over the matter quietly, since there would be no one else there apart from Lady Trenchard. Lawrence promptly accepted and he and the C.A.S. travelled down to Hertfordshire by the commuters' train Trenchard usually took, returning to London by a similar train next morning. Many years later Trenchard told Lawrence's brother Arnold: 'When he asked to join the Air Force in the lowest rank, though I tried to persuade him that he could achieve more in a more responsible position, he was so insistent that I eventually agreed.' It was also agreed that Trenchard would first have to obtain the permission of the Air Minister, Captain F. E. Guest, while Lawrence should find out from Churchill whether he had any objection to the move.

'Winston very agreeable', wrote Lawrence to Trenchard on 21 August. To which the C.A.S. answered next day: 'Yes my Lord was very agreeable, but can you leave it for me to see you until after August 1st? . . . The trouble about seeing you earlier is, as you will understand, with all this panic going on I am rushed off my feet. . . . Anyway give me a date for talking with you and a date for the final *plunge*.'[10] The panic to which Trenchard alluded was the possibility of Britain going to war with Turkey, owing to the Turkish leader Mustafa Kemal repudiating the Treaty of Sèvres which had been concluded between Turkey and the Allies in 1920.

Eventually Lawrence saw the C.A.S. at the Air Ministry on 14 August when Trenchard told him that the arrangements for his enlistment would be made by the Member of the Air Council for Personnel, Air Vice-Marshal Oliver Swann, to whom Trenchard introduced him personally, and that he would be shortly informed of the details from him. At the same time Trenchard sent Swann the following internal memorandum.

It is hereby approved that Colonel T. E. Lawrence be permitted to join the Royal Air Force as an aircraft-hand under the alias of

John Hume Ross
AC2   No. 352087

He is taking this step to learn what is the life of an airman. On receipt of any communication from him through any channel, asking for his release, orders are to be issued for his discharge forthwith without formality.

H. Trenchard
O. Swann   CAS[11]
AMP   16.8.22

Some correspondence subsequently passed on this and related matters between Lawrence and Swann, who incidentally was considerably embarrassed by the part he was obliged to play in the arrangements. 'One would think from the letters, that I was a close correspondent of Lawrence's, possibly even a friend of his,' he admitted afterwards. 'But, as a matter of fact, I never met him until he was brought to me at the Air Ministry and I was *ordered* to get him into the R.A.F. I disliked the whole business, with its secrecy and subterfuge; I discouraged communication with or from him. I handled all the matters of his entry and movements entirely myself. I don't think a soul in my department knew who Aircraftman No 352087 was, and his eventual discovery at Farnborough was solely due to carelessness at the Colonial Office and to Lawrence's unfortunate love of drawing a veil of mystery about himself.'[12]

2

Air Vice-Marshal Swann's instructions to Lawrence were explicit. He was to present himself at the Inspector of Recruiting Office,

4 Henrietta Street, Covent Garden, about 10.30 on the morning of 21 August 1922. (At Lawrence's request the date was subsequently changed to 30 August.) He was to say that he wished to see Mr Dexter, and Flight-Lieutenant Dexter would interview him and would fill up the necessary forms. 'You should tell him the particulars we have arranged upon. (Not the whole truth, nor your real name.) He will advise you as to the age to give and what trade to enter in. (Dexter knows you are being specially entered and will help, but does not know all the facts which do not concern him.)' Really all Dexter knew was that for some reason best known to the Air Ministry, the new recruit was to be entered as John Hume Ross. This alias appears to have been suggested by Arnold Lawrence after a Mrs Ross who was a friend of their mother's. ('He [T.E.] said that would do – he was looking for a short name.')

The prospective recruit was also told that he would have to produce two references as to character and previous employment during the past two years. 'I leave you to procure these,' Swann added. 'They will not be investigated but it is necessary for you to have them in order that someone may not say that your papers are not correct.' He would then be medically examined at Henrietta Street. 'Do not mention any disability. If you are passed all will be well. If you are failed, F/L Dexter will arrange matters. . . . No one will know about you after leaving Henrietta Street: but if any difficulty arises, as a last resort, ask that Mr Dexter of Recruiting Depot be communicated with by telephone.'

You will be sent to Uxbridge with a draft of recruits. At Uxbridge you will be attested and medically inspected. You will have to declare that what you have stated on the attestation form is correct and you will have to swear allegiance to the Crown. You will be given a slight educational exam if you are entering as an aircraft-hand.[13]

'God this is awful,' Lawrence wrote afterwards in his book *The Mint*, recalling the occasion of his original induction in Henrietta Street some years later. 'Hesitating for two hours up and down a filthy street, lips and hands and knees tremulously out of control, my heart pounding in fear of that little door through which I must go to join up.' Then he thought he would sit for a moment in the churchyard opposite, St Paul's, Covent Garden, the work of Inigo Jones and the first Protestant church of any size to be erected in London, where some great figures in the arts of the late 17th and 18th centuries lie buried – Samuel Butler, Sir Peter Lely, William Wycherley, Grinling Gibbons and Thomas Arne, among others. But Lawrence was not thinking of any of these great men, only what his architect friend Herbert Baker had told him about the cornice. Suddenly he had an acute urge to go to the lavatory and remembered there was one under the church.

'A penny; which leaves me fifteen. Buck up, old seat-wiper: I can't tip you and I'm urgent. Won by a short head. My right shoe is bust along the welt and my trousers are showing fringes. One reason that taught me I wasn't a man of action was this routine melting of the bowels before a crisis. However, now we end it. I'm going straight up and in.'[14]

Unfortunately things did not go according to plan. No doubt on his arrival he asked for F/L Dexter, but Sergeant-Major Gee who was on duty at the reception desk in the entrance hall brought him instead to the chief interviewing officer. This was Captain W. E. Johns, later well known as the author of Biggles, the character he devised in a long series of works of fiction for air-minded youngsters and whose exploits were to bring him fame and fortune as a writer. According to Johns, the sergeant, when he introduced the prospective recruit, made a signal which implied that the man was 'a suspicious character', since crooks often tried to hide in the Services and in co-operation with Scotland Yard the interviewing officer had in his desk photographs of criminals wanted by the police.[15]

Lawrence had no papers of identity with him. Nor did he have the references, one from his last employer and the other as to his moral character, which Swann had told him he would be required to produce. Lawrence did supply particulars of his birth but Johns told him that he would need to see his birth certificate as well as the references. Lawrence then departed ostensibly to obtain these documents. During Lawrence's absence, Johns was apparently unable to recognise him from any of the photographs of wanted characters in his desk. However, his suspicions having been aroused by Sergeant-Major Gee, Johns checked the records in the registry of births at Somerset House, and found there was no record of the birth of John Hume Ross on the date Lawrence had given. Presently Lawrence returned with the references which he handed to the interviewing officer, who quickly ascertained that they were forgeries. (No doubt they were fabricated by Lawrence himself.) Sergeant-Major Gee then showed him the door.

Lawrence thereupon went off to the Air Ministry, which was only about five or six minutes' walk away in Kingsway. He was soon back at the Recruiting Depot escorted by an Air Ministry messenger with a dispatch case. The latter, according to Johns's account, contained: 'a minute signed by a very high authority, ordering his enlistment', no doubt the minute from Trenchard to Swann quoted above. 'I accepted the order of course,' noted Johns afterwards, 'but there was still a stumbling block.' This was the medical examination.

Lawrence went in to face two doctors, one a Squadron-Leader named Valerie and the other a Scot, junior in rank, whom Valerie called 'Mac'.

'Ross?' the Squadron-Leader barked at him.

'Yes, that's me.'

'D'you smoke?'

'Not much, Sir.'

'Well, cut it out. See?'

In fact, it was six months since Lawrence had had his last cigarette, but since he felt there was no use giving himself away, he said nothing.

'Nerves like a rabbit,' said the Scottish doctor as his hard fingers hammered the recruit's ribs. After being made to go through a number of evolutions, he was told to turn round.

'Hullo, what the hell's those marks? Punishment?'

'No, Sir, more like peaceful persuasion, Sir, I think.'

'H...m...m... that would account for the nerves.' The Squadron-Leader's voice sounded softer now. 'Don't put them down, Mac. Say *Two parallel scars on the ribs*. What were they, boy?'

'Superficial wounds, Sir.'

'Answer my question.'

Lawrence muttered something about a barbed-wire tear, over a fence. But he refused to say exactly what the marks were.

S/L Valerie then left the room to fetch Captain Johns, who came in and looked at the marks on Lawrence's back, recognising them as scars caused by flogging. But Lawrence persisted in his refusal to say how he got them.

The medical officers were inclined to overlook this, but they could not pass him as fit on account of his obvious malnutrition.

'How long have you been short of food?'

'Gone a bit short the last three months, Sir.'

'More like six,' Valerie growled back.[16]

This is how Lawrence described the upshot of the medical to Swann.

My teeth never were any good, so the doctors threw me straight down stairs again. There Dexter caught me, and lent me what was no doubt his right hand to steer me past the medical and through other rocks of square roots and essays and decimals. However I was obviously incapable of getting through on my own, so he got another chit from you, and that did the trick satisfactorily. If I'd known I was such a wreck I'd have gone off and recovered before joining up: now the cure and the experiment must proceed together.

Captain Johns's account dovetails generally with what Lawrence wrote to Swann. Johns subsequently wrote:

The doctors refused to pass as fit a man who was not up to the medical standard laid down.

Upon this I took the case to the Commanding Officer, who spoke to the Air Ministry. When he had finished, he said to me, speaking very seriously: 'Watch your step. This man is Lawrence of Arabia. Get him in, or you'll get your bowler hat!'

I took this information to the doctors. It made no difference.

They refused to sign. The Air Ministry ordered them to sign. Still they refused, whereupon an outside doctor was brought in. He signed, I signed, and Ross was in.

By this time everyone on the station knew who Ross was. Certainly Lawrence knew that I knew, because I had a long talk with him while he was waiting for the train to take him to Uxbridge. When he went he left me with the memory of a cold, clammy handshake.

I then rang up F/L Nelson, my opposite number at Uxbridge, to warn him of who was on the way, for by this time Lawrence was making it clear that he had no time for junior officers. Lawrence himself soon saw to it that everyone else knew who he was.[17]

'Biggles' Johns certainly did not take to Lawrence, and there is no evidence to support the substance of the last sentence of his account. The secret was generally unknown among Lawrence's airmen comrades, but it got out in the officers' mess, no doubt due to the garrulity of F/L Nelson. Unfortunately for Lawrence it encouraged the unfounded rumour that he had been deliberately infiltrated into the ranks at Uxbridge in order to spy and report on the officers, some of whom at least determined to take it out on him accordingly.

The recruit's first night was spent in a hut full of other 'unsigned' airmen, who fought off their nervousness by noise, talk, playing 'Swanee River' on a mouth organ, and by japes and rough horseplay as they swiftly stripped for sleep, while: 'A reek of body fought with beer and tobacco for the mastery of the room.' Lights went out at ten-fifteen, but the night dragged and kept Lawrence awake with the sounds of the trams passing outside and: 'the cobbling tic-tac of the relief guard, when they started on their round in file past our walls. Next day breakfast and dinner were sickening, but ample.'

Testing and examination went on, intermittently. The R.A.F. standards were severe – more so than the Army's – and many of us found difficulties. The supervising officer was prompting his rejects to go up elsewhere for some regiment. Those who had passed came back to the hut but confessing their success with good-humoured rueful resignation: but in secret they were proud. Those who failed saw yellow and thanked their stars – too loudly to convince us. On the credit side was our laughing, our candour, our creeping obedience: on the other side the uncanny gentleness of sergeants and officers whenever we met them. Always I thought of the spider and its flies. Around us, for the rest, the unheeding camp lived its life to a trumpet code and a rhythm of bells like ships' bells.[18]

In the afternoon Aircraftman Ross was called, sat at a table, and was told to write an essay on his birth-place which he had not seen since he was barely a year old. So he improvised gaily. 'You'll do,' said the flight-lieutenant, liking his prose. The Education Officer also asked him: 'And you, Ross, what is the subject in which you feel particularly weak?' 'Polishing boots, Sir,' was the answer, whereas, as Lawrence later told Robert Graves, 'the others had babbled of French and geography and sums.'[19]

The Education Officer then passed him on to a bald-headed officer whose small eyes must have been paining him, since he had taken off his glasses and repeatedly pursed his eyelids in a tight grimace, while he put the recruit through a stiff catechism. London had told him that the formalities were over bar the swearing in, so he was taken by surprise, and shifting his feet stammered out parts of his history.

The officer got very impatient and shouted out: 'Why were you doing nothing during the war?'

'Because I was interned, Sir, as an alien enemy.'

'Great Scott, and you have the nerve to come to ME as a recruit – what prison were you in?'

'Smyrna, in Turkey, Sir.'

'Oh! What ... why? As a British subject! Why the hell didn't you say so directly? Where are your references, birth certificate, educational papers?'

'They kept them in Henrietta Street, Sir. I understood they signed me on there.'

'Understood?' the bald-headed officer barked at him. 'Look

here, m'lad. You're trying to join the Royal Air Force, so get it
into your head right away that you're not wanted to understand
anything before you're told. Got it?'

Then the officer's eye fell on the papers in the file before him,
where the acceptance Lawrence had stated was plainly set forth.
He waved him wearily away. 'Get outside there with the others
and don't waste my time.'

As we waited in the passage for the oath which would bind us
(we waited for two hours, a fit introduction to service life
which is the waiting of forty or fifty men together upon the
leisure of any officer or N.C.O.), there enwrapped us, never to
be lost, the sudden comradeship of the ranks; – a sympathy
born half of our common defencelessness against authority
(authority which could be, as I had just re-learnt, arbitrary)
and half of our true equality: for except under compulsion
there is no equality in the world.

The oath missed fire: it babbled of the King; and, with
respect, no man in the ranks today is royalist after the antique
sense in which the Georgian Army felt itself peculiarly the
King's. We do certainly observe some unformulated loyalty
with heart and soul: but our ideal cannot have legs and a hat.
We have obscurely grown it, while walking the streets or lanes
of our country, and taking them for our own.

When they had sworn and signed their years away, the sergeant
marched them back to the hut. There seemed a new ring about
his voice. 'We collected our tiny possessions and moved to
another hut, apart from the unsigned men. A sober-faced corporal
counted us in. His welcome was the news that henceforward, for
weeks, there would be no passes for us nor liberty to go through
the iron gates. The world suddenly went distant. Our puzzled
eyes peered through the fence at its strangeness, wondering what
had happened.' In the evening they began to talk about
'civilians'.[20]

The following day Lawrence wrote to Swann. 'I hadn't meant
to write,' he explained; 'but the mess I made of Henrietta Street
demands an apology.' He went on:

I'm not very certain of myself, for the crudities, which aren't as bad as I expected, worry me far more than I expected: and physically I can only just scrape through the days. However they are a cheerful crowd; and the N.C.O.s behave with extraordinary gentleness to us (there's no other word fits their tone – except on the square, from which Good Lord deliver us!) and I usually enjoy one hour of the sixteen, and often laugh in bed after lights out. If I can get able to sleep, and to eat the food, and to go through the P[hysical] T[raining] I'll be all right. The present worry is 90 per cent nerves.

'Please tell the C.A.S. that I'm delighted, and most grateful to him and to you for what you have done', he concluded. 'Don't bother to keep an eye on what happens to me.'[21] But that was just what Oliver Swann, not to mention the C.A.S. himself, was obliged to do, willy-nilly.

3

Lawrence spent a little more than two months at Uxbridge. His letters, mainly to Edward Garnett and Bernard Shaw, were largely taken up with the question of *The Seven Pillars*, altering, illustrating and abridging. 'The personal chapter clearly bothers you', he wrote to Garnett, no doubt alluding to the controversial parts of chapter LXXX describing his adventures at Deraa. On the other hand, his Oxford contemporary and friend Vyvyan Richards had read it and told him that: 'it stood out as the finest chapter in the book'.

I tend more to your opinion: it's not meant for ordinary intelligences, and *must* mislead them: but to set it out in plain English would be very painful. However six months away from it, and then a fresh approach may work a change in my feeling towards it: it may even give me the energy to re-write it. At present nothing sounds less probable. I don't even feel capable (though I'd love to) of writing a fresh book on this place. I've made some rather poor notes, which show me how hard it would be to bring off a picture of the R.A.F. Depot.[22]

The notes which Lawrence referred to were to form the basis of *The Mint*, a somewhat disjointed but brutally frank account of his life as an aircraftman at Uxbridge, with some later notes of his time at Cranwell written up while he was in India, the whole destined to remain unpublished until twenty years after his death. 'I am not frightened of our instructors, nor of their over-driving', he wrote in one passage which perhaps gives the key to this work, and certainly to its title. 'To comprehend why we are their victims is to rise above them. Yet despite my background of achievement and understanding, despite my willingness (quickened by a profound dissatisfaction with what I am) that the R.A.F. should bray me and re-mould me after its pattern: still I want to cry out that this our long-drawn punishing can subserve neither beauty nor use.'[23]

The picture which Lawrence drew in *The Mint* of the Uxbridge Commandant, Wing-Commander (later Air Commodore) Bonham-Carter, though he did not mention him by name, was harsh, even cruel, and it was to cause resentment among officers who had served with him, such as Sholto Douglas, afterwards Marshal of the R.A.F. Lord Douglas of Kirtleside.[24] A veteran who had fought with distinction in South Africa, India and in the First World War where he had been severely wounded, Ian Malcolm Bonham-Carter was a strict disciplinarian, but that (as Lord Douglas later remarked) was exactly the quality most needed in the Commandant at a Recruit Training Depot. But to Lawrence he was a bully who overdid it, particularly on P.T. mornings when he would drive over from his house in his little two-seater car to watch the recruits with the instructor.

He is only the shards of a man – left leg gone, a damaged eye and brain (as we charitably suppose), one crippled arm, silver plates and corsets about his ribs. Once he was a distinguished soldier: – and now the R.A.F. is his pitying almoner.

For P.T. he does not wear his artificial limbs: instead he crutches himself with empty trouser-leg to the cook-house wall, and props himself against a buttress, while with his arm he attempts to follow the instructor's movements. Magnificent, you say, of a cripple so to defy his disability? Theatrical swank, done at our expense. He, being always resentfully in pain, is determined that we shall be at least uncomfortable. His presence drags out the P.T. to its uttermost minute: and however hard the sky may weep on us, the exercises must be gone through. Then he drives home to change his clothes, if in his ruins there is a bone whole enough to feel the chill of damp. The airmen have to walk these their only trousers dry.

Once, after P.T., Lawrence was detailed as headquarters' runner for the day, which meant missing breakfast and then being in attendance on the Commandant wherever he went. After sitting for two hours on a bench and rising every few minutes to salute every officer who came past, the Commandant eventually appeared and sallied forth to inspect the kit of a trained draft about to leave the Depot.

Where he went I had to follow, like Mary's lamb, two paces behind him: and I was studying how to keep step with his dotting false leg when he swung round on me and shouted to know why the bloody hell I'd let the point of my stick droop towards the ground. The rage-distorted face was thrust down into mine, making me sick at the near squalor of those coarse hairs which bushed from his ears and nose, and the speckle of dark pits which tattooed his skin.

'What's your squad?' the Commandant barked at the offending aircraftman.
'I've not been squadded yet, Sir.'

Beaten, he faced round and stumped on. Not even the arch-punisher could punish an undrilled man for a fault in drill. To inflict misery pleased him, for his body so pained him that only tight lips and a scowl kept him going: and it was an alleviation to see the circle of terror widen about him.

During a kit inspection of one of the huts, the bullying went so far that Lawrence found himself trembling with clenched fists, repeating to himself: 'I must hit him, I must', and the next moment 'trying not to cry for shame that an officer should play the public cad'.

At last four-thirty came and the Commandant prepared to return home. Lawrence bore his attaché case and papers to his little car.

He struggled hardly in, unhelped: for we knew that he would swipe at an offered hand with his crutch. On the seat he made room for the dog, I swung the engine. He waved me away while he let in the clutch and backed her round: then roared, 'Now jump, you damned fool!' I took a flying leap to the sloping back, and clung there apelike between the hood and the luggage rack while he drove smartly across the park to his tree-bowered house by the golf course. He pulled up at its gate: and shouted to me, 'Attention!' I stood as if on parade. 'Carry your stick properly, next time. Fall out!' I turned to the right, saluted and marched off . . . Before I was out of earshot I could hear him loudly drilling his little children in the garden.

Lawrence's pen-picture of the bullying Commandant is devastatingly vivid, as is his summing up of Bonham-Carter's character.

One day he started to walk across with a leashed dog in each hand. The excited beasts sprang forward after a cat. Down went the cripple, fairly pulled over on his face. He would not let go the dogs. Nor could he raise his blaspheming self. The slopes thickened with airmen silently watching him struggle. The contagion of interest reached the squads, and drill stopped. At last the duty officer, seeing the derelict, rushed down and set him again on foot. 'Let the old cunt rot,' had muttered airman to airman.

Yet were we kinder to him than his next command. The day he first flew there, the aerodrome was ringed with his men almost on their knees, praying he would crash. Such hate of a brave man is as rare as it is hurtful to the service. His character was compounded of the corruptions of courage, endurance, firmness and strength: he had no consideration for anyone not commissioned, no mercy (though all troops abundantly need mercy every day) and no fellowship. He leaned only to the military side of the Air Force, and had no inkling that its men were not amenable to such methods. Partly this may have been honest stupidity. His officer friends urged that he was kind to dogs, and had the men's material interests at heart. It was that which hurt us most. We felt that we should be more considered than our food and our clothes. He treated us like stock-cattle: so the sight of him became a degradation to us, and the over-hearing his harsh tone an injury. His very neighbourhood grew hateful, and we shunned passing his house.

There were seemingly endless drills, the fatigues, the fire pickets, the menial and useless tasks, such as peeling potatoes with issue knives in the cook-house, the inspections, the unjust punish-ments, and the sense of comradeship among the enlisted men, in spite of their barrack-room language. Furthermore, the drilling had an unpleasant aspect which was not lost on Lawrence's per-ceptive observation. This he was to describe in *The Mint*.

I have been before at depots, and have seen or overseen the training of many men: but this our treatment is rank cruelty. While my mouth is yet hot with it I want to record that some of those who day by day exercise their authority upon us, do it in a lust of cruelty. There is a glitter in their faces when we sob for breath; and evident through their clothes is that tauten-ing of the muscles (and once the actual rise of sexual excite-ment) which betrays that we are being hurt not for our good, but to gratify a passion. I do not know if all see this: our hut is full of innocents, who have not been sharpened by my penalty of witnessing: – who have not laid their wreath of agony to induce: – the orgasm of man's vice.[25]

On the general question of sex among the airmen at the depot, Lawrence recalled the select preacher at an Oxford evening service speaking of venery: 'And let me implore you, my young friends, not to imperil your immortal souls upon a pleasure which, *so I am credibly informed*, lasts less than one and three-quarters minutes.' Of direct experience Lawrence went on to state that he could not speak, never having been tempted to imperil his immortal soul. 'Six out of ten enlisted fellows share my ignorance despite their flaming talk.'

Shyness and a wish to be clean have imposed chastity on so many of the younger airmen, whose life spends itself and is spent in the enforced celibacy of their blankets' harsh embrace. . . .
By general rumour troops are accused of common lechery and much licence. But troops are you and me, in uniform. Some make a boast of vice, to cover innocence. It has a doggy sound. Whereas in truth, with one and another, games and work and hard living so nearly exhaust the body that few temptations remain to be conquered. Report accuses us of sodomy, too: and anyone listening in to a hut of airmen would think it a den of infamy. Yet we are too intimate, and too bodily soiled, to attract one another. In camps all things, even if not public, are publicly known: and in the four large camps of my sojourning there have been five fellows actively beastly. Doubtless their natures tempted others: but they fight its expression as the normal airman fights his desire for women, out of care for physical fitness.[26]

Most of the recruits were too exhausted at the end of the day to do much more than roll into bed, particularly if the day had been spent in collecting and emptying refuse bins from the 'shit-cart'. 'Then to bed but not in my case to sleep', wrote Lawrence. 'Partly I was too tired: partly the smell of swill and refuse oozed slowly from my soiled things and stagnated into a pool over me. I lay staring into the black roof for hours, trying to forget the five days that must pass before my laundry went.'[27]
The airmen – 'irks', as they were known colloquially – had little contact with the officers on the station, except on ceremonial occasions such as inspection or when they were reported for some breach of discipline. Once when a Squadron-Leader, ex-Navy, was going round Lawrence's hut, not bothering too much about the kits but speaking to each man, his eyes lit on

Lawrence's books in his polished locker and he read some of the titles on their backs.

'What's that?' he asked, pointing to *Niels Lyhne* by the Danish novelist J. P. Jacobsen in the original. 'Oh, you read Danish: why did you join the Air Force?'

'I think I had a mental breakdown, Sir.'

'What, what? What! Sergeant-Major, take this man's name,' said the inspecting officer, passing on.

'Office, nine o'clock,' said the Sergeant-Major curtly, with a gleam in his eye.

The seemingly erring recruit was marched in to the Flight-Lieutenant's office under escort at the appointed time. The Flight-Lieutenant looked grave. He could only give the airman seven days and the crime of insolence to a Senior Officer demanded extreme rigour. At last he remanded him for trial by the Squadron-Leader he had apparently insulted.

When Lawrence finally faced the Squadron-Leader and the charge was repeated, the Squadron-Leader burst out laughing. 'Bless my Sowl, Sergeant-Major; bless my howly Sowl. I told you to take his name in case we wanted an intelligent man for a job. What damned fool drafted this charge? Get out!'

With that the Squadron-Leader gave Lawrence a friendly swipe across the backside with his stick. 'They say I'm the first man to dodge a charge laid by our S.M.,' noted Lawrence afterwards. 'Perhaps. I'm bobbing on not getting that intelligent job from him!'[28]

The recruits' worst tormentor was a sergeant called Pearson, who took a sadistic delight in humiliating the airmen on the parade ground, using the most filthy and insulting language. Lawrence knew that his turn must come. Eventually it did. 'He drenched my eventual dumbness with all the foul and hurtful names in his mouth: but they seemed not to soak through to the quick of my notice. I hung there more curiously miserable than indignant.'

'Answer him back, Cough-drop, answer him,' whispered another airman from the rear rank. 'He sees you stuck there like a cunt, shitting yourself, and that makes him go on. Blind him with science same's you do us in the hut.' Nevertheless, although

Lawrence could hold his own in verbal rallies with his peers, 'when I am standing to attention this obscure respect for duty intervenes'.

I fear the sight of me miserably squirming to dodge the goad does inflame Sergeant Pearson. 'Look at me!' he yells: but I can't. If I am angry, I can outface a man; but when this hyaena curses me I sicken with shame wondering if my authority, in the past, so deflowered myself and those under me. 'Look at me, look me in the face, you short-arsed little fuck-pig,' he is yelling again. If I meet his eyes for more than a moment, my sight reels giddily outward, and my focus loses itself in a guttering rim of tears. But for that my body's swaying would throw me down. 'Well, I'm fucked, the ignorant queenie' (of our adjectives, printable or unprintable, 'ignorant' is gauged the hurtfullest). 'Funks looking at me, an' thinks his equipment's right. Blood like fucking gnat's piss.'

It may be an infirmity of my eyes, that they cannot be intensely concentrated for more than a moment.[29]

In one of the most revealing passages in *The Mint*, Lawrence describes the Chief of the Air Staff and the new peacetime force he was trying to fashion on a tight budget.

This Royal Air Force is not antique and leisurely and storied like an army. We can feel the impulsion of a sure, urging giant behind the scurrying instructors. Squad 5 is today the junior unit of the service. There are twenty thousand airmen better than us between it and Trenchard, the pinnacle and our exemplar: but the awe of him surely encompasses us. The driving energy is his, and he drives furiously. We are content, imagining that he knows his road. The Jew said that God made man after his own image – an improbable ambition in a creator. Trenchard has designed the image he thinks most fitted to be an airman; and we submit our nature to his will, trustingly. If Trenchard's name be spoken aloud in the hut, every eye swivels round upon the speaker, and there is a stillness, till someone says, 'Well, what of Trenchard?' and forthwith he must provide something grandiose to fit the legend. 'I reckon he's a man's man,' said Jones, in laughing admiration, one day, after several fellows had been swapping yarns of Trenchard's short way with commanding officers, our superb tyrants. China, the iconoclast, revolted. 'And I reckon,' he said, 'that Trenchard's shit smells much the same as mine.' The others cried him down.

The word Trenchard spells out confidence in the R.A.F. and we would not lose it by hearing him decried. We think of him as immense, not by what he says, for he is as near as can be inarticulate: – his words barely enough to make men think they divine his drift: – and not by what he writes, for he makes the least use of what must be the world's worst handwriting: – but just by what he is. He knows; and by virtue of this pole-star of knowledge he steers through all the ingenuity and cleverness and hesitations of the little men who help or hinder him.

Trenchard invented the touchstone by which the Air Council try all their works. 'Will this, or will this not, promote the conquest of the air?' We wish, sometimes, the Air Council would temper wisdom to their innocent sheep. For instance, they have just decreed that the black parts of bayonets be henceforward burnished. That gives each man about twenty hours' work a year. Twenty hours is two and a half days for we work eight hours on average and find time, by hook or crook, in official hours for all such Air Council luxuries. Rack their brains as they will, the urks cannot connect polished bayonets with flying efficiency. The fault is on us. Yet how can this brightness dangling at our left hips as we go to church be worth half a week, five thousand pounds a year, to Trenchard? If it were Stiffy now! The Guards polish their bayonets. But what a mess the Guards'd make of our job.[30]

'Stiffy', an ex-Guards ranker, was the nickname bestowed by the recruits upon the drill-adjutant, whose prime responsibility was the supervision and carrying out of the twelve-week training course for the airmen recruits at Uxbridge. Thus when the news came through early in November from the Air Ministry that A/c2 Ross was being posted to a unit, the R.A.F. School of

Photography at Farnborough, 'Stiffy' was understandably incensed, although Lawrence was greatly relieved since he was able
to 'dodge the last weeks of Depot-training and the orgy of fitness
tests with which it closes'. A corporal appeared in Hut 4 with a
message that A/c2 Ross should report to the orderly room next
morning at nine o'clock. 'Old Stiffy's hopping mad at a man being
sent off before the end of training,' the envious corporal volunteered. 'Chewed my fucking balls up, something cruel.'

> So I went there knocking at the knees and gave Stiffy a won-
> derful salute, in palliation. He looked down at me as if I were
> ugly and ill-smelling.
>   'How long you here?'
>   I told him.
>   'How much drill d'you know?'
>   'Very little, Sir.'
>   'How's that?'
>   'First month's all fatigues, Sir: since, it's been all cenotaph
> practice.'
>   He heard me in silence and disgust.[31]

The relations between Aircraftman Ross and 'Stiffy' Breese
had never been harmonious. According to Breese, shortly after
he arrived at Uxbridge, Lawrence, of whose identity the drill-
adjutant was unaware, came to see him, since Breese used to
assure every new batch of recruits that they could see him privately about any personal worries they had. When Lawrence
appeared Breese asked him whether it was woman trouble. No,
it was not, said the recruit, vigorously denying the suggestion.
What he wanted, according to Breese, was a room in which he
could do some writing undisturbed. 'Stiffy' explained with more
than a touch of sarcasm that it was not possible to provide each
of 1100 recruits with such a room, but suggested that there was
an excellent writing room in the NAAFI which he could use if
he liked.

This information was contained in a letter Breese wrote many
years later shortly before his death in 1955 in a popular magazine,
praising an article Richard Aldington had written in the same

journal 'debunking' Lawrence. 'The next week he was up for disciplinary reasons', Breese continued, ' – for being consistently dirty, for being insubordinate to his hut sergeant, refusing to obey an order about his kit, and for being persistently late on parade. He would say nothing in his defence except that he had always felt a little tired in the early morning. I admonished him, but in subsequent weeks when he was up on disciplinary charges he was awarded a few days' loss of privileges, and finally recommended for discharge. It was only then that I learnt his real name.' At the same time he wrote to Aldington: 'I had the perisher, under his assumed name, under my direct command. I tried to get him out three times until I was ordered to headquarters and partially told the reasons for his recruitment. For years I have been trying to debunk him but have been howled down.'[31]

For some reason the drill-adjutant had conceived a violent dislike for Aircraftman Ross from the beginning, and no doubt it distorted his memory when he came to write about it more than thirty years later. There is no reference to these disciplinary charges in *The Mint* and they are not borne out by any other evidence, except perhaps by the recruit's tendency to be late for parade.

On his last night at the depot, his particular friends in Hut 4 gave him a party. Throwing their cleanest bed-sheet over the table and putting a form on each side they spread the top with food. There were 'Zepps in a cloud' (sausage and mashed), and 'Adam and Eve on a raft' (fried eggs on toast) as main dishes, with every available trimming of cheese, tomatoes and tea: 'for which they'd put up the every last copper of their joint pay.' Lawrence was greatly touched. 'It was their farewell to me, who surely must have been a little human here: no one ever ventured to banquet me before.'[32]

Aircraftman Ross arrived at South Farnborough on 7 November 1922, although his official posting was dated two days later. This may have been due to leave of which he did not take full advantage. His feelings after his first two months in the ranks at Uxbridge he noted at the time.

The R.A.F. for me is now myself: a vocation absolute and

inevitable beyond any question under the sky: and so marvellous that I grow hot to make it perfect. I have hated to see the bloom of the virginal recruits wasted by the inept handling here. My own injuries are risible always: every man's own injuries are risible always, only too easy for him to forgive, if, indeed, they ever earn that great word 'forgive'. Could a Pearson, however early he got up in the morning, collect enough subtlety to hurt me memorably? But when he offends the others I am indignant. He sins against the Air.[33]

4

'I expect my move here is your doing,' Aircraftman Ross wrote to Swann from Farnborough after he had reported for duty.

When the order came to Uxbridge I nearly burned down the camp with joy: – for Uxbridge is pretty miserable in its way: miserable and splendid at once, since the fellows rise to it so well. I'm awfully glad I went there and stayed a couple of months: and awfully glad to have got away. It will amuse you to hear that this place seems almost loose now to my depot-educated eyes! That's a great compliment to Uxbridge, for it never had a recruit less adaptable than myself. . . .

Will you tell the C.A.S. all's well: and that I'm going on?
. . . I'd like to have introduced him to Hut IV of Uxbridge. They are devout worshippers: and it's rather enviable, I think, their worship. At any rate if I was the God I'd feel pleased at them and it.

At the same time he asked Swann to have his photographic training expedited. Apparently the day before he arrived, the November class of photography had begun, and consequently the station commander had put him back until the next class which was not due to begin until 6 January 1923.

This irks me a little, because it is a nine months' course anyhow, and it seems a pity to make it eleven. I'd have no difficulty in joining even a class earlier than the November one, for except in enlarging and mosaic work, (learned in two of the later months) I'm already as good as the men passing out. My father, one of the pioneer photographers, taught me before I was four years old, and I've done the photographic work of several British Museum Expeditions, and exhibited a good deal at the Camera Club, regularly.

I asked, accordingly, if you could put me straight into the School, for my technical training. Except for that, Farnborough doesn't offer me much scope. The camp isn't quite the sort of R.A.F. I want to write about! At the same time the technical work is A.1. and I'd like to watch the growth of a class. It was the coming-into-being of the squad which was so exciting at Uxbridge.

I'm exceedingly glad to have got away from Uxbridge. The physical side of that was knocking me up, and this place is a jolly rest cure by comparison. I'm reading German and Spanish to keep myself busy; for my nature doesn't second the demands of discipline very well, and unless I keep working at something I get Bolshie![34]

After ten days or so during which Lawrence heard nothing from the Air Ministry, he was appointed to the Adjutant's office as orderly, his duties being to clean the office in the morning and act as messenger during the day. He struck the Adjutant, Charles Findlay, as an average type of recruit who performed his duties quietly and efficiently. 'Nothing about him suggested that here was the most amazing aircraftman ever to join the R.A.F.'[35]

The first hint of anything unusual came about the third week in November when the Station-Commander, whose name was Guilfoyle, called the Adjutant to his office. 'Air Vice-Marshal Swann has just telephoned from the Air Ministry,' he said. 'He wants to know why A/c2 Ross is not engaged in photographic training.'

The Adjutant was a little taken aback. 'You know the position, sir,' he replied. 'We only have a limited staff. We can't begin a class until we have a minimum of ten pupils.'

'Yes, I've explained all that,' said the C.O. 'I've told him that pupils arrive from the depot in penny numbers and that we have to keep them occupied until we have enough to form a class. But Swann was not at all sympathetic. He insists that Ross's training must begin at once.'

Since it was most unusual for a high-ranking officer like the Director of Personnel to telephone from the Air Ministry, both the Station-Commander and the Adjutant were frankly perplexed. 'Who is this Ross?' asked Guilfoyle, who had never met the new recruit. 'What's he like?'

In order to give the Station-Commander an opportunity of seeing the new recruit, the Adjutant sent for him on the pretext of giving him something to do. Afterwards the Adjutant recalled that he came into the room, a slight, short figure, about five feet four in height. 'He was thirty-four, but in his uniform he looked strangely younger. His blue eyes were set in a long, finely chiselled face. His jaw was square. But the most outstanding features were his long, sensitive fingers.' After the aircraftman had left the office the C.O. turned to the Adjutant with a look of amazement.

'Findlay! Do you know who I think he is? Lawrence!'

'Lawrence?'

'Yes, Lawrence of Arabia! I saw him once in Cairo early in the war, and this airman looks uncommonly like him.'

The Adjutant could scarcely credit that this was the same man who was now lighting fires in his office. 'What are we going to do, sir?'

'I don't know,' Guilfoyle replied. 'You see, I can't be certain, and I don't want to make a silly mistake. Say nothing about my suspicions for the moment.'

'Very good, sir. But what about starting his instruction?'

'It must be arranged at once. Get the Chief Instructor to come and see me right away.'

So it was that a few days later a class was formed, and A/c2 Ross began his photographic training. The Adjutant was on the look-out for anything unusual in the new recruit, and he was soon to find out. In order to ascertain individual standards, certain educational tests were prescribed at the beginning of each course. On this occasion, when the instructor scrutinised the mathematics paper, he noted with surprise that Ross's paper gave the answers without apparently working them out. On being questioned the pupil said he had worked out the answers in his head.

'All right,' said the instructor, who had his doubts, and gave him a more complicated problem to solve, saying as he did so: 'Find the answer to this one in your head.' Ross looked at it for a moment and then wrote down the correct answer. The instructor said no more, but he knew that he had found a bright pupil. In fact he was so bright that his knowledge of optics made him unpopular with the instructor who told the C.O. that Ross was telling *him* things. He was then transferred to the 'Neg' room, identifying war negatives, where he was 'a great success'.

But still the C.O. and the Adjutant could not be sure he was Lawrence. 'Mentally, he stood out from his fellows which only added to the mystery surrounding him,' Findlay noted. On one occasion the Adjutant had to reprimand him for his behaviour during an inspection of dress and arms before mounting guard, in the course of which the orderly officer told one of the airmen that he was not properly turned out. According to Findlay: 'The airman (it was Ross) replied to the officer in a foreign language, which elicited the inevitable titter from the other members of the guard. This was certainly not in keeping with his expressed desire to remain unnoticed.'

At last, however, the moment came when their suspicions were finally confirmed. A staff officer from the Air Ministry arrived at the school on a routine visit and, in the course of conversation, the C.O. asked him if he would recognise Lawrence of Arabia if he saw him.

'Certainly I would,' said the officer. 'I knew him quite well in Cairo.' He was thereupon taken to the classroom where several pupils were working, and he immediately picked out Ross as Lawrence. But beyond revealing this information to the Adjutant and the Station-Commander, the staff officer gave no sign of recognition, and Guilfoyle and Findlay resolved to do their best to keep Lawrence's identity secret.

'It was a heavy responsibility to have a world-famous character on our hands as an A/c2', Findlay was to recall later; 'and many times as I saw his slight, blue-uniformed figure engaged in some menial task I tried with difficulty to reconcile it with the romantic soldier who had inspired the grim, desert peoples to fight so audaciously.' Such menial tasks as he had to perform in addition to his photographic training, Lawrence described at this time in a letter to Bernard Shaw.

You ask for details of what I'm doing in the R.A.F. Today I scrubbed the kitchen out in the morning, and loafed all the afternoon, and spent the evening writing to G.B.S. Yesterday I washed up the dishes in the sergeants' mess in the morning (messy feeders, sergeants: plates were all butter and tomato sauce, and the washing water was cold) and rode to Oxford in the afternoon on my motor-bike, and called on Hogarth to discuss the abridgement of the Arabian book. It being Christmas we do fatigues in the morning, and holiday in the afternoon. Normally I'm an 'aerial photographer, under training': it doesn't mean flying, but developing the officers' negatives after they land: and the 'under training' part means that I'm a recruit, and therefore liable to all sorts of mis-employment. For three weeks I was an errand-boy. I've also been dustman, and clerk, and pig-stye cleaner, and housemaid, and scullion, and camp-cinema-attendant. Anything does for airmen recruits: but the life isn't so bad, when the first crudeness works off. We have a bed each, and suffer all sorts of penalties unless they are 25 inches apart: twelve of us in a room. Life is very common, besides being daily. Much good humour, very little wit, but a great friendliness. They treat my past as a joke, and forgive it me lightly. The officers fight shy of me: but I behave demurely, and give no trouble.[36]

The secret of Ross's identity could not be kept for long, and soon rumours began to spread both inside and outside the camp. Eventually the Press began to show interest, and the Station-Commander wrote to Swann accordingly.[37]

Farnborough
16.12.22

Dear Air Vice-Marshal,
    As you thought, some of the papers had evidently got wind

of Ross and 2 reporters – one from the *Daily Mail* and one from the *Express* – have been here.

They interviewed 2 of the junior officers and learning from them that Colonel Lawrence was not in the Mess and as far as they were concerned not on the Station, they then asked to see the Adjutant and requested permission to visit the airmen. This was not granted but they apparently waited outside the gates and were seen talking to airmen.

Do you think that all the conjecture and talk is in the best interests of discipline? As Station Commander I do hope that some definite procedure will be taken either way.

Do please forgive me for writing such a statement, Sir, but perhaps you will understand.

I am,
Yours sincerely,
W. Guilfoyle.

'Please see the attached,' Swann minuted Trenchard with the Station-Commander's letter. 'I understand you saw the Secretary of State on the matter and would be very glad to learn what he wishes done on this.'[38]

Swann was duly informed by Trenchard's personal assistant T. B. Marson that Sir Samuel Hoare, who had succeeded Captain Guest as Air Minister on the fall of the Lloyd George Coalition, had 'approved that the service of this airman should follow its natural course'.

'As rumours of Lawrence's presence at Farnborough grew,' wrote Findlay afterwards, 'so the press contingent outside our gates was increased day by day. Photographers waited to get a picture of the elusive Colonel. From my office window I could see the airmen passing out of the main gate, taking off their caps and hiding their faces. These tactics fooled the press for a while, and it was a grand game while it lasted.' Indeed the airmen played up splendidly and actually broke up the slides of a camera with which Lawrence had been photographed.[39]

'It was one of the beastly officers who gave me away,' Lawrence wrote to a friend shortly afterwards. He later told another friend, his future biographer Robert Graves, that the officer had recognised him and sold the information to a daily paper for £30. The paper was the *Daily Express* which thus 'scooped' its principal rival the *Daily Mail*.

5

On 27 December 1922, the *Daily Express* came out with the news on its front page:

'UNCROWNED KING' AS PRIVATE SOLDIER

LAWRENCE OF ARABIA

Famous War Hero becomes a Private

SEEKING PEACE

OPPORTUNITY TO WRITE A BOOK

The story was splashed over the centre pages as well and there was another sensational follow-up next day in the reporter's characteristic prose.

No one had any idea that Aircraftman Ross was the world famous man who united the wild Arab tribes, created two kingdoms in the east, and became the only white man ever made a Prince of Mecca. . . .
Sometimes in the evenings he would tell astonishing stories of the East, of wild tribes, and exciting fights, of tight corners, and marvellous marches over desert sands. . . .

After his identity became generally known in the station, he appeared to be less reticent, at least with the Adjutant. Although he told Bernard Shaw that the officers tended to fight shy of him, Findlay later recalled that he spoke to him many times and always found him willing to talk. The reason why the officers still

avoided him was due to the suspicion that he had been deliberately planted by the Air Ministry to spy on them. 'They little
knew old Trenchard, if they thought he would use a spy,' was
Lawrence's comment on this canard to Graves.

'Why did you enlist in the ranks of the R.A.F. ?' Findlay asked
him at this time.

'I couldn't batten on my friends any longer,' he replied frankly.
'I decided that the R.A.F., being a young, technical service,
offered the best opportunity of leading a quiet and interesting
life.'

'But surely you would have been more use to the Service as an
officer ?'

'That would have spoiled it for me,' he answered in language
suggested by that already quoted in *The Seven Pillars*. 'I wanted
to see the Service from the ranks' point of view, and I could only
do this by living with them and sharing the life in the barrack
room.'

At the same time he made it clear to the Adjutant that discipline
did not come easily to him. He complained that he found the drill
and P.T. at Uxbridge arduous and he did not like doing fatigues
and 'errand boy' jobs. He was keenly interested in photography
and he felt, a little unreasonably, so Findlay thought, that he was
being misemployed when engaged on any other task. And yet
once when a Flight-Sergeant saw him sweeping a passage in the
school and said he would get someone else to do the job, Lawrence replied: 'Am I not capable then, Flight-Sergeant ?'

On another occasion Findlay asked Lawrence why he had
recorded 'Nil' on his Service papers in respect of the item 'Previous Service'. Lawrence assured the Adjutant that this was
correct, that he had roamed as a kind of free-lance during the
war, with authority from the Colonial Office to assume any rank
which suited the exigencies of the moment. 'And he made the
point that John Hume Ross had no previous service.'

Findlay's assessment of Lawrence's character and personality
at this time is worth quoting.

The conversations I shared with him produced the impression
that he was searching for something new in life – but had not

yet found it. Participating in the life of the Royal Air Force was only a partial solution to his problem at that time, and he appeared to be still trying to shake off something. For what it is worth, a note I made at the time reads: 'I am convinced that some quality departed from Lawrence before he became the R.A.F. recruit. Lawrence of Arabia had died.' The man with whom I conversed seemed but the shadow of the Lawrence who was picked up by the whirlwind of events to become the driving force of Arab intervention in the war. . . .

It was difficult to believe that Ross was the same man. The only satisfactory explanation must be that he was suffering from nervous exhaustion, that the hypersensitive man had partially succumbed to the rough and tumble of the war and its immediate consequences, that the product, for the time being at least, was a personality less intense and hoping to shun the responsibility of making decisions.

Yet he could not escape the fact of being Lawrence; the end of the war was too recent for this to be unimportant. It was a form of vanity, I think, that made him draw mentally apart from his fellows, wrap himself in an aura of mystery, and rejoice in the excitement his presence created in the barrack room. His assumption of mental leadership among the rank and file mattered little while his identity was unrevealed. The position altered when the airman Ross was known to be Lawrence of Arabia, and there is little doubt that his presence in the camp had an unsettling effect upon all ranks. As Adjutant of the school, I was very conscious of this.[40]

After the Station-Commander had made several more representations to the Air Ministry to the effect that Lawrence's continued presence in the camp was prejudicial to good order and discipline, the Chief of the Air Staff suddenly paid a surprise visit. He had a private talk with Lawrence, telling him that he was 'an unusual person, and inevitably embarrassing to a C.O.'. But Lawrence did not agree. As he told Trenchard's personal assistant T. B. Marson: 'I've had a lurid past, which has now twice pulled me down, and of which I'm beginning to despair: but if my C.O. was a decent size he'd treat me as average, and I'd be average.'

The only condition on which the C.A.S. would allow Lawrence to remain in the Service was if he could accept a commission. 'I said I couldn't take it and begged to be left in,' Lawrence later recalled; 'but he couldn't do it: asked me to take my discharge as final: and he's not a mind-changer.'[41]

The Air Minister was also adamant. 'I was horrified at the disclosure,' Hoare wrote afterwards. 'The position, which had been an extremly delicate area when it was shrouded in secrecy, became untenable when it was exposed. The only possible course was to discharge Airman Ross. He had brought his discharge upon himself, for it was he who had given the story to the Press.'[42] (This was quite untrue: as noted above it had been sold to the *Daily Express* by an officer on the station.) Shortly afterwards instructions arrived for his discharge from the R.A.F. and he was sent on indefinite leave pending the completion of the necessary formalities. 'I had the task of telling him officially that the axe had fallen upon his career,' the Adjutant later recalled. 'He told me he was sorry to be sacked and would dearly have liked to continue his career in the ranks. I am sure he was genuinely miserable at leaving, and he told me he would make another attempt to get into the R.A.F.'

He first went to a small nearby hotel at Frensham well known for its large pond and bird life, where he could think things out. When his money ran out he moved back to his old quarters above Herbert Baker's architect's office in Barton Street. Meanwhile he had written formally to the Air Minister asking to be given a reason for his discharge. 'My Secretary of State tells me that you want to be given a reason for leaving the Air Force,' Trenchard replied for the Minister. 'As you know, I always think it is foolish to give reasons!! but this case is perhaps different. I think the reason to give is that you had become known in the Air Force as Colonel Lawrence, instead of Air Mechanic Ross, and that both you and the officers were put in a very difficult position; and therefore that it was considered inexpedient for you to remain in the Service.'[43]

Lawrence had not received this communication when he wrote to Marson from Frensham on 28 January 1923 correctly diagnosing the reason for his dismissal and asking for another chance, possibly by being posted to a more remote station like Leuchars: 'whose C.O. is a solid and masterful person', who could sack him if he found him 'inconvenient'. He went on:

> This is for the C.A.S., when he is not momentarily burdened with big politics I've been looking round these last few days and find an odd blank: – there is nothing I can think of that I want to do, and in consequence, nothing that I will do! And the further I get away from the R.A.F. the more I regret the loss.
>
> So I'm writing, not hopefully, to ask whether he thought (and turned down the idea) of giving me another chance? The Newspaper chatter I don't take seriously, (and you won't still it much by throwing them the fresh tit-bit of my discharge), so it seems the real difficulty must be the disturbance I caused, unwillingly and unwittingly at Farnborough. I can't help thinking it must have been in large part, because the finding me out happened there....
>
> As I say, this isn't hopefully written. I fear it's too late and the business closed.... The last thing I wish to seem is importunate: but I'm so sure that I played up at Farnborough, and did good, rather than harm, to the fellows in camp there with me, that I venture to put in a last word for myself.[44]

His fear was realised. It was too late and the die had been cast, as Trenchard wrote to him in a private letter next day.

> Marson has shewn me your letter. I am never burdened with big politics, it is always that the little politics are the burden to me.
>
> I would like to agree with all you have written but the trivial circumstances have been too much for me and for you. It is the smallness of it that has brought about the decision to finish it, and I know you will accept it however much you hate it.
>
> To my way of thinking, the only thing that would be of use would be an Armoured Car Officer – Short Service.
>
> One of the drawbacks to you is that you have been a bit of a friend of mine, and that has made it so hard for me to deal with.

I will think over things, and if you could come and see me I will talk over what I can suggest for you, provided my Secretary of State agrees, and you want it and after investigation it becomes feasible.[45]

But Lawrence did not want to be an officer again. 'You see I'm fed up with being called Colonel in this ridiculous year 1923: and am determined not any more to be respectable', he wrote to B. E. Leeson, an old friend who had been in the Royal Flying Corps in the Hejaz in the early days of the Arab Revolt, when they had taken a Crossley car through very difficult country to search for a missing plane. 'Besides I liked being an A.C.2 and would like to be something of the sort in future. However, they won't have me back, so that hope is vain.'[46]

[3]

Bovington

I

'I've now been sacked from the R.A.F. as a person with altogether too large a publicity factor for the ranks – and feel miserable about it,' Lawrence informed Bernard Shaw. 'I've only a few days' money so will do something decisive soon.'[1] From his Barton Street attic, he badgered several friends in high places for the kind of job he still wanted. The first was Leopold Amery, the First Lord of the Admiralty, whom he had known in the Middle East. What he needed, he told Amery, was some routine occupation without responsibility to prevent a nervous breakdown, such as a store-keeping clerk at Bermuda or some other quiet naval station. 'I tried to fix him up,' Amery has recalled in his memoirs, suggesting a coastguard or light-house keeper; 'but the Sea Lords were not too anxious to fit him in,' and nothing came of any of these projects.[2] One offer which he did get was from the Irish Free State army, no doubt on the strength of his previous acquaintance with Michael Collins, but this did not appeal to him much. 'No luck with the work-hunt, except in the Free State, which is willing, but from which I shrink a little,' he told the sculptress Lady Scott, who had designed a war memorial using his brother Arnold as the central theme for the British Empire Exhibition at Wembley. 'In fact I've postponed it for a week, in the hope that the British Army (to which I've made advances) may offer me a shilling. Light-houses seem to be all booked.'[3]

Fortunately for Lawrence an old friend from his desert days had recently been appointed Adjutant-General to the Forces at the War Office. This was General Sir Philip Chetwode, later Field-Marshal Lord Chetwode, who had commanded the Desert Column of the Egyptian Expeditionary Force during the desert fighting and later the XX Corps which took part in the advance on Jerusalem. Lawrence appears to have made the initial approach through Colonel Alan Dawnay, who had also taken part with Lawrence in the desert campaign. Asked by Dawnay why he wished to rejoin the army in the ranks, Lawrence jokingly replied: 'Mind-suicide!'[4] The Tank Corps was suggested and Dawnay backed his application with Chetwode, who sounded out Colonel Sir Hugh Elles, the Commandant of the Tank Corps Centre near Wareham. On 17 February 1923, Chetwode wrote to Lawrence: 'I have received this morning a letter from Elles who is prepared to consider your proposal and sees no very great difficulty about it. . . . He asks you to write to him at H.Q. Tank Training Centre, Bovington Camp, Wool, Dorset, marked personal. . . . If you come to a satisfactory arrangement, would you call here at the War Office to see [the Director of Organisation] General Vesey . . . as there are certain matters which he would have to arrange with you before the matter is carried through.'[5]

One of these matters was the name under which he should enlist, since that in which he had been discharged from the R.A.F. was in the circumstances considered inappropriate, and in the event he joined the Tank Corps as Thomas Edward Shaw. He told Robert Graves that he took the name Shaw because it was the first one-syllabled one which turned up in the Army List he picked up in the waiting-room in the War Office when he went for his interview. 'The Adjutant-General's secretary told me I mustn't use my former name,' he added, 'so I consulted the *sortes*. Later a deed-poll was made out, so the change is legal.'[6] According to another version, on the authority of Bernard Shaw's secretary Blanche Patch, shortly before he enlisted he went to call on the Shaws and there encountered a clergyman who remarked how 'very like his uncle' Lawrence was. Whereupon Lawrence exclaimed: 'A good idea! That is the name I shall take.' According to Bernard Shaw himself, Lawrence was once taken for his son by a clergyman who met Lawrence at Thomas Hardy's house in Dorchester. He was also thought to be Hardy's son by his first wife. The rumour that subsequently gained widespread notoriety that Lawrence was Bernard Shaw's illegitimate son has already been mentioned. It was a rumour which, so far as is known, Lawrence did not go out of his way to contradict, just as more recently the late Brendan Bracken made no attempt to deny that he was Winston Churchill's son, although there was no truth in this any more than there was in the rumour about Lawrence and Bernard Shaw. It is also possible that Lawrence's choice of his new name may have been consciously or even unconsciously suggested by his increasing veneration of Bernard Shaw and his wife, his appreciation of the help he had received from them with *The Seven Pillars* and his negotiations for its publication.[7]

Thus Lawrence enlisted in the Royal Tank Corps on a seven years' engagement with a liability to serve a further five years on the reserve. He was given the number, rank and name of No. 7875698 Private T. E. Shaw, and was posted to A Company of the R.T.C. Depot at Bovington with effect from 12 March 1923.

Meanwhile Trenchard had not forgotten him, for he had developed a strong affection for his wayward friend in the ranks. 'I hope before you join up in your new Tank Corps you will come and see me, so that you can say if there is anything you want me to do or look after', the C.A.S. wrote on 19 March. 'Mind you, at all times, you have only to write to me and I will do anything I can to help you in any way you require.'[8]

'Sorry, your letter was too late,' Lawrence replied on 28 March from Bovington. 'I've been here nearly three weeks, and am (as a recruit) too completely possessed by the authorities to get leave or anything.' He went on:

> It's like and unlike Uxbridge – a camp on a great heath, little less beautiful than the park round Hillingdon House, but unlike it in that the country round is nearly desert. We can't run up to London every evening – nor can we spend much money.
>
> It's run like Uxbridge, but in small squads, of twenty each. The training period is eighteen weeks, half as long again as yours. It is less urgent too: the standard not less, but the approach to it gentle: nor is there the same tightness of control over our walking about, nor as many penalties or threats as in your place.
>
> You will be glad to hear that the camp is more lavishly run than yours. Fuel, food, bedding etc. all plentiful. Also baths and libraries.

The education section is crudely run by N.C.O.s, who at Uxbridge would be taught themselves: but then that's accounted for by the very different class of fellows.

It's astonishing that. The fellows at Uxbridge had joined the R.A.F. as a profession – or to continue in it at their trades. They talked of futures and jobs all day, and were excited about life. These fellows have joined up as a last resort, because they had failed, or were not qualified, for anything else, and they take no interest in the Army, and hope no more from it than food, and not too much work, and pocket money. There is no wish, as there was at Uxbridge, to do better than the standard required.

There is one improvement I see. At Uxbridge when I joined I went straight to fatigues, all day, and often till 8 p.m. and heavy work too. Here there is practically nothing of that. The duty men, not the recruits, do the fatigues, and the camp is so arranged, with civilian contracts, that the balance of military work is very light. I do not think the average here is more than half the working standard of Uxbridge.

The officers too are different. They speak and act with complete assurance, believing themselves better than ourselves: – and they are: whereas in the R.A.F. I had an uncomfortable feeling that we were better than the officers: and this feeling was strengthened, if not founded on the fact that the officers were treated by the men, off parade, as rather humorous things to have to show respect to. The officers played up to this impression by avoiding all contact with us.

The Army has the better of you, in this only.[9]

Although it was obvious to everyone in the camp that he was no ordinary recruit, being over the maximum age and under the minimum height for enlistment, and that he must have been attested for service under special authority from the War Office (which was true), Private Shaw was treated in the usual manner, undergoing medical and dental examinations for physical fitness, and taking the educational test. One of the subjects of this test was to write a short essay on: 'Your first impressions of Bovington Camp.' Private Shaw's essay was indeed short. It consisted of a single line, very much to the point: 'I arrived in the darkness and have not yet had time to look round.'[10]

The fact that Lawrence did not arrive at Bovington until it was dark may have been due to the fact that apparently by prior arrangement he met in Bournemouth a friend named John Bruce, a tough young Scot, who had also enlisted in the Tank Corps. At all events they were together when they entered the guard room at Bovington and they were both assigned to Hut 12. Bruce, whose acquaintance Lawrence had recently made in London, seems to have constituted himself Lawrence's bodyguard. That a curious relationship, which may have had sexual overtones but which was not homosexual, existed between them will be described later. Bruce has recalled the atmosphere in the hut a few days after their arrival.

On the Friday evening some of the inmates had more drink than they could hold. The filth that followed before and after lights out has been adequately described by Lawrence himself, and he was not exaggerating. They didn't know who Lawrence was, but it was obvious some of the chaps in the hut wanted to pal up with him, and this could have led to trouble. . . .

By this time we had everyone in the hut sized up. It was the bad ones I had to keep my eyes on, especially the drinkers, who were continually touching Lawrence for money . . . I came into the hut and heard a fellow giving Lawrence a mouthful of filth because he refused to give him a pound. I jumped him there and then and one hell of a fight took place. We both spent the night in the guard room; seven days each next day.[11]

Lawrence has described his feelings about Hut 12 in his letters of this period to Lionel Curtis, which David Garnett has described as: 'the most revealing letters of Lawrence's' that he knew.[12] 'It's a horrible life and the other fellows fit it,' he wrote in one of these letters. 'I said to one "They're the sort who instinctively throw stones at cats" . . . and he said "Why, what do you throw?" You perceive that I'm not yet in the picture: but I will be in time. Seven years of this will make me impossible for anyone to suggest for a responsible position, and that self-degradation is my aim.

I haven't the impulse and the conviction to fit what I know to be
my power of moulding men and things: and so I always regret
what I've created, when the leisure after creation lets me look back
and see that the idea was secondhand.'[13]

And again:

I can't write it, because in literature such things haven't ever
been, and can't be. To record the acts of Hut 12 would produce
a moral-medical case-book, not a work of art but a document.
It isn't the filth of it which hurts me, because you can't call
filthy the pursuit of a bitch by a dog, or the mating of birds in
springtime; and it's man's misfortune that he hasn't a mating
season, but spreads his emotions and excitements through the
year . . . but I lie in bed night after night with this cat-calling
carnality seething up and down the hut, fed by streams of fresh
matter from twenty lecherous mouths . . . and my mind aches
with the rawness of it, knowing that it will cease only when the
slow bugle calls for 'lights out' an hour or so hence . . . and the
waiting is so slow . . .

However the call comes always in the end, and suddenly at
last, like God's providence, a dewfall of peace upon the camp
. . . but surely the world would be more clean if we were dead
or mindless? We are all guilty alike, you know. You wouldn't
exist, I wouldn't exist, without this carnality. Everything with
flesh in its mixture is the achievement of a moment when the
lusty thought of Hut 12 has passed to action and conceived:
and isn't it true that the fault of birth rests somewhat on the
child? I believe it's we who led our parents on to bear us, and
it's our unborn children who make our flesh itch.

A filthy business all of it, and yet Hut 12 shows me the truth
behind Freud. Sex is an integer in all of us, and the nearer
nature we are, the more constantly, the more completely a
product of that integer. These fellows are the reality, and you
and I, the selves who used to meet in London and talk of
fleshless things, are only the outward wrappings of a core like
these fellows. They let light and air play always upon their
selves, and consequently have grown very lustily, but have at
the same time achieved health and strength in their growing.

Whereas our wrappings and bandages have stunted and deformed ourselves, and hardened them to an apparent insensitiveness ... but it's a callousness, a crippling, only to be yea-said by aesthetes who prefer clothes to bodies, surfaces to intentions.

These fellows have roots, which in us are rudimentary, or long cut off. Before I came I never visualised England except as an organism, an entity ... but these fellows are local, territorial. They all use dialects, and could be placed by their dialects, if necessary. However it isn't necessary, because each talks of his district, praises it, boasts of it, lives in the memory of it. We call each other 'Brum' or 'Coventry' or 'Cambridge', and the man who hasn't a 'place' is an outsider. They wrangle and fight over the virtues of their homes. Of solidarity, of a nation, of something ideal comprehending their familiar streets in itself – they haven't a notion.[14]

'The R.A.F. was foul-mouthed, and the cleanest little mob of fellows,' he wrote in another letter to Curtis. 'These are foul-mouthed, and behind their mouths is a pervading animality of spirit, whose unmixed bestiality frightens me and hurts me. There is no criticism, indeed it's taken for granted as natural, that you should job a woman's body, or hire out yourself, or abuse yourself in any way. I cried out against it, partly in self-pity because I've condemned myself to grow like them, and partly in premonition of failure, for my masochism remains and will remain, only moral. . . .'

This sort of thing must be madness and sometimes I wonder how far mad I am, and if a madhouse would not be my next (and merciful) stage. Merciful compared with this place, which hurts me, body and soul. It's terrible to hold myself voluntarily here: and yet I want to stay here till it no longer hurts me: till the burnt child no longer feels the fire.[15]

'It will be a puzzle for my biographer (if I have one of those unprofitable things) to reconcile my joy in the R.A.F. with my disgust with the Army,' he wrote to Hogarth, his old mentor in archaeology. 'The R.A.F. is utterly unlike this place: the men are so different, and their hopes and minds and talk. They weren't happy: it used to be said at Farnborough that I was the only happy man there . . . but they were essentially decent: and the going has been rather a jerk to me. I feel queerly homesick whenever I see a blue uniform in the street.'[16]

2

There is no doubt that Lawrence was suffering from great nervous strain at this time. Nor was he at all happy during the first two or three months of his service with the Tank Corps. According to Alec Dixon, a corporal, formerly a tax clerk in private life, who became friendly with Lawrence at Bovington and was drawn to him by a common interest in literature and art, he disliked the routine of the depot with its seemingly endless drills and guard duties which he had not expected to find in a mechanised unit. 'Nevertheless he was a good soldier, although sorely tried at times by those whose delight it was to make life miserable for any recruit who showed more than animal intelligence.' On one occasion Dixon has recalled that he went to his hut after the last parade of the day and found Lawrence in bed.

> He looked haggard and seemed very depressed. When I sat down he apologized for his state and said he had a touch of fever. He explained, à propos of nothing, that his visit to the Hejaz in 1921 had been almost too much for him and that the mental strain to which he had been subjected during the negotiations had been worse than anything he had known during the [desert] campaign. He went on to discuss politicians, the War Office and, finally, the Army. He spoke bitterly of 'the stiff professional soldiers who expect their men to be accomplished housemaids'. Then he became critical of the Tank Corps, saying that it was run by a gang of superannuated infantrymen who overruled those who were trying to build up an efficient service. Tanks, as weapons of war, amused him; he thought them 'museum pieces' and a burden on the taxpayer.

He had a weakness for armoured cars, and thought well of the Rolls-Royce then in general use.

He also had a weakness for motor-bicycles, a weakness which was eventually to prove fatal to him. He favoured the Brough make and indeed the manufacturer George Brough was to design eight Brough Superiors for him over the years, although the last was destined never to be delivered. Dixon first met Lawrence outside a garage where he had stopped to fill up with petrol and suggested that the Brough must be a difficult machine in slow traffic. 'Yes,' said Lawrence, grinning; 'a wild beast! But it gives me an opportunity to see Dorset in my spare time.'

Shortly afterwards in an off-duty period he took Dixon to Salisbury in the side-car which he also had as an attachment to the vehicle. It was on this occasion that Dixon, who was unaware of Private Shaw's identity, brought up the subject of Lawrence of Arabia and asked his companion whether he thought that Lawrence's enlisting as an aircraftman was some kind of 'stunt' on the part of the Air Ministry to encourage recruiting. This idea struck Lawrence as amusing. However, he remarked that he did not think it could have been that kind of stunt. Then after a brief pause, in which he looked Dixon straight in the eye, he said: 'That was a difficult question. You see ... I *am* Lawrence!'[17]

Private Shaw also found relief from his nervous tensions by driving his 'bike' at very fast speeds. The maximum figure on the speedometer was 100 miles an hour, but Lawrence once broke the instrument by exceeding this figure. On another occasion, just outside the camp, he ran over a broken glass bottle at speed, burst the front tyre, ran up a bank and turned over. 'Damage to self nil: to bike somewhat,' he told Hogarth. 'There goes my power of breaking bounds.'[18]

He was always willing to take other men for rides on his machine. Once he took one riding pillion to Corfe Castle, where he stopped to make some purchases in a shop. While he was there, two military policemen appeared and arrested his companion for being improperly dressed, namely, not carrying a walking-out cane. With great presence of mind, the delinquent shouted out, 'Sir, sir, I'm being arrested!' Lawrence, who was wearing dun-

garees, immediately appeared from the shop and said to one of
the military police: 'Oh, it's all right, Corporal, he's with me.'
The two policemen thereupon saluted smartly and walked away.[19]

He found relief too at this time in a more questionable manner,
with the co-operation of his friend John Bruce, whom he is said
to have first met early in 1922 while he was still working in the
Colonial Office. This meeting allegedly took place in the Mayfair
flat of a man called Murray, who was a friend of Bruce's family
doctor in Aberdeen and was trying to get Bruce, then a youth of
nineteen, fixed up in a job. Lawrence is supposed to have paid him
a small weekly retainer of £3 to do odd jobs for him when called
upon, and in fact did so even when Bruce went home to Aberdeen. In July 1922, shortly before he enlisted in the R.A.F.,
Lawrence sent for Bruce and told him that an uncle whom he
called 'The Old Man' but never referred to by name was annoyed
at his throwing up a good job in the Colonial Office and refused
to help him financially unless he allowed his affairs to be controlled
by 'The Old Man' and that he would be subject to discipline
including corporal punishment. According to Bruce, his (Bruce's)
initial reaction was to tell Lawrence that the whole thing was
ridiculous and that he should tell 'The Old Man' to go to hell.
'Too late now,' Lawrence is said to have replied. 'I've agreed and
it must be done . . . I had to agree with him or he would expose
the circumstances of my birth. I have my mother to consider and
she comes first whatever happens to me.'

After Lawrence's basic training at Bovington had been completed, he was assigned a relatively easy job, in charge of the
Quartermaster's stores, and here was quickly trusted by the
Quartermaster to work without supervision. One day, according
to Bruce, Lawrence asked him to come and see him in the stores.

He was nervous and upset. He said he had heard from The
Old Man and that he was in disgrace. He had failed to attend
church parades and had been a disappointment in many
ways.

Lawrence said The Old Man had decided he must be
punished, and the sentence was to be twelve strokes of the
birch. He handed me an unsigned, typed letter which he said
was from The Old Man. It was on blue paper. It said that a

birch had been despatched to a nearby railway station and I was to administer the punishment with it. I would be paid for it. Afterwards I was to report in writing if I had done so, and I was to describe Lawrence's demeanour and behaviour under punishment. I said I wanted nothing to do with it, but Lawrence said it would have to be done, 'otherwise The Old Man will publish my ancestry to the world'. In the end I said I would be a willing party only because Lawrence was a willing party.[20]

Consequently Lawrence was beaten by Bruce, and these birching rituals were to be continued from time to time over the next dozen years. Shortly after Lawrence's death in 1935, according to Bruce, he (Bruce) met Charlotte Shaw, who seems to have known about these flagellations. The meeting took place in a solicitor's office. At all events she is supposed to have told Bruce that Lawrence's relations and personal friends were 'very concerned and they were endeavouring to get people to give an undertaking not to publish confidential matters concerning Lawrence'. She is supposed to have asked Bruce if it was his intention to publish his story and if this were the case would he not consider Lawrence's mother? 'I said that publishing my story had never entered my head,' Bruce states he replied; 'and if it was his mother they were all concerned about, then I would give my word of honour that I would publish nothing while she was alive.'

Bruce kept his word. However, some years after Mrs Lawrence's death he sold his story to the London *Sunday Times*, where a series of articles based upon it appeared, written by Philip Knightley and Colin Simpson, and subsequently expanded into a book entitled *The Secret Lives of Lawrence of Arabia*. Although Mrs Lawrence was dead, her youngest son Professor Arnold Lawrence was very much alive, and in a letter to *The Times* which appeared shortly after the publication of *The Secret Lives* he pointed out several inconsistencies in Bruce's story, and he expressed the belief that with one conspicuous exception 'Bruce's narratives should be regarded with considerably greater caution than the authors of the recent book suggest'. Thus, he went on, 'I accept only one significant ingredient in Bruce's story, the basic fact that my brother, while in a state of extreme physical and mental distress, invented the myth of an implacable uncle's demands and induced Bruce to execute them.'[21]

And with that statement it is perhaps as well to let the matter rest. 'Do you think there have been many lay monks of my persuasion?' Lawrence asked Lionel Curtis in what he described as 'a nice neurotic letter!'[22] Penitential flagellation was frequently practised in the Middle Ages both by monks and nuns on themselves and each other. In Lawrence's case the beatings may well be regarded as a penance rather than a form of sexual deviance. In this context it should not be forgotten that the righteous Mr William Gladstone, four times Liberal Prime Minister of Britain, on the evidence of his diaries often scourged himself, particularly after visiting prostitutes in their lodgings for the purpose of reclaiming them, encounters which aroused lustful desires in him which he felt deserved to be expiated by self-inflicted physical punishment.

3

In the autumn of 1923, shortly after finishing his basic training in the Tank Corps and settling into his job in the Quartermaster's stores at Bovington, Lawrence found a derelict cottage on the slopes of Clouds Hill, about a mile and a half across the heath – the Egdon Heath of Thomas Hardy's Wessex stories. He told Robert Graves that it was the cottage where Eustacia Vye lived with her father the Captain in Hardy's novel, *The Return of the Native*, where it is called 'Mistover Knap'.[23] It was built in 1808 and Lawrence was able to rent it for the modest sum of 2s 6d a week from a distant cousin on his father's side, who lived nearby. 'Quaint how these people are settled all about here,' he wrote to his mother at this time. 'The daughter of the rector of South Hill parish it was who knew all about us.'[24] It had been derelict for years and needed a lot of attention in the way of repairs, which Lawrence put in hand. 'This I'm fitting up with the hope of having a warm solitary place to hide in sometimes on winter evenings. This district is unusually desolate (of good company) and I covet the idea of being sometimes by myself near the fire.'[25] He also needed a room in which to work on revising and re-writing the text of *The Seven Pillars of Wisdom*, which was to appear two years later in the de-luxe subscribers' edition and in which the author was to give full rein to his lavish idea on typography and illustrations.* Two Greek words, which Lawrence inscribed over the front door, he took from a tale by Herodotus expressing indifference to worldly advancement. He freely translated them as 'Why worry?' As he put it to the wife of the artist Eric Kennington: 'It means that nothing in Clouds Hill is to be a care upon its habitant.'[26]

'A tiny brick cottage, with old tiled roof, very high pitched,' was how he described Clouds Hill to Hogarth. 'It stands in a thicket of laurel and rhododendron, with oak trees and a huge ilex stretching arms over its roof. Damp? Yes; for the cottage dates from pre-damp-course days, and the trees drip great raindrops on the roof after each storm. They patter across the tiles like the first notes of the [Beethoven] Fifth Symphony. Only two rooms, the upstairs of the cottage, are habitable. They have three-foot walls, and nine-foot roofs, all open. A great deal of oak and chestnut on show: but my repairs to the roof had to be in deal, which we creosoted to bring it to an ancient colour. My gold Meccan dagger paid the repair bill, and left something over for furniture.'[27]

'I don't sleep here,' he told Chambers, who had served with him at Farnborough and was now stationed at Duxford; 'but come out 4.30 p.m. till 9 p.m. nearly every evening, and dream or write or read by the fire, or play Beethoven and Mozart to myself on the box. Sometimes one or two Tank Corps slaves arrive and listen with me ... but few of them care for abstract things.'[28] Corporal Dixon has recalled how he spent every weekend and two or three evenings a week there with Lawrence and what 'a very happy time' it was for him.

Two or three other men – sometimes more – of widely differing types were among the regular visitors to Clouds Hill in

---

* He consulted Bernard Shaw and his wife throughout, frequently accepting their criticisms and taking their advice. It was at Bernard Shaw's suggestion that Lawrence's original introductory chapter was omitted from the published edition. It eventually appeared in Lawrence's posthumously published volume of miscellaneous writings, *Oriental Assemblies* (1939), edited by his brother A. W. Lawrence.

those days. T.E. was an expert at 'mixed grills' where men were concerned.

He presided over the company, settling arguments, patiently answering all manner of questions, feeding the gramophone, making tea, stoking the fire and, by some magic of his own, managing without effort to keep everyone in good humour. There were many picnic meals (stuffed olives, salted almonds and Heinz baked beans were regular features) washed down with T.E.'s own blend of China tea. Some of us used chairs, others the floor, while T.E. always ate standing by the end of the wide oak mantelshelf which had been fitted at a height convenient for him.

Our discussions were many and various and T.E. invariably had the last decisive word. One day, when we were talking of Communism, T.E. shocked the troops by remarking, casually: 'When history comes to be written, Lenin will probably take his place as the greatest man of our time.' To a cavalryman who was bemoaning the passing of horses from the Army, T.E. pointed out that such animals were out of date – 'their acceleration is bad,' he explained solemnly. Once the talk came round to women, and someone sought T.E.'s opinion. 'Ah!' he said with a grin, 'women are like horses: they need a large field.'[29]

Later, when the novelist E. M. Forster came down for a week-end, Dixon and the others were all 'impressed' to spring-clean the cottage and chop firewood. In the midst of their hustle, Lawrence sat at a table in the upstairs room fiddling with a primitive radio set. At first Dixon said nothing, although he knew that Lawrence was rather contemptuous of the 'wireless'. But when he put up an aerial and installed the set on a corner table, Dixon's curiosity got the better of him and he asked: 'What's the idea of the wireless, T.E.?' Lawrence looked round with a grin and said: 'It's for Forster . . . it occurred to me that he might like to hear Big Ben strike while he is shut out of the world down here.'[30]

In 1938, Professor A. W. Lawrence presented Clouds Hill and its contents to the National Trust as a memorial to his brother. To mark the occasion E. M. Forster broadcast a talk in which he described the place, its owner (for Lawrence later bought the cottage), and its visitors, as he remembered them.

In those days the two bottom rooms were full of firewood and lumber. We lived upstairs, and the sitting room there looks now much as it did then, though the gramophone and the books have gone, and the fender with its bent ironwork has been remodelled.* It was, and it is, a brownish room – wooden beams and ceiling, leather-covered settee. Here we talked, played Beethoven's symphonies, ate and drank. We drank water only or tea – no alcohol ever entered Clouds Hill . . . and we ate – this sounds less romantic – out of tins. T.E. always laid in a stock of tinned dainties for his guests. There were no fixed hours for meals and no one sat down. If you felt hungry, you opened a tin and drifted about with it . . . T.E. slept in camp, coming out when he could during the day, as did the rest of the troops. It was fine being alone in Clouds Hill at night: so silent . . .

I don't know whether I'm at all conveying in these trivial remarks the atmosphere of the place – the happy casualness of it, and the feeling that no one particularly owned it. T.E. had the power of distributing the sense of possession among all the friends who came there. When Thomas Hardy turned up, for instance, as he did one sunny afternoon, he seemed to come on a visit to us all, and not specially to see his host. Thomas Hardy and Mrs Hardy came up the narrow stairway into the little brown room and there they were – the guests of us all. To think of Clouds Hill as T.E.'s home is to get the wrong idea of it. It wasn't his home, it was rather his pied-à-terre, the place where his feet touched the earth for a moment, and found rest.[31]

---

* The EMI gramophone has been restored to the upstairs room, now known as the Music Room. The books, or the majority of them, are now preserved in the principal downstairs room, the Book Room, which also contains a large leather-covered divan with a cushion designed by Lawrence and his sleeping-bag marked *Meum*. A list of the books has been published in *T. E. Lawrence By His Friends*, edited by A. W. Lawrence (1937), pp. 476–510.

Before leaving London for Bovington, Lawrence had asked Robert Graves for an introduction to Dorchester's most distinguished literary inhabitant. 'We are near Dorchester and I run about Dorset on wheels (when they take their eyes off us) . . . do you think old Hardy would let me look at him? He's a proper poet and a fair novelist, in my judgement, and it would give me a feeling of another milestone passed if I might meet him. Yet to blow in upon him in khaki would not be an introduction. You know the old thing, don't you? What are my hopes?'[32]

Graves immediately wrote to Hardy who replied that Lawrence would be very welcome at his house, Max Gate. Graves felt that the two would get on well together, which they did. After he had been at the camp for less than three weeks, Lawrence wrote to Eric Kennington, who did a portrait of Lawrence for *The Seven Pillars*: 'I saw Hardy yesterday: paid for seeing him too, for it meant cutting a parade! However it was worth it, and I'm going down again, if ever he asks me. His weakness in character-drawing is a reflection of himself. A very sensitive little man: faded now: with hope yet that mankind will give up warfare. He felt incredibly old to me.'[33] (He was 83.) Lawrence returned to Max Gate a week later, and frequently thereafter, while the Hardys visited him at Clouds Hill. 'Dear Mrs Hardy,' he wrote in reply to an invitation to tea to meet Walter de la Mare: 'I'm afraid I'll come on Saturday next at tea-time! De la Mare is known to me only by his books – but he should be delightful, if he lives up to them: and most good people are better than their books. It sounds greedy always to come when you ask me: but your house is so wonderfully unlike this noisy room that it is difficult to resist, even for its own sake: and then there is Mr Hardy, though you mustn't tell him so, for the thrill is too one-sided. He has seen so much of human-kind that he must be very tired of them: whereas for me he's Hardy, and I'd go a long way even to see the place where he had lived, let alone him living in it.'[34]

On another occasion Lawrence invented an excuse to come over again. He had copies of the thin paper editions of Hardy's *Poems* and *The Dynasts* and he wondered whether the author would inscribe them for him if he turned up with them. 'I know it's a vulgar desire; but I live in vulgar company: and they would be very precious possessions.'[35] The sage of Max Gate obligingly inscribed the latter volume: 'Colonel Lawrence from Thomas Hardy', underneath which the inscription's recipient wrote characteristically on his return to Bovington: 'To T. E. Shaw for his comfort in camp from Lawrence.'[36]

To Robert Graves, who had given him the original introduction, he conveyed his impressions in detail.

Hardy is so pale, so quiet, so refined into an essence: and camp is such a hurly-burly. When I come back I feel as if I'd woken up from a sleep: not an exciting sleep, but a restful one. There is an unbelievable dignity and ripeness about Hardy: he is waiting so tranquilly for death, without a desire or ambition left in his spirit, as far as I can feel it: and yet he entertains so many illusions, and hopes for the world, things which I, in my disillusioned middle-age, feel to be illusory. They used to call this man a pessimist. While really he is full of fancy expectations.

Then he is so far-away. Napoleon is a real man to him, and the country of Dorsetshire echoes that name everywhere in Hardy's ears. He lives in his period, and thinks of it as the great war: whereas to me that nightmare through the fringe of which I passed has dwarfed all memories of other wars, so that they seem trivial, half-amusing incidents. . . .

For the ticket which gained me access to T.H. I'm grateful to you – probably will be grateful always. Max Gate is a place apart: and I feel it all the more poignantly for the contrast of life in this squalid camp. It is strange to pass from the noise and thoughtlessness of sergeants' company into a peace so secure that in it not even Mrs Hardy's tea-cups rattle on the tray: and from a barrack of hollow senseless bustle to the cheerful calm of T.H. thinking aloud about life to two or three of us. If I were in his place I would never wish to die: or even to wish other men dead. The peace which passeth all understanding; – but it can be felt, and is nearly unbearable. How envious such an old age is.

However, here is enough of trying to write about something which is so precious that I grudge writing about it. T.H. is an experience that a man must keep to himself.[37]

On 23 May 1923, the day after Baldwin had become Prime Minister for the first time, Bernard Shaw addressed a memorandum to him expressing considerable concern at Lawrence's poverty, showing it first to Hogarth for his comments and amendments. It ran in part:

> The fact remains that he [Lawrence] is serving as a private soldier for his daily bread: and however much his extraordinary character may account for this, it strikes all who know about it as a scandal that should be put an end to by some means. They feel that the private soldier business is a shocking tomfoolery and are amazed to find that Lawrence is not in a position of a pensioned commanding officer in dignified private circumstances.[38]

The Prime Minister took no action in the matter, although Shaw continued to press him from time to time. It was not until Baldwin's defeat at the General Election in the autumn that Lawrence learned of Bernard Shaw's efforts on his behalf. 'It seems I'm to regret the fall of Mr Baldwin: and to thank you very much for the attempt at a pension,' Lawrence wrote to Shaw on 20 December 1923. 'Hogarth gave me no idea of it. Why did you think I wouldn't take it? It's earned money which sticks in the throat: – that a man should come down to working for such stuff. . . .'

> You suggest that I'm not genuine in the ranks: but I am: just as good, now, as the others. Not very good, I'm afraid (I will be if I can) since I'm slow, having to learn to do all the daily trifles which others used to do for me. If it wasn't that I've been somebody or something else the authorities would have a fair opinion of what I am.[39]

Armistice Day in 1923 fell on a Sunday, and Trenchard, who was due to represent the Air Force at the Cenotaph ceremony in Whitehall, thought he would give a dinner at his club in the evening, and he wrote to Lawrence at Bovington, inviting him to join the party. Lawrence replied:

I'd like to very much: but there are two difficulties already in my view: –
(a) It is Armistice day, and I do not know if leave will be given.
(b) I have a decent suit, but no dress clothes at all.
The leave I will ask for, but till Thursday next (Nov. 8) there will be no answer to the application. The clothes are beyond my power to provide: and I fear that Lady Trenchard might not approve a lounge suit at dinner. It depends on the other company probably. Please ask her before you reply. . . .
The Army and Navy Club at six or six-thirty would suit me excellently, and I hope it may come off. Undiluted Tank Corps is a disease . . . [40]

However, the dinner did come off, since he was told that it would be in order for him to wear his private's uniform. Asked by one of the other guests how he managed to obtain such a well fitting suit of khaki, he replied that it was to the fact that he worked in the Quartermaster's stores.[41] Three days later, on his return to camp he wrote to Hogarth: 'Saw Trenchard on Sunday. He said something about a month's leave for me. I said no, since returning here would be unpleasant after so long a holiday. The Army does not improve upon longer knowledge.'[42]
Trenchard thought that Lawrence should have some more leave and he sent Lawrence a telegram inviting him to meet him at the Air Ministry on a certain day. It so happened that Private Shaw had been ordered to be confined to barracks for some contravention of military regulations, possibly for missing parade by going to see Thomas Hardy. In the event he replied: 'Unable to comply with request as am a defaulter.' Trenchard was furious and after having a word with Chetwode at the War Office the military authorities at Bovington were instructed to arrange for him to be sent on leave without delay.[43]
'The Adjutant-General has arranged your leave most carefully,' Trenchard wrote to him early in December. 'At the same time, you must not be a defaulter or you will be kicked out. Don't be an ass! If you start being a defaulter it will be impossible for me to help you or for you to help yourself.' The C.A.S. ended his

letter on a milder note. 'I wish I could see you again and have a talk with you. Do not forget that I am always ready and anxious to help you. Best of luck. . . . Come to the Air Ministry midday on Monday next – before you return to Wool.'[44]

Lawrence spent Christmas alone in the cottage, having excused himself to the Hardys who had invited him to celebrate the festival with them. ('I refused Max Gate. It's not good to be happy too often.') Instead he did 'rations and coalyard' to set the other men 'free for their orgy. . . . Xmas means something to them. My pernickety mind discovers an incompatability between their joint professions of Soldier and Christian.' Otherwise it was 'a quiet time of simply thinking' for Lawrence, as he told R. M. Guy, one of the friends he had made at Farnborough. 'It seems that I've climbed down very far from two years ago: and a little from a year ago. I was in the guard room at Farnborough that night, and the next day the newspapers blew up and destroyed my peace. So it's a bad anniversary for me.'[45]

The Shaws were spending their Christmas in a hotel at Bournemouth, and they all met at Max Gate with the Hardys for lunch on the last day but one of the year. 'Will you come to Clouds Hill?' Lawrence had written to G.B.S. 'I'd like to have you, though it's little worthy of your coming . . . and I'm afraid Mrs Shaw will find it unclean.'[46] However, they did come, as Shaw was later to recall in connection with Lawrence's work on *The Seven Pillars*, which both the Shaws and the Hardys had read and praised.

As a tanker-ranker soldier living humbly with his comrades (though I must confess that when they invited me to tea he looked very like Colonel Lawrence with several aides-de-camp) he directed the manufacture of the *Seven Pillars* even to ordering a different binding for every copy, so that there might be no 'first edition' in the collector's sense, meanwhile refusing any position in which he would have to give an order, and making me wonder whether he ever did anything else.[47]

4

Whatever Mr Baldwin may have felt about Lawrence's rejoining the R.A.F., the Minister Sir Samuel Hoare had been implacably opposed to the idea. However, with the Conservative defeat at the polls and Baldwin's resignation, when Parliament met in January 1924, the first Labour Government led by Ramsay MacDonald took office. The new Air Minister was a particular friend of the Prime Minister's, Brigadier-General Christopher Thomson, a former sapper officer and military attaché in Rumania, who had joined the Labour Party after the war and whom MacDonald now raised to the peerage as Lord Thomson of Cardington, since he had failed to get elected to the House of Commons. Lawrence had little better hopes of finding Thomson any more sympathetic, since they had had a row at the Peace Conference and both men now had little liking for each other. Nevertheless, this did not deter him from trying again with Trenchard. At all events, when his first year in the Tank Corps was nearly up he saw Trenchard, and the following day he addressed a strong plea to the C.A.S. for his position to be reconsidered, one hitherto unpublished, like most of Lawrence's other letters to Trenchard in this book.[48]

1.3.24

Dear Sir Hugh,

Forgive me this letter. I'm ashamed of it already, since I know that you sacked me for good, and it's perverse of me not to take it so. Yet the hope of getting back into the R.A.F. is the main reason of my staying in the Army. I feel eligible, there, for transfer or re-enlistment. You once took over some Tank Corps fellows: and lately the change of Ministry heartened me: and I've served exactly a year in the Army now, and been found amenable to discipline. Don't say that the Army can more easily digest an oddity than can the R.A.F. It isn't true. The Air has twice the vitality – with good reason.

Whenever I get one of your letters I open it excitedly to see if your mind has changed. It seems to me so plain that the presence in the ranks of a man as keen on the air as myself must be generally beneficial. Yesterday however you told me plainly, for the first time, that it was my gaiety which got me into trouble at Farnborough. I didn't know of it, and doubt it yet. Guilfoyle's neurasthenia made him imagine things. He didn't amuse me – rather he made me sick and sorry. I don't like saying so (since part of the game is to take what happens in C.O.s) but I fancy he injured me out of deliberate fear. It wouldn't happen again, for not one in a hundred of your Squadron-Leaders is a nerve-wreck.

However on the whole I was happy at Farnborough, and as perhaps I did, unawares, walk about smiling. Surely not a great fault, and one easily put right. The superiors have lots of power over the ranks, in every service, including yours, and Guilfoyle could have made me cry (if he'd wished) by some sentence less than indefinite years in the Army. I don't mind the present discomfort (as long as I can hope to reach the R.A.F. at the end): but the filth is a pity, for no fellow can live so long in it and keep quite clean. I feel I'm not worth as much to your people as I was a year ago . . . but as I said before, I'm still worth having. It was a stimulant to the other A.C.s to have a man, relatively, so experienced as me, content among them: and I liked them, which shows that it was all right. I still hear from many of them.

It's all difficult to write. If you'd been a stranger I could have persuaded you: but my liking for your Force and its maker make it impossible for me to plead properly. Do think of the many hiding-holes there are (India, Egypt and Mespot and seaplane-ships) before you tear this up!

Yours sincerely,
TEL.

Trenchard passed this letter with Lawrence's personal files to Air Vice-Marshal Philip Game, who had succeeded Swann as Air Member for Personnel. Game, later to become like Trenchard Commissioner of Metropolitan Police, minuted on one file that he saw no objection to Lawrence's return to the Service and suggested that: 'He should be sent to a good squadron commander, abroad for preference, who should be informed of Lawrence's identity.'[49] Trenchard took the matter up with the new Secretary of State, but the minister would not have Lawrence back in the ranks at any price. The truth was that Lawrence, as he himself wryly observed at the time, was not popular with the politicians of whatever party. 'The Labourites think I am an Imperial spy, and the diehards thought I was a Bolshie and Lord Thomson says I am a self-advertising mountebank.' Trenchard himself was as disappointed as Lawrence, and he looked around for another possible opening in the Service for him, if Lawrence would not insist on rejoining as an aircraftman. A few weeks later an opportunity presented itself which the C.A.S. thought might appeal to Lawrence's literary skills. This was to complete the official war history of the air force, *The War in the Air*, the first volume of which had been written by Sir Walter Raleigh, Merton Professor of English History at Oxford.

Having finished the first volume, a scholarly and most readable book, in which he described the origins of British aviation and the early days of the Royal Flying Corps – Lawrence had a copy of this work amongst his books at Uxbridge which he used to lend to any airman who was interested in the subject – Raleigh had set out for the Middle East in the spring of 1922 to collect material for the second volume. Unfortunately he contracted typhoid in Iraq and died a few weeks after his return to England. First, Hogarth 'did a little and then threw it up'. Next, Trenchard offered the job to Maurice Baring, who had written an excellent account of his experiences at R.F.C. headquarters during the war when he was Trenchard's personal assistant. But Baring turned down the offer because he did not feel capable of dealing with the vast mass of documentation involved in the preparation of an official history. After several other names had been considered, including that of Hilaire Belloc, and for various reasons rejected as unsuitable, Trenchard turned to Lawrence.[50]

On 9 May 1924 Lawrence wrote to his mother from Bovington.

Lord Trenchard sent for me the other day, hoping to hear something about my getting back to the R.A.F. But all that he wanted me for was to offer me the writing of the R.A.F. history of the war ... the thing of which Professor Raleigh did one volume, and whose continuation Mr Hogarth lately laid down. Of course it's a very difficult thing to do, and D.G.H. has been a sick man lately. The diabetes opened the way to all sorts of minor ailments, so that he is now feeling fully his age: indeed I suspect he will never be quite right again: and in the circumstances he was wise to give up so exacting a job. Of course it is out of the question that I should take it over.[51]

When Trenchard put the idea to him, Lawrence had asked for a night to think it over, and he then went off to see his namesake's play *Saint Joan*, which was running at the New Theatre. (G.B.S. later presented him with a published copy of the play inscribed to 'Private Shaw from Public Shaw'.)

'I took thought for a night and then declined,' Lawrence told Hogarth on the same day as he wrote to his mother. But his reasons for doing so were different from Baring's.

The job is a hazardous one (T. wants a 'literary' history, the C.I.D. a 'technical'); attractive, very, to me by reason of its subject. The terms (three years) compare unfavourably with the six which the Army offers: and the responsibility is one which I'd regret as soon as I had shouldered it. Also it's no use, having gone through the grind of climbing down to crowd-level, at once to give it up for three years decent living. It would leave me older, less strung up to make another effort at poor living. If I can complete my seven years in the Army I should be able to slip quietly into a job of some sort at the end. There is a garage near here which might take me on.

I hope you are fit again: much of the illness which you have had lately I put down to the plague of that ungrateful book. You must feel like a reprieved prisoner.

Here at Bovington I seem to sit still: so still that often I fancy the slow passing of time about me can be *heard*. Isn't it rare for a person, who has been as unsparing as myself, to be purged quite suddenly of all desire? Even the longing or regret for the R.A.F. sleeps now, except when I come suddenly at a turn in the road, on its uniform. *That* was another bar to the job:

because I'd have had to visit aerodromes, and each time the homesickness would have made itself felt afresh.[52]

Lawrence then wrote to Robert Graves in case he might be interested in taking it on. 'It's a three year job, worth £600–£800 a year. See Hogarth if you are tempted. He would tell you how to put in for it. My aim is to prevent, at all costs, its becoming an "official" history: and the Air Ministry are on the same side.'[53] But Graves likewise turned it down. The job eventually went to Raleigh's principal research assistant, Mr H. A. Jones, an industrious and conscientious civil servant, who completed the work in five more volumes over the next dozen years, making it just the kind of 'official' work which Lawrence feared in contrast to Raleigh's admirable initial 'literary' volume.

Much of Lawrence's spare time in the year 1924 was spent in his cottage working on his own literary interests. He translated a short work by the French writer Adrien Le Corbeau for Cape which was published as *The Forest Giant* under the name J. H. Ross. He also set about collecting subscriptions for the privately printed edition of *The Seven Pillars of Wisdom* limited to 100 copies. There were to be fifty illustrations and he provisionally estimated the cost of block-making and printing at about £3000. Hence he asked subscribers in the circular letter which he sent out that they should pay thirty guineas (£31·50) a copy. 'Type, paper, and illustrations will be decent of their kinds (I hope!) and the complete work, as sent to subscribers, will not be re-issued in my lifetime.' Certain people who were partners with him in the Arab Revolt would receive copies of the text at his expense with such illustrations as immediately concerned them: hence their copies would not be complete and he would only give them to such of those as he thought fit. The work would be copyrighted in Britain and the United States, but no copies would go to libraries, if he could prevent it. 'I'm bound to say that I think the book is exceedingly dear, an unjustifiable purchase either as investment for resale, or as a thing for reading: and I hope no one will decide to get it unless he is in the position to (mis)spend thirty guineas without a regret.'[54]

The initial response was encouraging. 'Subscribers roll in for my book, which lately has been praised by H. G. Wells!' he told Lionel Curtis in August. But the costs of production soon considerably exceeded Lawrence's estimate, and these were eventually met by an overdraft provided by Lawrence's banker friend R. V. Buxton, secured upon the royalties of *Revolt in the Desert*, the abridged version which it had been arranged should be published by Cape.

Meanwhile life in the camp grew progressively worse for Lawrence, since Bruce was no longer there to act as bodyguard. 'My face was damaged and my lately broken rib rebroken (I think) by four drunks in the hut', he wrote on 27 July 1924 to Alan Dawnay, who had originally been instrumental in getting him into the Tank Corps. 'Night terrors after proof-correcting had revived war memories. I kept the barrack room awake five nights running. They gave me a sort of barrack court-martial to keep me quiet. This was humiliating and rather painful.'[55]

He felt happier next month after he had escaped to Clouds Hill. 'Yesterday was an occasion', he wrote to Charlotte Shaw on 17 August. 'I celebrated a birthday. By my pay-book (full of queer statements about me) it was my twentieth. By my attestation it was my thirtieth. By truth it must have been my thirty-sixth ... The day justified itself splendidly. Salmond, an Air Marshal ... took me off to dinner with his wife and brother ... it's rich to eat at a table whose top does not physically remind you of its past meals.'[56] No doubt Lawrence took the opportunity of impressing upon both the Salmond brothers, particularly the Air Marshal, Sir John Salmond, who had just returned from Iraq where he had commanded the R.A.F. for two years and was temporarily attached to Trenchard's staff at Adastral House, his great desire to get back to the service.

[4]

Cranwell

Towards the end of his second year in the Tank Corps, Lawrence addressed a final appeal to Trenchard.[1]

> Clouds Hill
> Moreton
> Dorset
> 6.11.25

Dear Sir Hugh

February is 'supplication' month . . . so for the third time of asking – Have I no chance of re-enlistment in the R.A.F., or transfer? It remains my only hope and ambition, dreamed of every week, nearly every day. If I bother you only yearly it's because I hate pestering you on a private affair.

Last year I said all I could in my favour, and have no eloquence left. My history hasn't changed. Clean conduct sheet since then, which (in a depot) shows that I have been lucky as well as decent. I've kept my job as storeman in the recruits' clothing store, except for intervals of clerking (for the Q.M.), a Rolls-Royce Armoured Car Course, and a month in Company stores. Official character (from the Q.M. who is good to me) 'Exceptionally intelligent, very reliable, and works well.' A descending scale, you will note: but I so loathe the Army that I might not work at all. Even in better days I was not laborious. 'Intelligent' was because I got 93% on my Rolls course: the highest marks ever given. 'Reliable' because when a company stores went wrong they borrowed me to enquire, check, make new ledgers, and wangle deficiencies.

I've lived carefully, and am in clean trim, mind and body. No more value, as an Aircraft Hand, than I was. Last Sunday I rode to Yorkshire and back, averaging 44 m.p.h. just for fun.

The war-worry and middle-east are finished: and I'd be peaceful and moderately happy if I wasn't always seeing the R.A.F. just out of reach.

Your objections to me lay on the point of discipline. Yet I pass [paper torn] all right and the R.T.C. being weekly, can less afford exceptions than the R.A.F. [They] don't say that I fit in, exactly: – any more than I did at Uxbridge or in Arabia or at All Souls or in any Officers' Mess. But I'm not the only misfit one meets (and is usually sorry for). There is nothing portentious about my small self. If I had the greatness you alone see in me would I write you begging letters year after year? It's true I wasn't brought up as a mechanic; but I've learned the way (nearly three years, you know) and can pass muster, and avoid their dislike. Being 'bottom dog' isn't a whim or phase with me. It's for my duration, I think.

Please don't turn me down just because you did so last year and the year before. Time has changed us both, and the R.A.F. since then. I could easily get other people to help me appeal to you: only it doesn't seem fair, and I don't really believe that you will go on refusing me for ever. People who want a thing as long and as badly as I want the R.A.F. must get it some time. I only fear that my turn won't come till I'm too old to enjoy it. That's why I keep on writing.

Yours very apologetically,

T E Shaw

Ex TEL)⎱
THR) ⎰

By this date the Conservatives were back in office and Baldwin had become Prime Minister for the second time, while Hoare had returned to the Air Ministry and Churchill had, somewhat surprisingly, become Chancellor of the Exchequer. At the end of March Lawrence wrote to Churchill's secretary Eddie Marsh, urging him to do what he could to get him transferred by persuading Churchill to use his influence with Hoare to this end, since if Churchill moved in on Hoare, Hoare would 'run obediently'. He had now, he told Marsh, reached the stage of writing begging letters. 'Trenchard has had three . . . and now here is

No. 4 to you – but with compunction, since Winston doesn't approve of me hiding in the ranks. He was born for power: whereas I got suddenly afraid of the openness of the world, so that the R.A.F. became a refuge.'[2] Meanwhile after talking the matter over with Philip Game, Trenchard expressed himself willing to take Lawrence back as an airman, provided Hoare agreed. But no immediate decision was possible since the Minister was on a tour of the Middle East with Amery. When Hoare eventually got back and gave his decision, Lawrence told Garnett that he was in such deep despair that he intended to take a truly desperate step after he had settled up his affairs.

> Trenchard withdrew his objection to my rejoining the Air Force. I got seventh heaven for two weeks: but then Sam Hoare came back from Mespot and refused to entertain the idea. That, and the closer acquaintance with *The Seven Pillars* (which I now know better than anyone ever will) have together convinced me that I'm no bloody good on earth. So I'm going to quit: but in my usual comic fashion I'm going to finish the reprint and square up with Cape before I hop it! There is nothing like deliberation, order and regularity in these things.
>
> I shall bequeath you my notes on life in the recruits' camp of the R.A.F. They will disappoint you.[3]

This was not the first time that Lawrence had threatened to commit suicide. Once, when staying with Trenchard at his home in Hertfordshire when he was still in the Tank Corps, he had spoken with a theatrical gesture of 'ending it all', if he could not get back into the R.A.F. 'All right,' said Trenchard quietly; 'but please go into the garden. I don't want my carpets ruined.' This brought a smile to Lawrence's face, and thenceforward the incident was treated as a private joke between them.[4]

On another occasion, in March 1925, according to Bruce, he had threatened to do the same at Clouds Hill when Bruce was staying there. Bruce removed his cartridges. This led to a scuffle for the weapon in the course of which Bruce bashed his hand against the wall until Lawrence dropped it. 'Then he cried like a child', Bruce wrote afterwards. 'I got him up the stairs but I'm afraid there was no sleep for either of us that night. There is no doubt that he planned to end it, because the next day we destroyed eighteen letters which he had written to various people before I arrived, including one to his mother in a very large envelope.'[5]

Apparently he had never made the threat to such an intimate friend and confidant as Garnett. In the event, Garnett became thoroughly alarmed and wrote to Bernard Shaw, who also took the threat seriously. 'I have sent on your letter to Downing Street with a card to say that some decision should be made,' G.B.S. replied, 'as there is a possibility of an appalling scandal, especially after Lowell Thomas's book.'[6]

The novelist and historian John Buchan also appealed to the Prime Minister on Lawrence's behalf. Buchan, who lived near Oxford, had first got to know Lawrence at All Souls. A chance meeting in the street one Sunday in April, a few weeks before Lawrence wrote to Garnett, followed up by a letter in which Lawrence repeated his request for help in getting back to the R.A.F., determined Buchan to act with characteristic vigour. His intervention on top of Bernard Shaw's letter tipped the balance, and Baldwin decided to intervene and overrule Hoare, which he did.

On 5 July 1925, Lawrence gave Buchan the good news in a letter from Clouds Hill.

The oracle responded nobly. I was sent for by Trenchard on Wednesday last (horribly inconvenient, for my revolver course did not finish till Saturday, yesterday) and was told that I was acceptable as a recruit.

The immediate effect of this news was to put me lazily and smoothly asleep: and asleep I've been ever since. It's like a sudden port, after a voyage all of our reckoning.

I owe you the very deepest thanks. I've been hoping for this for so many years, and had my hopes turned down so regularly, that my patience was completely exhausted: and I'd begun wondering if it had ever been worth waiting and hoping for. Odd, that the Air Force should seem to me (after trial too!) as the only way of getting across middle age. I wish I could make you some sort of return.

Formalities will take some weeks: but I should change skins in September at latest.

Please inform your family that the bike (Boanerges is his name) did 108 miles an hour with me on Wednesday afternoon. I think the news of my transfer has gone to its heads: (cylinder heads, of course.)[7]

Eleven days later, Trenchard signed the order approving of Lawrence's transfer to the R.A.F. and Lawrence was instructed to put in an application for his transfer through his Commanding Officer at Bovington.[8] This he did and after a week he was ordered to proceed to the R.A.F. camp at West Drayton for the first stage of his processing as a recruit. ('They set me sums: which I solved as fast as they brought them.') A Flight-Sergeant came along and recognised him. 'Hallo, Ross,' he greeted him, and was immediately corrected by a dynamo-switch-board attendant behind him who said: 'Garn . . . that ain't Ross. I was at Bovington when he came up, and he's Colonel Lawrence!'

The usual medical examination followed. When he was asked if he had ever broken any bones, Lawrence recited such a catalogue of fractured fibulae, radii, metatarsals, phalanges, cosyes, clavicles and scapulae that the medical orderly yelled at him to stop, while he made clumsy efforts to write them all down. He was then sent to Uxbridge, where no one would sign for him. Eventually he was taken before the Adjutant, and the following dialogue ensued.

'What are you?'

'Yesterday I was a Private in the Royal Tank Corps.'

'Today?' the Adjutant asked with a snort.

'I think I'm an A.C. twice in the R.A.F.?'

Another snort from the Adjutant. 'Will you be in the Navy tomorrow?'

'Perhaps,' replied the recruit.

'I can't sign for you,' said the Adjutant. 'I don't want you.'

'I don't want anyone to sign for me.'

'Damned silly . . . who the hell are you?'

At this point Lawrence's patience gave way. 'If your name was Buggins and I called you Bill . . .' he began, only to be interrupted by a shout of joy from the Adjutant, who promptly recognised the names by which he was known among the airmen and then gave him tea.[9]

A little later a message arrived that A/c2 Shaw was to report to the Cadets' Training College at Cranwell in Lincolnshire after he had been 'kitted out' suitably. Then he: 'walked round Uxbridge very new in blue', having blancoed his equipment and polished his bayonet. He arrived at Cranwell on 24 August to enjoy a bath and a heavenly sleep.

'Well, you're in luck here: this place is cushy,' said the airman who welcomed him to Hut 83. 'Any bed you like: there's no one but us two. I'm sort of hut-orderly. Spot of grub in the canteen? Righto ... Roll-call? Yes, they do have a sort of a one, I fancy, down in the lines: but the corp won't tool all the way up here. Your next stop will be the Adjutant tomorrow. I'll tool you along.'

'I've seen you before,' said the Adjutant. 'Were you at Depot three years ago?'

Lawrence admitted it in a tone which checked his asking for more. 'You'll go to "B" Flight. Just book his particulars, Sergeant-Major, and send him down.'[10]

To Mrs Hardy he wrote:

You see, it has happened! Quite suddenly at the end: so that I was spared a visit of farewell. It is best to go off abruptly, if at all.

I never expected the move to be so drastic. Cranwell is not really near anywhere (nor is it anything in itself): and the disorder of falling into a new station is yet upon me. The R.A.F. is a home to me: but it is puzzling to find the home all full of strangers who look upon me as strange. My known past always rouses curiosity in a new station. Probably in a few days things will be comfortable.

Alas for Clouds Hill, and the Heath, and the people I had learned in the two years of Dorset![11]

Also he thanked John Buchan again. 'I feel like a person home at last,' he wrote, ' – to find everyone else grown up, or changed, and the house open to all manner of other people beside myself. A new camp is always such a plunge into the unknown. This is a very comfortable, peaceful, cleanly camp, and will be glorious when I have settled into it.'[12]

2

The Commandant at Cranwell Cadet College was Air Commodore A. E. Borton, generally known as 'Biffy', who had flown with the Royal Flying Corps in the desert and had known Lawrence there. He had ended the war commanding the Air Force in Palestine. But Borton had no idea that Lawrence was being posted to Cranwell until he happened to catch sight of him a few days after his arrival. 'I walked in one day and saw Lawrence in an airman's uniform,' Borton later recalled. 'I was furious with Trenchard for not letting me know. Fortunately I kept my head and didn't say anything, but being taken by surprise like that I could easily have let the cat out of the bag. I went to my quarters and sent for him.' No doubt they began by talking about their first meeting in the desert when Borton arrived in a Handley-Page bomber and Lawrence laughingly told him that 'the Arabs said the war was as good as over because the biggest aeroplane in the world was on our side'.[13]

The vignettes of the life at Cranwell, which Lawrence gives in *The Mint*, are much shorter and happier than his account of his experiences at Uxbridge as Aircraftman Ross in the earlier part of the work. The 'explanation' as he called it, of what he had written about Uxbridge, he first sent to his friend Edward Garnett with the manuscript of the work, of which it forms the beginning of Part Three and which is devoted to Cranwell. 'But I cannot leave the tale at this point,' he wrote from India in 1928 when he was arranging the notes which were to form the core of the work. 'The Depot I knew was a savage place. That is now changed: so for fairness' sake I've picked out the few following extracts, mainly from letters to my friends: in the hope that they may give an idea of how different, how humane, life in the Cadet College was. There is no continuity in these past pages – and a painful inadequacy: but perhaps some glint of contentment may shine from between my phrases into your eyes.'

'How can any man describe his happiness?'[14]

The personnel of 'B' Flight, excluding the officers and cadets, consisted of a sergeant, a corporal and fourteen airmen, of whom A/c2 Shaw was one, and were accommodated in Hut 105, into which he shifted his kit after he had seen the Adjutant.

The hut is so small for the sixteen of us: a row of beds down each long wall, a table and two forms in the narrow middle, a square stove. In the centre of each short wall, a door: one gives on the open air, one to a wash-house–shower-bath–lavatory annexe, which makes a porch to the eastern or wintry side of the hut.

. . . Our beds are of iron sheeting, and slide in. Very hard they feel, for the first nights. The mattresses are three little square brown canvas cushions, rammed solid with coir. Biscuits they call them.

The next bed is only an arm's reach from mine. It is odd to have the other man's whispering breath so near my pillow all the night. His name is also Ross: a Scotchman from Devonshire, just married, a nice fellow: which is good fortune since a rough bedfellow is exhausting. Riches wholly deliver a man from bedfellows: – a privilege, and a loss, too: for the intimate jostling of like and like is often as fertile as it's disconcerting.

Airmen sleep very restlessly, always. Partly it may be due to the hard beds, on which a man cannot turn without a groan and half-waking up to lift the hip: yet turning is needful because the hardness cramps our bodies, if we do not constantly shift them. So the night to one who, like me, lies much awake is never fully quiet. There are groans and mutterings and dream-words. They all dream, always: and sometimes they say beastlike things in their sleep. . . .

I get up soonest of all, and nip over in the running vest and shorts which are my sleeping suit, to 83 Hut, of the opposite lines, across a grass meadow. There I bath. Such a funny little bath, a square brown earthenware socket, like a drain, in the cement floor. Fortunately I'm little, too, and if I tuck up like a tailor I can just squat in it, as if I were a dirty dish in a sink, with six inches of warm water round me: and there I splash, and shave, and splash again. This is heaven on a cold morning: and Cadet College faces the North Sea and can be colder than any spot in England. Indeed we are particular to score the low temperature record every winter.

About seven I run back to the hut and enter noisily, for a signal to the others, who begin to exhort one another to get up. We make our beds, heaping the three biscuits in a column and wrapping four blankets in a fifth, with an intervening sandwich of sheets. Then boot-cleaning, button-polishing, sweeping out the bed-area and doing my weekly one of the fourteen jobs into which hut-maintenance is divided. If it's stove-black-leading, another wash. Then I grab knife, fork and mug and run over to the mess-deck for breakfast.[15]

He was happy again now that his wish had been realised. As he told Trenchard: 'I've got everything I want: and nearly every morning when I wake up a little rush of delight comes over me, at finding myself still in the R.A.F. The only regrettable thing is that I have this feeling of delight at 6.30 a.m. in winter. It would be more moving if they let us lie in till 8.'[16] But there was a great consolation in the summer when 'we race over in the first dawn to the College's translucent swimming pool, and dive into the elastic water which fits our bodies as closely as a skin: – and we belong to that too. Everywhere a relationship: no loneliness any more.'[17]

At Cadet College the R.A.F. officer comes back to his own, in the foreground of authority, with the flight commander as the absolute fore-head. Our fifteen-man flight has three or four officers. Can they help meeting us, speaking to us, knowing us? We are the hands who actually push their machines about: on our vigilance and duty the officers' lives depend, for hours every flying day.[18]

'When opportunity permitted,' Sergeant Pugh, Lawrence's flight-sergeant in 'B' Flight, told Robert Graves, 'he made a point of flying with all the officers in the flight so that each knew him well and in my opinion were proud of the fact, the way they used to smile when he climbed in with them. . . . He even used to leave the office at times, shove overalls on, and away out into the hangar, scrubbing and washing machines down, although there was never any need to do so. Just to feel that he could do any job that came along.'[19]

Two incidents in particular which Lawrence described in *The Mint* are worthy of mention, each sharply contrasting with the other. The first was the late arrival in Hut 103 of a fellow airman who had been to a dance. Lawrence was still awake when he returned, having run the five miles so as to get back before lights out. 'Do you know what happened to me tonight?' he whispered to Lawrence. 'I met a girl . . . or she wasn't a girl, really . . . and we . . . clicked and went off together. Remember that dollar I borrowed off you, Monday? Well, that just did it.'

The airman threw his hard weight across the narrow bed and went on eagerly: 'Made me jump, this did, like two hundred volts . . . I can't ever do it the first time again: but Christ, it was bloody wonnerful.' Then, after a pause for reflection, he asked his confidant: 'I say, what've I got to do now? Wash it, I s'pose. Got any dope?'[20]

The other incident was the parade service on the November day that Queen Alexandra was buried beside her late husband in St George's Chapel at Windsor. 'Our distrusted chaplain preached one of his questionable sermons,' Lawrence noted. 'He spoke of the Dead Queen as a Saint, a Paragon: not as an unfortunate, a long-suffering doll. With luscious mouth he enlarged upon her beauty, the beauty which God, in a marvel of loving kindness, had let her keep until her dying.'

Lawrence thought of the day when he and others who had taken part in the Palestine campaign were received by her at the end of the war.

My thoughts fled back sharply to Marlborough House. The yellow, scaling portal: the white-haired footmen and door-keepers, whiter than the powder of their hair; the hushed great barn-like halls: the deep carpet in which our feet dragged unwillingly to the ceiling-high fireplace which dwarfed the whispering Miss Knollys and Sir Dighton [Probyn].* She incredibly old, wasted, sallow: he a once huge man, whose palsied neck had let down the great head on the breast, where its gaping mouth wagged almost unseen and unheard in the thicket of beard which overgrew the waistcoat. Sir Dighton had won the first V.C. in the Crimea: and he was so old, and Miss Knollys so old that this seemed a cruel duty which kept them always on their feet. We whispered with them: everybody whispered in that charnel-house.

We had to wait, of course: that is the prerogative of Queens. When we reached the presence, and I saw the mummied thing, the bird-like head cocked on one side, which the famous smile scissored across all angular and heart-rending: – then I nearly ran away in pity. The body should not be kept alive after the lamp of sense has gone out. There were the ghosts of all her lovely airs, the little graces, the once-effective sway and movement of the figure which had been her consolation. Her bony fingers, clashing in the tunnel of their rings, fiddled with albums, penholders, photographs, toys upon the table: and the heart-rending appeal played on us like a hose, more and more terribly. She soon dismissed us.[21]

These memories lost Lawrence much of the boring sermon. Once more Lawrence had to listen to the story of how the Prince of Wales in the House of Lords had warned Lord Granville that he must miss part of his speech because he had promised to take his daughter to the circus. 'This was the domestic picture and example which the Prince and Princess of Wales set their adoring people,' the padre droned on. 'Balls!' Aircraftman Shaw heard someone hissing savagely behind him. After more rolling of drums and last posts the parade dismissed and went off to dinner. 'Fall in at two for work!' shouted the orderly sergeant. 'Not even a half-holiday for the old girl,' one airman grumbled.

Most week-ends Lawrence would dash down to London on his

* Charlotte Knollys was the Queen's lady-in-waiting and General Sir Dighton Probyn her Comptroller. They had both entered her service in 1872 when she was Princess of Wales.

motor-bike, usually sleeping the night in the Union Jack Club for other ranks. Francis Rodd, son of the diplomatist Lord Rennell, lent him the keys of his flat while he was away exploring the Sahara, but Lawrence only used the place once for four nights. 'Four, you will say, is too few to justify my holding those keys all the weeks,' he wrote thanking Rodd for his hospitality, 'but consider the quality of those nights. The place so quiet, so absolutely mine, and the door locked downstairs, so that it was really mine. Why there isn't a lock in my power at Cranwell, not even on the shit-house door! The happiness and security of those nights were very keen.'[22]

He was also in London on the week-end before the special church-parade for Queen Alexandra, when he had called on King Faisal, whom he found 'lively, happy to see me, friendly, curious'.

He was due for lunch at Lord Winterton's [he wrote to Charlotte Shaw] (Winterton, with me during the war is now our Under-Secretary of State for India). We drove there together, and had lunch in Winterton's lovely house, a place of which I'm specially fond, because it has been his for hundreds of years, so carelessly cared for. Winterton, of course, had to talk of old times, taking me for a companion of his again, as though we were again advancing on Damascus. And I had to talk back, as though the R.A.F. clothes were a skin that I could slough off at any while with a laugh.

But all the while I knew I couldn't. I've changed and the Lawrence who used to go about and be friendly and familiar with that sort of people is dead. He's worse than dead. He is a stranger I once knew. From henceforward my way will lie with these fellows here, degrading myself (for in their eyes and in your eyes and Winterton's I think it is a degradation), and the hope that some day I will really feel degraded, be degraded, to their level. I long for people to look down upon me and despise me and I'm too shy to take the filthy steps which would publicly shame me, and put me into their contempt. I want to dirty myself outwardly, so that my person may properly reflect the dirtiness which it conceals . . . and I think from dirtying the outside, while I've eaten, avidly eaten, every filthy morsel which chance threw in my way.

I'm too shy to go looking for dirt. I'd be afraid of seeming a novice when I found it. That's why I can't go off stewing into the Lincoln or Navenby brothels with the fellows. They think it's because I'm superior, proud, or peculiar, or 'posh', as they say; and it's because I wouldn't know what to do, how to carry myself, where to stop. Fear again: fear everywhere.[23]

There is certainly no suggestion on the part of Sergeant Pugh, who slept in Hut 103 with the airmen in the flight, that any of them considered his manner at all superior or that his behaviour was in any way that of a 'posh' person. Here is the flight-sergeant's summing up.

It seemed his sole purpose was to be an airman of the lowest grade and rank and to be left alone with his Brough at 'B' Flight, Cranwell. He was hero-worshipped by all the flight for his never failing cheery disposition, ability to get all he could for their benefit, never complaining, and his generosity to all concerned till at times it appeared that he was doing too much for everyone and all were out to do their best for him. Quarrels ceased and the flight had to pull together for the sheer joy of remaining in his company and being with him for his companionship, help, habits, fun and teaching one and all to play straight.[24]

3

Many years later, in the course of an interview, 'Biffy' Borton, by then a retired Air Vice-Marshal, was asked how Lawrence had behaved when Borton was Commandant at Cranwell.

'He was extremely tactful and never did anything to call attention to himself,' Borton replied. 'I think he liked publicity and shunned it, but while he was in the Air Force and I knew him, he did nothing to court it.'

'Some people complained about his "spy" activities,' his questioner remarked, 'saying that it was unfair to officers to have

someone under them who could skip the chain of command and
talk to authority above them.'

'He only ever did this when he felt there was some abuse which
could not otherwise come to light,' Borton explained. 'I felt it
was very useful and it helped me to avoid mistakes.'

'What did you feel like having him under your command?'

'I was delighted,' said Borton. 'He did a lot for the library at
Cranwell, and of course he gave them the proof copy of *The
Seven Pillars* which was bound together with all sorts of papers
and things, in a very special binding.' Borton was also presented
with a copy for himself, but unfortunately this was stolen afterwards with other valuables.

Borton added that he often invited Lawrence to his private
quarters at Cranwell and they spent many enjoyable evenings
together, but that Lawrence 'always arranged things very dis-
creetly'. Of course, Borton went on, 'by this time everyone knew
who he was, but it did not worry them, and he certainly did not
remind anyone.' According to Mrs Borton, she usually left them
on their own on these occasions because she felt he was very shy
in women's company. Nevertheless he had no apparent difficulty
in overcoming this shyness when he wished.[25]

At the end of 1925 Wing-Commander Sydney Smith arrived
at Cranwell with his wife Clare to take up the post of Chief
Staff-Officer. They had previously met Lawrence at the Cairo
Conference in 1921 when Sydney Smith commanded the R.A.F.
station at Heliopolis and Aircraftman Shaw was Colonel
Lawrence. They had all three become friends then and Lawrence
was very pleased to see them again at Cranwell. According to the
Bortons' daughter, Lady Cunningham, Clare was adept at providing the right kind of company for Lawrence. 'She was very
clever at being just what was wanted. Her interest in music must
have made her interesting to him.' However, the first time he
came to tea with them in their married quarters at Cranwell,
Clare noticed that he had changed considerably over the past
four years.

Although physically he looked the same, he was far more rest-
less than when I had met him in Cairo. Sitting on his chair he

would rub his sides with his hands, up and down, up and down, and he would sometimes pass two fingers over his mouth and chin, or rumple up the crest of fair hair which was still unruly and refused to lie down.[26]

According to Flight-Sergeant Pugh, the Bortons, who were apparently going to be away, invited Lawrence to spend Christmas in their house, but he gratefully declined, preferring to stay with the other airmen in his flight in their hut. As the flight-sergeant put it: 'He was an Aircraft hand and as I've said before he kept his place as such, never allowing anything to break him from his position in the R.A.F.'[27]

'My R.A.F. character has been assessed (for last year) as "exceptional",' he wrote to Charlotte Shaw on 15 January 1926. 'This is the highest grade. It shows you how I can behave for four months. Down with the Sam Hoares!'[28]

Lawrence thought that Pugh's contribution to Robert Graves's biography were the best thing in the book: 'written in sergeant language,' as he told Charlotte Shaw, 'but so simply and kindly and delightfully. It is ridiculously too favourable: but like Morris when he saw good work my diaphragm is warmed by it.'[29] Here, for example, is a typical story as told by Sergeant Pugh during the General Strike in May 1926, when coal issues were stopped and 'B' Flight had only a lot of coal dust and slack.

S[haw]'s sheer cheek got to work, and calmly filling a huge bucket with dust he inquired the name of a Big officer who had stopped the issue. Walking point blank to his office, he found that the officer had not stopped his own coal ration, so he exchanged his load for some wonderful pieces of coal as big as himself. No one has found out who changed the dust yet. His comments were a broad grin and silence.[30]

'So far we have not been done anything with,' he wrote to Charlotte Shaw on the seventh day of the strike. 'All leave is cancelled and we just wait in camp till the Government want to use us. Everyone is passive. You know the Services are built of old crusted Tories: more Tories in the ranks than in command.'[31]

Charlotte Shaw was interested in Queen Eleanor of Castile, Edward I's wife, whose funeral procession from Lincoln to London was marked by a series of crosses, of which Charing Cross is the best known. There was a statue of the Queen in a niche above the chantry in Lincoln Cathedral, and Charlotte asked Lawrence if he could get a picture of it and send it to her. Lawrence did so on a picture post-card on the back of which he wrote: 'She is exceedingly lovely: just the sort of woman you meet at tea, constantly. Interested faintly, in church work, and has a pet dog.'[32]

Sunday he cycled over to Nottingham on Boanerges, as he called his Brough machine, and saw large crowds going into a Wesleyan Mission Hall. 'I went instead to a Lyons teashop and ordered tea,' he told Charlotte Shaw.

> The only friendly person was a black cat, who sat beside me, and was exceedingly insistent upon the point of food. I bought an eclair, and split it open down its length, like two little dug-out canoes. The cat flung itself upon them, and hollowed out all the pith with its grating tongue. When it got down to the brown shell it sat back on its hind legs and licked its face lovingly. A man on the opposite seat also had cream on his cheek and tried horribly to lick it. Only his tongue was too short. Not really short, you know only for that . . .
>
> The cat was a very excellent animal. The human beings were gross, noisy, vulgar: they did the same things as the cat, but in a clumsy blatant way . . .
>
> Heaven knows why I've bothered to write you this nonsense. The moral spoils it.[33]

While out riding on his motor-cycle one evening in the spring of 1926, he came upon a smash between a pedestrian and a car driven by an elderly man. When the pedestrian had been safely disposed of, the driver of the car asked Lawrence to crank it up. Unfortunately, nervousness and excitement caused him to leave the ignition fully advanced, with the result that when Lawrence swung the handle it flew back and broke his right arm. 'Without so much as a sign to show what had taken place,' Sergeant Pugh's account of the incident continues, 'Shaw asked if he would mind retarding the offending lever, and swung the car with his left hand. After the car was at a safe distance Shaw got an A.A. Scout to 'kick over' his Brough, and with his right arm dangling and changing gear with his foot, Shaw got his bus home, and parked without a word to a soul of the pain he was suffering. Through some unknown reason the M.O. was away and it was next morning before his arm could be "done". That is a man – Shaw, I mean.'[34]

One result of the accident was that he was obliged to write with his left hand in 'a drunken script', as he explained by way of excuse to Charlotte.[35] 'The tip of the radius was cracked off and the wrist dislocated,' he told his mother two months after it happened. 'Now they have put it nearly straight again: but it still cramps me badly after a few minutes in one position holding anything small like a pen or a knife. They say that in another month it will be quite fit; though I have lost the power of twisting my hand round very far. It goes about half way now.'[36] In fact, he made a complete recovery and his right-hand script was eventually as clear and neat as before.

The Medical Officer was an old Wing-Commander who looked after Lawrence well, and having heard about *The Seven Pillars*, asked if he could borrow a copy of the revised text, which Lawrence lent him. 'Pathetic,' Lawrence told Charlotte Shaw. 'He lit a candle after 11.20 p.m. when the electric current is cut off to carry on reading it. He is 70 odd: ex-surgeon to the King as a civil practitioner. Courtly: a wonderful bedside manner – so sympathetic. Rather nice too. He has been very good to me.'[37]

According to Sergeant Pugh, Lawrence was held up on three separate occasions by the same policeman on point duty in a traffic muddle at Sleaford, the nearest town to Cranwell. 'He pointed out that police were the servants of the public, paid by the public, and he did not think that the "copper" on point duty knew his job, that he was decidedly inefficient and a *"Swede"* (Airman's term for villager). The Super and S had a grand argument, but S's eloquence floored the Super and left him wondering what the R.A.F. had enlisted. That "copper" is now permanently excused traffic-control.'

He took all the flight and their wives to Hendon by charabanc to see the annual air display, although he told Pugh that he would have preferred to charter an Imperial Airways machine to 'do' it by air. Then when the summer leave came round he told Pugh and the others on the flight that he had been offered a job as steward on board a liner going to the United States but after carefully thinking it over had turned it down to work on revising *The Seven Pillars* and its abridgement. 'Wish this had come off,' noted Pugh.[38]

Lawrence himself made the abridgement, which became *Revolt in the Desert*, in seven hours with the aid of two airmen friends at Cranwell in March 1926, ignoring Garnett's earlier attempt. He took a set of the subscribers' sheets of *The Seven Pillars* and, with a brush and Indian ink, boldly obliterated whole slabs of text. The first seven chapters he dropped in their entirety, while consecutive pages would be removed wholesale in the later cuts and occasionally a whole chapter. The result was that the original 652 pages of *The Seven Pillars* were reduced by 211, which were cut out altogether.[39] 'The abridgement is better than the complete text,' he told Garnett when he had finished the cutting job. 'Half a calamity is better than a whole one. By excising heights and depths I have made a balanced thing: yet I share your difficulty of seeing the shorter version's real shape across the gaps.'[40] Yet remarkably his cuts required very few linking interpolations.

The editor of the college magazine asked Lawrence for permission to make a substantial quotation from *The Seven Pillars* which he proposed to preface with a short biographical appreciation of the author. This he sent Lawrence for his comments. Lawrence replied giving permission to quote at length from the abridged version:

> Thank you very much. I hope you will cut out 'Prince of Mecca', for that is an American invention and impossible in fact. 'Emir Mekky'= Prince of Mecca, and denotes actual temporal overlordship. It could not be an honorific – and King Hussein was never in the mood to honour me. We did not get on together.
>
> Also I was not among the first to enter Damascus; indeed

my position was very equivocal. I found an empty will amongst our leaders, when they got there – and knowing there were things urgently required I compelled them to do as I wanted. That was all.

Otherwise there is nothing which is not a fair expression of opinion. Of course I do not share your view of the literary merit of the book. It seems too literary for a memoir, and too truthful for literature. However that doesn't much matter.

The A.O.C. asked me for a copy for the C.C. library, and this I've sent him. So you will be able to look at it, when you wish.

The facts about publication are that this full text will not be published in my lifetime: but about 150 copies are going to friends of mine, without reservations: so knowledge of it will soon get about. They will be distributed in the end of November. An abridgement is to be published by Cape in March 1927 and the serial publication of 40,000 words of this abridgement can be begun by the *Daily Telegraph* after Dec. 15 next. So your long quotation shouldn't appear before the D.T. has had its whack. After that do anything you please. Other people will be doing the same.

T.E.S.

'Cranwell is not a good winter station,' Lawrence told Charlotte Shaw after he had been there for six months. 'Yet technically it is so good and peaceful that I hope they will leave me here a long time.'[41] But it was not to be.

4

It was a combination of circumstances produced by *The Seven Pillars* and its abridgement for commercial publication as *Revolt in the Desert*, that prompted Lawrence to volunteer during the earlier part of the summer for the average airman's customary spell of overseas duty. On 6 July 1926 he wrote to his mother.

I've been waiting for sure news before writing to you: but the

Air Force authorities drag too slowly. So here it is. I'm to go to India this winter: perhaps in September, perhaps in November, perhaps in February. It's the ordinary overseas draft, of the R.A.F. pattern. Most airmen do a turn abroad in their seven years' service. The Mesopotamian term is 2 years, the climate being bad. Egypt is 5 years: India is 5 years. I'm glad I'm not going to Egypt, for there is the risk of trouble there.

In a way I'd rather have stayed in England; but the warmth, if there is any, will be welcome: and it is good to be out of England when Cape brings out that abridgement of my Arabian book. I made the abridgement myself, and it is a severely plain one, but to sell it Cape must advertise it, and his best way of doing that will be to rake up all the old silly stories about me. I shall be glad this autumn when the real book is finished and distributed. All the work of the little book is done already: a good thing, for with this uncertainty about going abroad I do not want more liabilities than I can help. . . .

They wanted me to go out on a Commission of Enquiry to China, the other day! I told them I was happily engaged in the R.A.F.[42]

Lawrence said nothing to Trenchard, but inevitably the C.A.S. heard that Aircraftman Shaw was being posted to India, and he told him that it was not necessary for him to go if he did not wish it. 'It is good of you to give me the option of going overseas or staying at home,' Lawrence wrote back by way of explaining his action: 'but I volunteered to go, deliberately, for the reason that I am publishing a book (about myself in Arabia) on March 3, 1927: and experience taught me in Farnborough in 1922 that neither good-will on the part of those above me, nor correct behaviour on my part can prevent my being a nuisance in any camp where the daily press can get at me.'

Overseas they will be harmless, and therefore I must go overseas for a while and dodge them. After a few years the bubble will be either burst or deflated, and I can serve again at home. England seems to be much the best place to be anyway!

I'm sorry you should have been unnecessarily troubled. It

had been my ambition that you shouldn't hear of or from me, after my readmission to the R.A.F. I'm perfectly happy in it, on the ordinary terms: and if the other fellows knew that I used to know you, my character would be ruined.[43]

The subscriptions for the privately printed limited edition of *The Seven Pillars of Wisdom*, which had started slowly, had gathered momentum and by the end of 1925 it was clear that the edition would be over-subscribed. Some fellow-writers sent in their subscriptions and Lawrence told his banker Robin Buxton to return them if they subsequently thought better of it. One such was Compton Mackenzie. 'It's rather a compliment his wishing to subscribe,' the author told Buxton. 'What a gallery of them ... Wells, Shaw, Walpole, Hardy ... '[44] The other subscribers, to his surprise, included King George V, whose cheque was sent to Lawrence's friend J. G. Wilson, the manager of Bumpus's bookshop in Oxford Street, through Sir John Fortescue, the Royal Librarian at Windsor. 'The Windsor copy will be duly sent,' Lawrence wrote to Wilson: 'but I'm an old-fashioned person, to whom it seems improper that Kings should buy and sell among their subjects. You told me that the advance cheque was from Fortescue: and I mean to return it gently to him with the book when it is ready. F[ortescue] is decent, and will not tell his owner: for I should prefer Him to think He is paying for it, since that is His notion of propriety.'[45] For some reason Mrs Hardy was told she was getting two copies, but neither the British Museum nor the Bodleian were getting any, though they wanted them. ('Somehow they feel dehumanised, those places.') However, he gave the original MS. to the Bodleian, acting 'perhaps unhumourously', as he told Sydney Cockerell, and 'taking myself a little too seriously as a classic'.[46]

Being so-called copyright libraries entitled to a free copy of any book published in the United Kingdom, the British Museum and the Bodleian may not have realised that the work was being privately printed and distributed. 'Much fun lately with the copyright people, who ask for copies for the public libraries', Lawrence wrote to Buxton after the appeal for subscriptions had gone out. 'I've replied regretting that circumstances prevent my complying with the Copyright Act. They are hopping mad: and pretend that perhaps I've made a mistake, and don't intend to defy the Act. But I do: and will get away with it!'[47] Needless to add that he did.

The text and decorations were printed by a jobbing printer named Manning Pike and an assistant C. J. Hodgson, in a small room at the back of Whiteley's stores in London. It is significant that Lawrence's name was printed on the original title page, but he struck it out in the proof, his reason being a typographical one in that the page looked 'cleaner' without the author's name. Also, and significantly, copies he inscribed for friends bore the initials T.E.S. and not T.E.L. Altogether 128 complete copies were subscribed at 30 guineas each, in addition to which a further 36 complete copies and 26 incomplete copies, i.e. without all the plates, were given away by the author. Besides these, 22 copies without plates, with two variant passages and no introductory matter or appendices, were printed for the George H. Doran publishing company in New York to secure American copyright. Under his agreement with the author, Doran was to keep four copies and Lawrence six, two were to be deposited in the Library of Congress to meet the statutory copyright requirement, while the remaining ten were to be offered for sale at the prohibitive price of $20,000 per copy.[48]

Baldwin and Trenchard each received incomplete copies. Baldwin's was sent through John Buchan. 'This copy is one of those which I am giving to the fellows who did the Arab revolt with me,' he wrote in the covering letter to Buchan, requesting him to ask the Prime Minister whether he would care to accept it. 'He did me the best turn I have ever had done to me,' Lawrence added, 'and I think gratefully of him as often as I have leisure to think about my contentment. It is no great return . . . but I am hardly in the position to make any great return, and if he likes books, as I am told, he may prefer a broken copy to none at all. The thing is, anyhow, a rarity.'[49] Some years later he wrote to Bernard Shaw, who had been a pallbearer with Baldwin at Thomas Hardy's funeral: 'I wonder if he's ever looked at his *Seven Pillars*? He earned a copy by sitting on Sir Sam Hoare, and so getting me back to the R.A.F.'[50]

Trenchard's specially bound copy in air force blue was sent direct to its recipient with a covering letter, in which Lawrence wrote:

It is not the right blue of course: but then what is the right blue? No two airmen are alike: indeed it is a miracle if the top and bottom halves of one airman are the same colour. So perhaps you are not particular.

I told the binder (ex-R.A.F.) who it was for. 'Then,' said he, 'it must be quite plain and very well done.' And it really isn't badly done. Of course it's the first copy, and the later ones will profit by its experience.

You will see it marked 'Incomplete copy'. There are three plates missing: that's all. They make a tremendous difference in value, as you will find out if you try to sell it. Complete copies cost thirty guineas, and it would not be seemly (or financially possible) for me to give any of them away. This is the best I can do.

As I told you, it isn't given you to read: but merely as a sign that all is well. . . .

Let's hope this is my last letter till March 1930, when you are to be asked to prolong my engagement.[51]

Trenchard's copy was inscribed by the author:

Sir. Hugh Trenchard
from a contented, admiring
and, whenever possible, obedient
servant.

5·XII·26   T.E.S.

This gratified and amused the Chief of the Air Staff as 'being a delightful touch from the most disobedient mortal I have ever met'. In the same letter, in which he acknowledged the gift of the book, Trenchard wrote kindly and considerately.

I hope you keep fit but if you get seedy you may get sad and *if you do*, do write and *let me know*, so that if necessary I can bring you home.

You say you hope I shall not receive a letter from you until March 1930. By then I shall have gone and others will be here, but I will promise you that as far as possible I will see that you can get out if you want to.

I would very much like to have seen you before you actually sailed, but I suppose that is not possible, and perhaps it would be inadvisable from your point of view: but if you want to be put up for a night, my wife and children would be delighted to see you before you went out at Dancers Hill. Let me know.[52]

'Many thanks,' Lawrence replied: 'but I will not trouble Lady Trenchard.' He continued:

It wouldn't do in uniform: and I've no other clothes fit to wear. Also the last four or five years of low life have reduced my never very high social sense.

I'm always obedient when things go well. They have gone very well the last 18 months.

You say 'I shall have gone (by 1930) but so far as possible I will see that you can get out of it if you want to.' You have misread me. Getting out is easy. They would send the band to play me to the station. All my efforts are to stay in. If you can do anything to persuade your successor to prolong me, I'll be grateful to both.

This has been a hard-working, rushed month for me: and yesterday I had a crash on my bicycle. Broke the poor thing, and scratched my knee! First crash for 11 months. Hard luck.[53]*

*A former telegraph boy, who worked in the station post office at Cranwell fifty years ago and is still there, was asked by the present writer what he remembered about Lawrence. 'The large number of telegrams addressed to A/c Shaw which I had to deliver to him at his hut,' was the reply. 'He would give me a shilling for each one – and that meant a lot to me as my wages then were only half-a-crown a week!'

5

Indeed he had much to do during his month's embarkation leave. For one thing, he had to go down to Clouds Hill and arrange to let the cottage (to two service friends for 12 shillings a week) and also collect some of his books for reading in India. During this visit he went over to Max Gate to say good-bye to the Hardys. 'Hardy was much affected by this parting, as T. E. Lawrence was one of his most valued friends,' wrote Mrs Hardy afterwards, describing the scene. 'He went into the little porch and stood at the front door to see the departure of Lawrence on his motor-bicycle. This machine was difficult to start, and, thinking he might have to wait some time Hardy turned into the house to fetch a shawl to wrap round him. In the meantime, fearing that Hardy might take a chill, Lawrence started the motor-bicycle and hurried away. Returning a few moments after, Hardy was grieved that he had not seen the actual departure, and said that he had particularly wished to see Lawrence go.'[54] Perhaps each had a premonition that he would not see the other again, as indeed it was to prove.

'It was my doing,' Lawrence wrote by way of apology to Mrs Hardy, having heard what happened from E. M. Forster. 'The afternoon was raw and miserable, like the day, and when T.H. turned back into the house to get a shawl (as I guessed), instantly I ran the bicycle out into the road and away, so that no possible reproach might lie against me for having helped him into the danger of a chill.'

The knowing you and having the freedom has been a delight-ful privilege of mine for nearly four years. I cannot tell you how grateful I am to you both: and how much I look forward to finding you there when I come back. Eighty-six is nothing of an age, so long as its bearer is not content with it; in fact it is still fourteen years short of a decent score in cricket.[55]

On returning to London Lawrence took leave of the Shaws a few days before he was due to sail. G.B.S. gave him a proof copy of *Saint Joan* to take with him, as he did not like to take the copy inscribed to: 'Private Shaw from Public Shaw', but both copies were to disappear, no doubt stolen, as was a copy of the original acting edition, which Lawrence had lent a comrade in the Tank Corps. Later G.B.S. was to present Lawrence with another copy of the original Constable edition 'to replace many other copies until this, too is stolen'. To Charlotte he wrote on 2 December: 'We managed that good-bye occasion very well, I think. They are so difficult.' He told Lady Astor that he would rather visit the Shaws 'than read any book or hear any music on earth'; 'Charlotte,' he added, was 'as wise as 10,000 of you and me.'[56]

By this date about twenty copies of *The Seven Pillars* had gone to subscribers; most of the remainder were to be dispatched about Christmas time – 'my Christmas pudding', he called it, while a few special copies were to stand over until the New Year. 'I think my experience is almost a conclusive demonstration that publishing is not a suitable hobby for an airman,' he told his friend Francis Rodd, while to Dick Knowles, his neighbour at Clouds Hill, he wrote: 'It is a strangely empty feeling to have finished with it after all these years.'[57] His mother's copy he had sent to Arnold to await her return from China. 'Getting it over has been a big relief,' he told her. 'I have spent £13,000 on it altogether, and the responsibility of that has been heavy, since my own resources would not meet the liability.' He added that he was relying on the abridgement to bring in enough to cover the deficit.[58]

When she heard from him that he was going to India, Mrs Lawrence suggested that he should leave the R.A.F. and live quietly somewhere. 'I cannot be quiet, and so the bustle and enforced duty of the R.A.F. is good for me,' he replied. 'I wish it were not India – an experiment which has lasted too long, and where we are failing – but that is no great matter. The rank and file have nothing to do with politics.' At the same time he lectured his mother and brother in China on the folly of all 'endeavours to influence the national life of another people by one's own', foreseeing with remarkable accuracy the end of 'foreign' influence in that country and its replacement by complete political independence. 'The English, with their usual genius for beginning on the wrong side, are fighting the Nationalists, the party which must in the end (this year, next year, fifty years hence) prevail.'

The truth was that T. E. Lawrence had no use for missionaries, even of the medical variety, and he urged both his mother and Bob to leave China before events forced them to do so. As for Bob, 'there cannot be any conception of duty to compel him to stay', he counselled. 'In olden days doctors and medicine were respectable mysteries; but science is rather out of fashion now: and it seems to me that the fate of everyone upon earth is only their own concern.'[59]

As for himself, as he told T. B. Marson, 'the R.A.F. is still my spiritual home, and I'm awfully sorry to leave Cranwell, where I've had the best year I ever remember to have had. . . . However parts of that book of mine are to come out with Cape & Co. in the spring and people sort of agree that I'd better dodge out of reach of the daily press before that happens.' Marson had just retired from the Air Ministry, where he had been Trenchard's tactful Personal Assistant and Private Secretary, to take up farming in Scotland. He had a son John who was a cadet at Cranwell, but Lawrence had not seen much of him as he was in another squadron. 'Birds are wiser than us, in their habits of ruling their young ones out of the nest, so soon as they have done their first solo!' was Lawrence's comment. 'We make the weaning too slow. I hope he will like the R.A.F.* From my point of view it is the perfect existence: but then I've been battered so much elsewhere.'[60]

* John Marson became an Air Vice-Marshal, holding several commands, and was Director of Technical Services at the Air Ministry at the time of his retirement in 1958. His father Thomas Bertrand Marson served as a trooper in the Leicestershire Yeomanry in the Boer War. He joined up again in the First World War in which he lost a leg at Gallipoli, after which he was seconded to the Royal Flying Corps where he served under Trenchard in the Independent Force in France. When Trenchard became C.A.S. for the second time after the war in 1919 he appointed T. B. Marson his Private Secretary, and Marson served in this capacity until he retired in 1926. In his autobiography, *Scarlet and Khaki*, which Lawrence helped him to get published by his own publisher Jonathan Cape in 1930, Marson described Trenchard in the war: 'An inspired man himself he inspired those under him. He gave unstintingly of his best, and spirit and courage, moral and physical, permeated all ranks. He was beautifully served by a small but efficient staff, between whom and his command there was complete liaison and sympathy . . . The pilots trusted him implicitly, for he never asked of them impossibilities and he never let them down.' *Scarlet and Khaki*, p. 158.

India

I

Lawrence sailed from Southampton for Karachi on 7 December 1926 in the *Derbyshire*, a troopship overcrowded with a complement of 1200 officers and men. 'As you know my expectations were not good,' he wrote to Charlotte Shaw from Port Said: 'but I have been surprised at the badness of our accommodation and the clotted misery of our crowd on board. Nature has been kinder to us than mankind, and has given us calm seas and a moderate temperature.'¹ At Port Said he went ashore and spent the day with an old friend from the war, Colonel Stewart Newcombe, and his wife; the former, according to Mrs Newcombe, Lawrence had told as far back as 1914 that his parents were not married and he 'had no right' to the name Lawrence, adding six years later that he was seriously thinking of changing his name 'to be more quiet' and wished he could also change his face 'to be more lovely, and beloved!'² The Newcombes gave him dinner and a large tin of toffee as a parting present. The voyage was better from Port Said to Basra, where he did not land, since 300 had left the ship at Port Said, but from Basra to Karachi it was again overcrowded. 'Your improper department has ruled that at sea three airmen can be packed into the air-space of two sailors,' he wrote to Winston Churchill's secretary Eddie Marsh at the time. 'Kindly meant, no doubt, to keep us warm and comfortable. But in the Red Sea and the Gulf we grew sick of each other's smell.'³

Lawrence later recorded a few impressions of the voyage, which he seems to have intended as a kind of tailpiece to *The Mint – Leaves in the Wind*, he called it. 'The wash of the water, the *Derbyshire* swaying in a long slow swell, going over so far, swinging back: ever and again going further, with a muffled musical clash of crockery far away in her depths, oscillating back again – now and then an upward heave, and the slow sinking back. My eyes began to swim, and to see gassy clouds in the corridor, between the blobs of the dim safety lamps. They twinkled so electric blue. Wave upon wave of the smell of stabled humanity: the furtive creeping by rushes along the alley-way of the women to their latrine, fending themselves from wall to wall with the right arm, while the left held the loosened dress across the body.'[4]

John Buchan considered that Lawrence's power of depicting squalor was uncanny, and that there was nothing in *The Mint* which equalled the later passage describing the troopship on its way to India. ('That fairly takes the breath away by its sheer brutality.')[5] The passage which Buchan had in mind was Lawrence's experience as Married Quarters sentry during the night watches. It made his poor little ex-apprentice relief so sick that 'after fifteen minutes they had to help him up to the air'.

Swish swish the water goes against the walls of the ship – sounds nearer. Where on earth is that splashing. I tittup along the alley and peep into the lavatory space, at a moment when no woman is there. It's awash with a foul drainage. Tactless posting a sentry over the wives' defaecations, I think. Tactless and useless all our duties aboard.

Hullo here's the Orderly Officer visiting. May as well tell him. The grimy-folded face, the hard jaw, toil-hardened hands, bowed and ungainly figure. An ex-naval warrant, I'll bet. No gentleman. He strides boldly to the latrine: 'Excuse me' unshyly to two shrinking women. 'God', he jerked out, 'flooded with shit – where's the trap?' He pulled off his tunic and threw it at me to hold, and with a plumber's quick glance strode over to the far side, bent down, and ripped out a grating. Gazed for a moment, while the ordure rippled over his boots. Up his right sleeve, baring a forearm hairy as a mastiff's grey leg, knotted with veins, and a gnarled hand: thrust it deep in, groped, pulled out a moist white bundle. 'Open that port' and out it splashed into the night. 'You'd think they'd have had some other place for their sanitary towels. Bloody awful show, not having anything fixed up.' He shook his sleeve down as it was over his slowly-drying arm, and huddled on his tunic, while the released liquid gurgled contentedly down its re-opened drain.[6]

The airmen disembarked at Karachi exactly a month after leaving England. They were then conveyed to the R.A.F. Depot, Drigh Road, some distance from the town. 'A dry hole, on the edge of the Sind desert, which desert is a waste of land and sandstone, with plentiful stubble and cactus on its flat parts, and of tamarisk in its valleys. Over it blow hot and cold winds, very heavily laden with dust. We eat dust and breathe dust and think dust and hate dust on the days when dust-storms blow. At present, in the nominal winter, that is not often enough to be less than remarkable. In summer, they tell us genially, a little breeze arises every midday, blows a dust-gale every afternoon, and dies into a mere dust-soup at sunset.'[7]

Life at the Depot, where he was assigned to the engine repair shops, Lawrence described as 'cushy'. Every morning they paraded in overalls at 7.30 and knocked-off at 1 p.m., after which they were free for the rest of the day. Every day was a half-day, except Thursday and Sunday which were 'whole holidays'. There was no P.T. and he was only on guard duty once every two months. 'No bugles in camp. Also no hot water, till I won a blow-lamp and a dope can, and began to boil myself every three days. Food excellent. Canteen vile. Karachi (place of limited amusement) seven miles off. No occupation for spare hours, and the spare hours make up 15/16 of life apparently. No roads, fortunately, so I do not wish for a Brough. . . . No pay either to speak of. They keep you short on 5 rupees a week.' By putting two weeks' pay together Lawrence was able to buy three gramophone records, including the Largo of Bach's Concerto for two violins in D and Boccherini's Sonata in A. These astonished his fourteen fellow airmen with whom he shared a room, since they cherished 'very fondly a preference for *Rose Marie*'. Often in the evening he would go out to listen to the music of the camel bells on Drigh Road, and hang his topee on a cactus branch, and sit down under it and weep, remembering Cranwell and the Great North Road. 'The camel-bells sound just like a water-tap dripping, drop, drop, drop, into a deep cistern. When they condescend to cease (which is when one or other camel in the string, feeling a natural urge in him, straddles his hind legs and drags or bumps his fellow camels to a standstill) the quietude of the night smooths itself out like heaven.'[8]

'The camp is comfortable: new stone-built and spacious,' he wrote to his mother on 24 February 1927; but he complained that the airmen worked too short hours each day and were bored with an excessive leisure. 'My big book is now all distributed,' he added. 'The Cape abridgement appears in March. Financially I have done well: and all my liabilities at my Bank are safely covered. Any surplus there may be will be paid to a R.A.F. charity. The pictures are now being exhibited in London, with a very excellent preface to the catalogue by Bernard Shaw.' The exhibition, assembled by the artist Eric Kennington, who was also a prominent contributor, and put on at the Leicester Galleries for a fortnight in February, consisted of the original paintings, pastels, drawings and woodcuts which had been used to illustrate *The Seven Pillars*. Incidentally it gave Bernard Shaw a good opportunity to say some of the things he had in mind about Lawrence in the preface to the catalogue, from which the following passages are in character.

The limelight of history follows the authentic hero as the theatre limelight follows the *prima ballerina assoluta*. It soon concentrated in its whitest radiance on Colonel Lawrence, *alias* Lurens Bey, *alias* Prince of Damascus, the mystery man, the wonder man, the man who . . . did, when all the lies and all the legends are subtracted, authentically and unquestionably in his own way and largely with his own hands explode and smash the Turkish dominion in Arabia and join up with Allenby in Damascus. . . .

. . . Any country with a Valhalla or a spark of gratitude would have rewarded him with a munificent pension and built him another Blenheim. The British Government left him to pension himself like an ex-minister by writing a book about it all and living on the proceeds.

Now it happened that Lawrence's genius included literary

genius: and that his maddeningly intense conscientiousness obliged him to write the book. . . . It was a prodigious task; and the result was a masterpiece of literature. Commercially it was worth to the author a very large sum. . . .

Shaw went on to describe how Lawrence made up his mind to lose money by the book and how in fact he did so, with the help of a mortgage on the profits from 'the popular abridgement' in the form of *Revolt in the Desert*. Finally, 'having made up his mind to run away to India from the book and its inevitable re-kindling of the Lawrence limelight, he ordered his regiment (or whatever they call a regiment in the Air Force) thither, and is now out of reach of this exhibition and this preface, which is perhaps lucky for me, as I am able to say all these things behind his back'.

'What will happen in India next,' G.B.S. concluded: 'Heaven only knows.'[9]

Revolt in the Desert was published by Cape in two editions on 10 March 1927. The first was a limited edition of 300 copies priced at five guineas, and the other was the trade edition for general sale at thirty shillings. Both were illustrated, and the limited edition included some of the colour plates which had appeared in *The Seven Pillars*. The book had a remarkable success, encouraged no doubt by the mystique surrounding the production of *The Seven Pillars*. By June over 30,000 copies had been sold, which caused Lawrence to send instructions to the publishers to withdraw it since this was the number he had calculated as sufficient to clear his debts. However, when *Revolt in the Desert* was finally withdrawn it had sold 90,000 copies in the English market alone and contributed to an increase in Jonathan Cape's profits from £2000 to something in the region of £28,000 which, according to the firm's official history, was a distinct embarrassment since 'the Inland Revenue became excited, and required a long and cogent memorandum to explain this sudden opulence'.[10]

The reviews which various friends sent him he considered to be 'mostly slobber'. But he strongly objected to being accused by Leonard Woolf, Virginia's husband, of imitating Doughty, to an edition of whose *Arabia Deserta* he had once contributed a preface. 'I think (despite Woolf) that there is very little of Doughty in my style, and less in my matter,' he wrote to the Regimental Sergeant-Major at Bovington, who had asked him whether he had seen Woolf's review which had come out in the *Nation*. 'But Doughty was keen only on death and life, and I was keen on psychology and politics. So we quarter different fields.'

By way of compensation for Woolf's criticism, John Buchan wrote in the *Saturday Review* that the author had 'none of Doughty's biblical or Elizabethan anachronisms', while H. W. Nevinson in the *Manchester Guardian* praised the 'scholar's style, simple direct, and free from ornament'. Bernard Shaw summed it up as 'positively breezy'.[11]

'My dear Lawrence,' Trenchard wrote from the Air Ministry on 7 June. 'How are you? I hear you are at Karachi, and I hope you are well and enjoying yourself.' He went on:

Have read your book [*The Seven Pillars*] and I must say that once I took it up, I didn't put it down again until I had finished it, or nearly did. It is splendid, I could see the blowing up of the bridges you describe! I have insured it and left it to my little son in my will. I hear the abbreviated edition has had a phenomenal sale and is doing extraordinarily well.

Iraq seems to go on its usual way – every now and then Faisal getting down in the dumps and then getting above himself. I suppose we all do this, but on the whole it has gone extraordinarily well and continues to do so.

No time for more, but let me know how you are, and if you are happy and contented, or if you would care to come back to the Air Force in England for a bit and enjoy yourself in the cooler climate. I could do it quite easily if you want to. It would be better for me if you did, I think.'[12]

Lawrence replied to this letter on the same day as he received it.

Karachi. 30.vi.27. When I opened your letter I gasped, expecting something of ill omen. However all's well...

...Your wading through all my book astonishes me: also your insuring it, and leaving it to Hugh II. You'll leave him worse things, perhaps: things which he can't sell. Titles. Having a child is exciting. He may turn out a poet, or a labour M.P. or a mere admiral. I hope not the last. Beatty's gone now, which is one of your troubles done with. I suppose that brings your going nearer. Coming off guard is a wonderful feeling, but I shall be very sad when you finally do. It will mean that the R.A.F. is of age, and I prefer being looked after. Alas it isn't yet of age, nearly.

The last sentence approaches danger. I keep on unconsciously working round to shop. There is surplus energy here. A cool climate, like Devonshire, and working hours only 5 a day. What am I to do with so much leisure? Write books? Name again. They let a fellow in for trouble. 'Revolt' is rottenly written, worse than the 'Seven Pillars'. (Aren't you glad I stood out against the idea of finishing your war-history?) but it has sold 30,000 copies in England, and 130,000 copies in America. Good, in a way, for I was heavily in debt, and am now clear: but bad, for it has drawn new attention to me, and there is to be another 'life' of me this autumn, written by a friend, Robert Graves, who consented, to keep the job out of worse hands. Not in any way my fault, as you can imagine, for I hate being abroad, and the more they talk the longer I must stay.

Yet I'm sure I was wise to come overseas. There is no local press, and I rouse no interest in camp. Karachi I haven't visited, so nobody outside the depot has seen me. Service character still good, and I've not yet been in real trouble: nor sick. So probably I'll pass the M.O. when I apply to extend service this time next year.

Let me remind you on that point that you agreed to consider it, if still C.A.S.: and to mention it to your successor, if you have taken your freedom before then. It will be the subject of my next letter to you, I hope.

Meanwhile I'll wander round E.R.S. logging the events of each engine's overhaul, or doing what else they give me to do. It's not happiness, but marking time till the public forget me. As a rule they forget pretty quickly.

Iraq has had five years of peace out of us; if it went up in flames tomorrow, yet that five years would win forgiveness on doomsday for Winston and yourself, the sponsors of its scheme. It was a little demon delightedly rubbing his hands in the background. Surely my share in helping settle the Middle East atones for my misdeeds in the war. I think so, anyway.

Give Hugh II my best regards. I look forward to seeing him in 1930 or 1932 or 1935, or whenever it will be.[13]

The enormous success of *Revolt in the Desert* enabled Lawrence while serving in India at this time to promote a charitable project which had Trenchard's warm approval. In 1919 the Royal Air Force Memorial Fund, subsequently renamed the Royal Air Force Benevolent Fund, had been founded by Trenchard with the object of providing assistance in one form or another to all R.A.F. personnel in need, being run from three rooms in Iddesleigh House, Westminster, where Aircraftman Shaw was in the habit of calling from time to time when he was in London to see how things were going. Now, with the royalties from *Revolt in the Desert*, Lawrence established a £20,000 trust, known as the Anonymous Educational Fund to produce an income for the education of the children of disabled or deceased *officers*. It might be thought that, because he was serving in the ranks, Lawrence would have devoted his fund for the benefit of airmen. However, he argued that because of the high ratio of officers to airmen, and because flying was mostly carried out by officers, casualties among officers were disproportionately large and the main Benevolent Fund aimed at achieving fairness among all ranks and branches of the service.

At all events Lawrence was soon labouring in the knowledge that he was educating the children of deserving Royal Air Force officers with a preference for those who had lost their lives or been invalided out of the service. By the time he died in 1935, his trust had paid £4142 towards school fees and he was educating thirteen children in that year. After his death the trust was renamed the Lawrence of Arabia Educational Fund, although its objects remained unchanged, and it still exists in that form as a subsidiary of the main Fund.

2

Lawrence's amount of leisure time during the two years he spent in India, in which he voluntarily confined himself to camp and did not once venture into Karachi, greatly facilitated his literary activities. During this period he wrote over one hundred long letters to various correspondents, probably more than during any other two-year period in his life. In addition he collected all the notes he had made at Uxbridge and Cranwell and used them as the basis for the text of *The Mint* which he completed at this time, while he also began to make an English prose translation of Homer's *Odyssey* for an American typographer named Bruce Rogers, eventually to appear in 1932 under the imprint of the Oxford University Press in New York. Of course, he had other chores in addition to his work in the Engine Repair Section, which overhauled the aero-engines after they had done so many hours service in the squadrons on the frontier. 'They have given me a semi-clerical job,' he told his mother, 'to follow the various engines as they pass through the shops, and record what changes and repairs and adjustments each requires. That is my main job, but it is supplemented with others. . . . In India the R.A.F. un-fortunately is part of the military establishments, so there are many stupid ceremonies and public performances for which we have to turn out and pretend to be soldiers. That causes a lot of bad feeling amongst the airmen.'[14]

'Otherwise – Karachi is tolerable,' he told Marson at the same time as he answered Trenchard's letter. 'Not good: how can exile so far from London be good? But I am attempting a hard thing: to make the camp suffice for my needs. I haven't been out-side its bounds since I arrived: a sort of voluntary permanent C.B. But I shall be wildly glad when I reach England again.'

I was wise to come out [he went on], for my books stirred up quite a lot of trouble in the English press: and there is to be a new 'life' of me (before I'm dead, too!) this autumn. Had I stayed in England, Cranwell would have been terrible. But I'm only hoping that after this year the public, knowing all there is to know, will be sated, and will forget me: so that I can come home when my term runs out, and have another year or two of home service before discharge. I like the R.A.F. so much that it's hard to waste abroad living down a book-folly! Especially hard when every day I become more hopelessly decrepit and disgusting.

This is not cheering you up: but if yours had been my achievements, you would not have found them much of a mental meal ten years after. You would long all the more to recover the young time of which the war years had cheated you. It's hard to have got to the top of the tree, without the fun of swarming about the middle branches![15]

The Air Officer commanding the R.A.F. in India at this time was Air Vice-Marshal Sir Geoffrey Salmond, whom Lawrence had known since 1916 when he was appointed to command the Middle East brigade of the old Royal Flying Corps, and whom he liked and admired immensely for his knack of maintaining good human relationships wherever he served. Salmond first appeared at Drigh Road about five months after Lawrence had been there, as Lawrence related to Charlotte Shaw.

It is his distressing duty to inspect Karachi Depot, and every other R.A.F. station in India, every year. The coming of an A.O.C. always troubles the smaller fishes. We have to clear up all the confusion of twelve-months work, and offer him a swept and garnished, and thoroughly ornamental camp. We did it.

I didn't see him, for I am subtle at dodging heavy projectiles. Yet he remembers me. He said to the C.O., 'By the way how's Shaw getting on?' The C.O., aloof always and Olympian as a ship's captain, said, 'Shaw? Shaw? I do not think we have here any officer of that name.'

That evidence of my propriety of conduct delighted Salmond: but I'm afraid that the C.O. was probably the only man in the Depot who had not heard of me: though few yet know me by sight, since I do not appear at football matches and entertainments.[16]

'He is quite all right and does not want to be moved,' Salmond reported to Trenchard after he had seen Lawrence a couple of times. 'He is a very good influence in the Depot and the men are devoted to him. He is just the same as ever.'[17]

3

It was not until several more months had passed that Aircraftman Shaw came to the attention of the Camp Commandant, W/C Reginald Bone, c.b.e., d.s.o. 'The Wing-Commander met me for the first time, the other day, and tròd heavily on my harmless, if unattractive face,' Lawrence wrote to Marson on 20 January 1928. 'I think he must have been reading Robert Graves, and felt that I was a worm.'

> Fortunately Salmond happened along next day, and told him that I was all right. So my sheet remains clean. I have a terror about that sheet: if I get a mark on it someone will hoof me out into the street again: and I am too old to go wandering any more.
>
> Incidentally don't take that remark about oldness as a moan. For my rackety life and generally damaged condition, I enjoy the most astonishing health, and it surprises myself when I think about it. In India I am better than in England. Perhaps my lubricating oil is a bit heavy, and it takes a wisp of sunlight to get it circulating freely. Anyway I see myself signing on to convert my 5 reserve into 5 active, next winter. . . . believe me, St Anthony isn't in it with me now. There is that sheet to be considered. It was different at Cranwell, where I know that Biffy trusted me. So the old cat could pretend to be a kitten.
>
> I enclose you my last letter [from Trenchard]: 'cause I can't tear 'em up: and it would put me into the guard room to be found with it by the C.O. You can destroy it for me. The yarn about Faisal isn't true; he never asked me for one [a copy of *The Seven Pillars*].[18]

Lawrence's brush with the Commandant was apparently the

result of a request by the C.O. to the Adjutant. 'I fancy he writes to Headquarters,' said the C.O. about Aircraftman Shaw. 'Will you try to find out?' The Adjutant, 'being bull-honest', in Lawrence's words, immediately went to Lawrence and asked him. Lawrence, in describing the incident, wrote to Trenchard: 'I showed him the letter you had sent me, and the one Salmond sent me about the same time...both obviously private affairs. Person II was pleased. V.I.P. was not yet feeling safe, so I was sent for, cursed, and condemned to go up-country as a Bolshevik. This made me miserable, for a bad name in the Service sticks for years; and both here and at Cranwell I have been a plaster saint.' Then Salmond suddenly appeared.

> He inspected us, saw the tears not dry on my cheeks, and asked why I was not happy. So now I am to live here happy ever after. Do not allow any newspaper reports or lives of me (there are four of these) to persuade you that I am not the most inoffensive little creature alive. I've sacrificed a comparatively promising career to join the R.A.F. and I'd sacrifice any thing else I may have to keep in it...My service character is still spotless; and my officer here is very decent. In return I do quite a lot of work... [19]

A copy of Trenchard's letter, which Lawrence showed the Adjutant and then sent to Marson, who presumably destroyed it as asked, was preserved among Trenchard's private papers, so that it has been possible to reproduce it here.

Air Ministry, Kingsway, W.C.2.   28th November 1927.
How are you? I hope well.

We at home, owing to Faisal being home, have been having interesting times talking about Iraq. Of course, a lot of people want to run before they can walk, and I keep pointing out that it will be another 10 or 15 years before new Empires are sound, if then.

Then the other day I came across people who know you by going down to visit Oxford and I made a speech, and the Vice-Chancellor made one and went into legend and talked about

'Icarus' and 'Daedalus'. I, for once, replied impromptu that we had one more renowned – an aristocratic forbear in the Air Force, namely, the 9th King of Britain [Bladud]. Result – I was considered very learned by some of the Oxford undergraduates, which is the first time I have been considered learned.

But there I heard you had made away with all the profits from your valuable books, and therefore you became dependent, in your old age, on those whom you would hate to be dependent on. I hope anyhow, you can put this right, either with my aid or without it, if you wish.

Next, sorry to hear you have not left the camp. It will make you see all the people in authority with jaundiced eyes. When I don't leave this office, I see all those under me in a very red light.

I expect your fingers are itching to write again, in spite of your saying they are not. If they are, write an answer to this letter.

I was told the other day that Faisal had asked you for a copy of *The Seven Pillars* and that you had refused to give it to him.

I notice in the cheap evening papers lately (there are no expensive ones!) and in other papers that you have been attacked by Arnold Wilson and Philby.* I don't know how you like it. All the summer I was heavily attacked by my friends Groves, Sykes and all those people.† It is like a savoury to me – it gives me an appetite for more – it pleases me! I hope it does you.

---

* Sir Arnold Wilson had been a Political Officer in Mesopotamia during the Arab Revolt and in common with others who were attached to the India Office was highly critical of the work of Lawrence and the Arab Bureau. He reviewed *Revolt in the Desert* unfavourably in the *Journal of the Royal Central Asian Society*. St John Philby, who likewise served as a Political Officer in Mesopotamia, shared Wilson's view and felt that Ibn Saud and not Hussein should have been supported by Lawrence and the Arab Bureau. In Philby's opinion the only monument to Lawrence's work were the destroyed remains of the Hejaz railway.

† Brig.-General Percy Groves, British Air Representative at the Peace Conference in 1919, wrote a variety of articles and books on air matters critical of official policy, as also did Sir Frederick Sykes, M.P., a former Chief of the Air Staff, who was also a strong critic of Trenchard.

Well, I am still in office, having a certain amount of work and various things going wrong.

I expect what you would like to do is to get in one of Cave-Browne-Cave's boats and go flying round the world, but I fear it can't be.*

No more news at present. If you care to answer this you can but if not, I shall understand.[20]

Lawrence replied on 22 December.

Indeed my fingers do not itch to write; only in your case it is a different thing. You see, I have for you one of my unreasonable regards. So when a letter from you turns up, the border line between my chest and stomach gets suddenly warm; and it would take an uncommon convulsion of nature to stop me from answering you. . . .

I am glad you remain patient with the tantrums of Irak (or Iraq). All babies try to walk before their legs are really strong. It's the best way of strengthening them. Even in the case of infant Hugh . . .

Not guilty of refusing Faisal a *Seven Pillars*. He did not ask for one; and I was relieved by his decency. Otherwise he'd have had to have it and he's not the reading sort of man, nor would he have liked my freedom towards his father. Arabs are so filial. The only thing I have ever refused Faisal is myself . . . and he had a very useful loan of that, occasionally.

Arnold Wilson and Philby are all right in their place and time; but of their good graces I am not ambitious. My political manners are not Corsican. Just as well for them. As long as I get all I want they can do their pleasure, and say their pleasure. As a matter of fact, to pursue a personality is the best way to

* Wing-Commander T. R. Cave-Browne-Cave was an expert on aeronautics, particularly airships and flying boats. He was a member of the Departmental Aeronautical Research Committee and at the time Trenchard wrote was preparing to make a solo flight in an R.A.F. machine to Singapore and Japan, which he successfully accomplished in 1928, thus demonstrating Trenchard's argument that the R.A.F. should be given more say in overseas defence than the rival Chiefs of Staff would allow.

lose a principle and a campaign. Sometimes I want to show them how they could achieve their aim, if they would be just a bit cleverer. Ditto with Sykes, Groves, Grey* and Co.

Never, since it began, have I made one brass farthing out of my part in the Arab show. I would not feel so sea-greenly incorruptible otherwise. . . . In 1930, or whatever is the happy day on which the humblest airman (A.C.1 now; Records pushed me up a grade on Oct. 10) disembarks at Southampton, the heavy book [his copy of *The Seven Pillars*] is to be sold to provide him with a Motor-bike and its maintenance for five years at £1 a week. That means I see my way clear till 1935. After that, presumably, you mean me to 'become dependent on those I hate'. I hope not. Any God's quantity of fellows less healthy and particular than me make their own living. Don't judge me unfitted for life because a scruple makes me refuse the honour and rewards of one particular incident in my history.

I gave the cash to the R.A.F. fund because the R.A.F. gives, and has given me a great deal of good life and peace to me. Of course there are . . . V.I.P.s who have given me enough of the other side of things to value the good when I get it . . . but the credit balance is infinitely on the T.E. side. I shall always be in debt to the R.A.F. Nor was the disposable cash very much, after the debts of the big book were paid. I am never likely to regret what I've done with it. When people ask me 'But why the R.A.F.?' (They being more interested in the Battersea dogs' home) I grow portentiously serious and point out that I am quite likely to be a distressed airman one day. I suppose some idiot has repeated his remark to you as a serious one.

Last month I refused an American offer of 100,000 dollars for a seven weeks lecture tour in the States; last week an offer of £5000 for one of the five copies of my proof-printing of the *Seven Pillars*. So it is not only in respect of the pay of Lieut. Col. and some decorations, and the profits of *Revolt in the Desert* that I have been consistently wise or foolish. All this is of course for your private comfort. Do, PLEASE, not feel

* C. G. Grey, editor of *The Aeroplane*.

responsible for me. I have done fairly well for myself, so far, for forty years, and I want to remain in charge for the rest. When I want a thing, I know it, and peg away till I get it. If you see Sir Samuel Hoare, ask him to tell you how hard it was to keep me out of the R.A.F.

The death of Hogarth was, as you will have imagined, a blow to me.* I have had the fortune to serve three great chiefs: Allenby, and Winston, and another, more recently [Trenchard]. I did a lot for (1) and for (2) and have done little for (3); but Hogarth was not a chief but a friend, and he did for me more than I will ever be able to do for anyone. It was because he lived there that I liked Oxford. And now I shall be afraid to go back to it.

Enough of this stuff. I'm sorrier about Hogarth going than I've been about anything.[21]

Ironically, Hogarth, the scholar-traveller and archaeologist, who had given Lawrence his chance as a youngster at Carchemish in 1911, on the strength of a senior history demyship at Magdalen, was working on an article on Lawrence for the *Encyclopaedia Britannica* at the time of his death. 'I had (and perhaps still have) a hedge full of trees,' Lawrence wrote to a newly acquired pen-friend, H. S. Ede, who worked in the Tate Gallery and first wrote to Lawrence after seeing the exhibition in the Leicester Galleries. 'They are old: and whenever one falls I miss something of what used to be the shapeliness of that hedge. So Hogarth is part, a great part, of Oxford, the concrete thing for which Oxford stood in my mind. Now Thomas Hardy has followed him into that very rich company. I am sorry for T.H.'s going, too, though less so, for T.H. had perfected himself in his work, and went into the grave very poor in spirit. Whereas Hogarth put so much of his force into the act of living.'[22]

Lawrence was lying on his bed in camp on the Sunday after Hardy's death on 11 January 1928 listening to Beethoven's last quartet when one of the airmen came in with the news. 'We

---

* D. G. Hogarth, who was President of the Royal Geographical Society, died in his sleep at Oxford on 6 November 1927, aged 75.

finished the quartet, because all at once it felt like him,' Lawrence
wrote the same day to Mrs Hardy. 'I am well off, having known
him: you have given up so much of your own life to a service of
self-sacrifice . . . T.H. was infinitely bigger than the man who died
three days back – and you were one of the architects. In the years
since *The Dynasts* the Hardy of stress has faded, and T.H. took
his unchallenged – unchallengeable – place. . . . He is secure.
How little that word meant to him.'[23]

Hardy's ashes were laid to rest in Westminster Abbey, the pall-
bearers including Baldwin, who was then Prime Minister, his
cousin Rudyard Kipling, J. M. Barrie, Edmund Gosse and Bernard Shaw. Charlotte sent Lawrence a detailed account of the
ceremony. Baldwin, she thought, was the only one in the Abbey
who looked unimpressed by the pomp and dignity of it all. She
was put off by Kipling's appearance. 'So Kipling looked sinister,
did he?' commented Lawrence. 'The silly little man annoyed me
by smally refusing to be decent to old T.H. who did quite a lot
for him when he first came to London, but whom he dropped
after *Jude the Obscure*. So he probably was under Baldwin's dress.
Baldwin I am sure is very good . . .'

It is worth noting here that a few weeks previously Lawrence
had sealed his friendship with Charlotte Shaw when she had sent
him her common-place book of private anthology of meditations
and he had responded by sending her a volume into which he had
copied over the past decade more than a hundred poems which
had caught his fancy and which he called *Minorities*. 'Some are
the small poems of big men: others the better poems of small
men,' he wrote to her with the volume. 'One necessary qualifica-
tion was that they should be in a minor key.' He went on:

> The worst is you do not like minor poetry: so that perhaps
> the weakness of the spirit in this collection will only anger you:
> and then my notebook will not be a fair return for your note-
> book. In my eyes it is: for I'm not so intellectual as to put
> brain-work above feeling: indeed as you know, I don't like
> these sub-divisons of that essential unity, man.[24]

4

Two of Lawrence's contemporaries at the Karachi Depot later recalled some memories they had of him there. One was the Adjutant, Squadron-Leader W. M. M. Hurley, and the other was Leading-Aircraftman B. V. Jones, who occupied the next bed to him in the airmen's Room 2.[25]

The Adjutant, who had learned of A.C 2 Shaw's identity in a private note from R.A.F. Headquarters in Delhi, was quick to notice that he spent most of his spare time writing in the E.R.S. Office. He therefore offered him the facilities of his Orderly Room with the use of the typewriter on Thursdays, which Lawrence accepted, as Thursday was a holiday and the Adjutant himself found that this day was the only one upon which uninterrupted work could be got on with in his office. Consequently they saw a good deal of each other, although even in the intimacy of their relatively long acquaintanceship Lawrence: 'never allowed himself to depart from the strict attitude which he had accepted for himself as an essential accompaniment of his adopted position'. The Adjutant particularly noted that he did not smoke or drink and indeed ate very little, and that all the time he was at Karachi he was very much the airman. Also 'he had a very soft voice which he never found necessary to raise even when his feeling upon a subject or in a situation demanded biting sarcasm or pitiful denunciation. In appearance his head was everything, a noble feature indeed with a lofty forehead, very soft blue eyes and a strong chin. His body was small and wiry and must have framed a splendid constitution, when we consider the trials and the actual brutality which had been part of his share in the Arabic campaign'.

On the whole Hurley considered that he was happy at Karachi, since everyone in camp played up to the question of leaving him alone, if he wanted to be alone, which was pretty often, though people outside the camp who heard he was there were always asking about him. Moreover, he was pestered by unwanted gifts from unknown admirers, some seeking his autograph and others offering him well-meant sympathy for what they imagined he had 'had to come down to', and requesting information about his exploits in Arabia. The only packages he would accept from the Post Office were books and gramophone records, and the Adjutant was amused to receive the following note which was passed to him by the local Indian postmaster.

> Postmaster, Drigh Road.
> Please take notice that I am not able to sign receipts for parcels addressed to me.
>   T. E. SHAW 338171
>   9.11.27

There was quite a good library at the depot, but it was very much better by the time Lawrence left, since he had acted as a kind of unofficial librarian not only suggesting books for it but presenting many of his own. 'On looking back on those days spent in his company,' the Adjutant was to recall, 'the most definite characteristic of the man seems to have been his quiet unobtrusiveness. It was as if, outside any private conversations with him, we agreed to ignore the fact that he had any previous existence.' Yet little incidents did occur from time to time which suggested 'qualities which could not be dispersed by merely a formal adoption of a new name and identity'. Incidentally it was at this time that he changed his name by deed poll to Shaw, although he had been known as Shaw since he enlisted in the Tank Corps. Once at the annual pistol course on the range, when Lawrence happened to be range orderly, only Lawrence, the Adjutant and the Armament N.C.O. were left behind. Then, suddenly and quietly, Lawrence picked up a pistol and put six 'bulls' on the target.

On another occasion, which Hurley has recalled, the aircraftman's previous knowledge as an Arabist was put into use, when the Persian Government had declined to allow British civil aircraft to land in their territory, and it became necessary to organise an R.A.F. survey of an alternative route along the eastern coast of Arabia and that side of the Persian Gulf. The party, led by Squadron-Leader C. H. Keith, whose book *Flying Years* gives a vivid picture of service in the Middle East at this period, duly arrived at Karachi, which was to be the terminus of the air route from England, bringing with them various reports from Political Officers and photographs of tribal personalities encountered on the way. The British Resident in the Persian Gulf also arrived, and a conference was arranged in the Depot Commandant's house. According to the Adjutant, A.C. Shaw proved very useful in his identification of the Arab sheikhs and his assessment of their influence, although he did not have an intimate knowledge of that part of Arabia. After he was satisfied that there were no females in the party, before whom he would be an interesting exhibit, Lawrence was brought in from the garden where he had been waiting dressed in his aircraft hand's overalls, and in this garb he attended the conference.

Although Aircraftman Shaw's religion appeared in his personal file as 'C. of E.', he asked to be excused church parades, since, as he told the Adjutant, it was an unbearable strain for him to have to sit and listen to sermons with which he did not agree and not being allowed to challenge them in argument and request foundation for what was being said. The Adjutant therefore arranged that he should be given a routine duty in the Orderly Room on Sunday mornings, since 'it was obvious that his continued attendance at the services was not likely to lead to benefit or conversion'.

It was about this time that his mother and elder brother left China on account of the civil struggle which had broken out between the Kuomintang and the Communists and which was characterised by considerable anti-British feeling. 'I sincerely hope that they will not return,' he told a friend. 'The Chinese are waking up, at last – and the fewer foreigners they have there the better – well-intentioned foreigners, that is. Foreign enemies do no harm to a race just beginning to feel national. By their opposition they inflame the race-consciousness of the local people: but foreign friends! Oh, they are a disaster.'

After they were back in England, Lawrence wrote to his mother and Bob, pointing a lesson which no doubt they failed to appreciate.

The civil wars will last for a while yet, and after that a violently national Government will want to restore Manchuria and Korea. So for a long time China will look after itself: indeed I think probably there will not be much more missionary work done anywhere in future. The time has passed. We used to think foreigners were black beetles, and coloured races were heathen: whereas now we respect and admire and study their beliefs and manners. It's the revenge of the world upon the civilization of Europe.[26]

Lawrence particularly endeared himself to the other airmen, and also to the Adjutant, by volunteering for guards and pickets on any special occasion when the average airman wanted to be free, and Hurley distinctly remembered him on Christmas Day 1927: 'absent from the feast in the dining-hall but very prominent as sentry at the main guard-room'.[27] This was confirmed by Lawrence in one of his letters to H. S. Ede. 'My Christmas passed quietly in the guard room, where I was one of four on guard,' he wrote. 'The camp was drunk, as a body: so the guard room was a good place. I often go there on a holiday, swapping turns with some convivial fellow.'[28]

One such fellow was Leading-Aircraftman Jones, who occupied an adjacent bed and whose acquaintance began when Lawrence asked him for the loan of an india-rubber, which he was able to supply, remarking as he returned it that he was not in the habit of using a rubber as he had: 'made a study of being precise both in his speech and his writing.' Mention has already been made of the books which he collected, many of them complimentary copies sent out by English publishers, which he would lend round the airmen or present to the library. They included reprints of William Blake, Thomas Malory, Bunyan, Plato, and James Joyce's *Ulysses*. He kept his copy of *The Seven Pillars* in a small tin box under his bed, and obligingly allowed Jones to read it. Jones has also recalled that when he asked Lawrence, after he had become aware of his identity, what were the world's five greatest books, he replied without hesitation that they were, in the following order: The Old Testament, Tolstoy's *War and Peace, Don Quixote, Moby Dick*, and C. M. Doughty's *Arabia Deserta*. Often while he was darning socks, he would discourse on such subjects as Woolley's finds at Ur or the exploits of Charles XII of Sweden. 'Shaw's advent among us did much to awaken an interest in literature; an airman who had been accustomed to read penny dreadfuls could be seen struggling with such a book as Churchill's *History of the Great War*.'[29]

There was a strange quality of impishness in Lawrence's make-up which appealed to Jones. Due to the poor lighting of the barrack rooms, many airmen had followed his example by rigging up reading lamps which had leads connecting to the fan switchboxes. The Camp Commandant on one of his periodical rounds of inspection commented on the increase of 'these pirate fittings' and on the ground of economising in the use of electricity ordered their removal. Aircraftman Shaw's lamp, however, continued to burn with its accustomed brightness. 'On the next inspection Shaw stood rigidly to attention. The C.O., his Adjutant and the Regimental Sergeant-Major proceeded to investigate, only to make the exasperating discovery that the leads were not connected to the camp supply as had been anticipated, but to a separate source of power in the form of a large battery under Shaw's bed. This battery was, in reality, an artistically contrived dummy, and cleverly concealed leads which found their way circuitously to the forbidden switchbox.'

In Jones's view, Lawrence's personality was best interpreted to many of the airmen through his choice of music. By reason of their spaciousness, the barrack-rooms at Karachi had very good acoustic properties, and often from tea-time to lights out, Lawrence would run through the classical masters from Beethoven and Schubert to Wagner and Delius. But Mozart was always his favourite. 'Music at first so strange and unintelligible to many of us, by its constant reiteration, impressed something of its significance, until there was born, even to those who had voted it an unsufferable "bind", an apprecation of the immortal masters.' However, he did have some popular records, one of which was of the American vocalist Sophie Tucker singing some of her cabaret numbers. The fate of this record he described in a letter to Robert Graves on Christmas Eve 1927.

I have given away Sophie Tucker. She was worn to the bone,

after about two hundred playings; and I find her just as intel-
lectually suggestive when she comes down the wind to us from
the next barrack-block ninety yards away. A splendid woman,
doubtless, but she inclines me against matrimony. Imagine her
greeting you at breakfast, day after day.[30]

About this time the London *Daily Express* ran a feature on
Lawrence's activities in camp allegedly obtained from its Karachi
correspondent. Instead of visiting Karachi, according to the
correspondent: 'He goes when off-duty to the edge of the desert
with a pocketful of cigarettes purchased out of his daily pay of a
few shillings. There he chats with the villagers, and joins in their
profound Eastern meditations.'

Lawrence cut out the piece from the paper and sent it to the
editor, R. D. Blumenfeld, who was an old friend of his, annotating
it with characteristic comments. For one thing, he pointed out,
they were not on the edge of the desert but in the middle of it.
Secondly he never smoked, and as for the chats with the villagers,
he did not know a word of any Indian language, but he supposed
they talked English. But if there was a village anywhere near, he
had not seen one. 'Villagers in all countries have their thoughts
centering on those parts of their bodies which lie, as the Arabs
say, between the navel and the knees,' he went on. 'Food and
sex: and I don't meditate, not even profoundly about either.'
Consequently he adjured the editor to 'tell your bright young
thing that it's a rotten effort. I could do better than that in my
sleep. I hope he'll be content, however, to forget it. I'll promise,
in return, not to write fancies about him'.[31]

When he departed from the depot for an up-country posting,
as he was to do in the spring of 1928, Lawrence left his fellow
airmen in Room 2 his gramophone, most of his records, and
many of his books as a parting gift, an action remembered with
especial gratitude by one Leading-Aircraftman called B. V. Jones.

5

By mid-March 1928 Lawrence had completed the final draft and

fair copy of *The Mint*, which were laboriously transcribed in a
notebook from his original notes and earlier drafts, and he posted
the notebook to Edward Garnett. This he had specially bound in
air force blue. 'It is the blue we wear,' he explained to Garnett:
'and you can imagine the tooling is our brass buttons.' If he had
thought of it, he went on, he would have had six buttons down
the front like his uniform. He added that he had sent the volume
'by an official by-pass, for safety, as there is no copy, and the
making of this long manuscript has hurt my eyes exceedingly'.

The notes eventually worked out at 70,000 words: the Uxbridge part was 50,000: and I added 20,000 on Cranwell, (built
up out of contemporary letters and scraps of writing which I'd
hoarded against such a need) to redress the uniform darkness
of the Depot picture. Cranwell was a happy place.

Will you let me hear of their safe arrival to your hand? If the
first receiver does not put on stamps, and you have to pay, let
me know that also. I have no English stamps here, and this is a
gift to you: a very overdue gift. Was it 1923 I promised you
the things? So very sorry.

This afternoon I am going out into the desert with some
paraffin and the original draft, to make sure that no variant
survives, to trouble me as those two editions of *The Seven
Pillars* do. So before you get it your copy will be unique. . . .

I want it offered to Cape, for publication, in extenso, without
one word excised or moderated. Can you, as his reader,
arrange this? I'd rather no one read it but you (and David G.
who feels rather like your second edition, revised and corrected
by the author, but less spontaneous): and I want him to refuse
it, so as to free me from the clause in his contract of the *Revolt
in the Desert*, tying me to offer him another book. I hate being
bound by even an imaginary obligation.[32]

The 'official by-pass', referred to by Lawrence in this letter was
Charlotte Shaw, to whom he had already sent a typescript of part
of an earlier draft. '*The Mint* has been impossible to write all these
years,' he told her: 'for six years I have had its pieces in my bag,
and it was not till England was away behind me that I could take

it up and work on it. It is not easy, either, in this place and climate, and in service conditions to write seriously. You'd have laughed, I think, if you'd seen me working away with a pencil, as I sprawled on my bed afternoon and evenings, while the crowd chattered and wrangled over my head.'[33]

He now asked her to send on the typescript, within ten days, to Edward Garnett in a plain wrapper, and with no indication of who was forwarding it to him. The Shaws were spending a holiday in North Wales at the time, and so as to give no clue to the sender Charlotte tied up the script in a plain parcel with a second wrapper addressed to her husband's secretary Blanche Patch, who sent it on to Garnett correctly stamped. Miss Patch found the mystery in which Lawrence enveloped the dispatch of his manuscript puzzling, and she regarded Lawrence's remark to Garnett about the stamps as indicating his views upon 'the unreliability of womankind'.[34]

Lawrence now thought he had better let Trenchard know what he had done and what *The Mint* was all about and how he had come to write it. So he wrote to the C.A.S.:

Karachi. 17/3/28. . . . In 1922, when you let me enlist, I promised that the C.A.S. should see, first, any book I wrote on the R.A.F. I don't think it's a book: – but I posted something rather like one yesterday to Edward Garnett: and you'd better hear about it.

In those days I hoped to turn as much of me as had survived the war into a writer; and I thought the R.A.F. was a subject. So I made full and careful notes of Uxbridge. Afterwards, at Farnborough in 1923, I had a look at the printed *Seven Pillars* and realised I should never write well. So pop went that ambition; and the notes popped into my kit-box.

In the midst of that misery I was kicked out of what had become my profession: and so re-met Garnett, whose name you probably know as a critic of genius. Of course he's more than that; but that's only his reputation. I explained to him that the reason had fallen out of my existence – and so there wouldn't be another book. He remained curious. If not a book, what of the notes? I sort of grinned, and said 'I'll give 'em you, for keeps'. But they'd been left at S.O.P. in one of the fellows' lockers; and they banged about the earth for years, occasionally coming into my hands. They felt unbearably vivid and meaningful to me, like a part of myself (for private reasons) and I didn't want to lose them: but at last you let me back again, and then I cared for them no more.

Garnett used to hint at his unfulfilled present, from time to time. So in Karachi I took them up, at last, to send him: but time had blurred their original pencil into unintelligibility, except for me. They'd been written nightly in bed! So they had to be fair-copied; and I sweated on them for months, till they were all out straightly in a little note-book of 176 pages (70,000 words) called *The Mint*. *The Mint*, because we were all being stamped after your image and superscription.

This note-book it was which I posted yesterday. Last night I made a lovely bonfire of the originals. Up came the orderly sergeant, and asked silly questions: wanted to know what I was burning. 'My past,' said I. But suddenly I thought – perhaps they'll say I've written another book. Do you think so? If you care to see it you may. This letter will catch up, and I am sending Garnett a copy to show him it's your right to see it. That will explain the typing of an A.C.H., afraid to type well for fear they promote him into a soft-boiled clerk. It also shows devotion to duty, to send two Air-Mail letters in one week. Twelve annas gone west.

Garnett will not hawk the thing about; only his son will read it. After I'm dead someone may censor out of it an edition for publication. I shall not care, being dead; and the R.A.F. will be different and indifferent. Quite wrong of it; doesn't know its mercies: may be years before it has another A/C like me.

I don't advise even Garnett to read it; much less a man of action. 170 pages of my handwriting. It's a worm's eye view of the R.A.F. – a scrappy uncomfortable thing. I've been an uncomfortable thing while I wrote it. The ranks, even of your imcomparable force, don't make for easy living or writing. Every word of this has been done in barracks. Any word used in barrack rooms has been judged good enough to go in; wherefore Scotland Yard would like to lock up the author. The general public might be puzzled, and think I didn't like the R.A.F. whereas I find it the only life worth living for its own sake. Though not the Depot. Uxbridge was bad, and I'd have written and told you so, only that it seemed implicit, in your letting me join, that I should take my stuff quietly.[35]

A few days later he wrote to Garnett again, enclosing a copy of what he had written to the C.A.S.

The Trenchard letter will explain itself to you. If he asks for the notebook, it will be out of curiosity only. My handwriting will easily defeat him. Probably you're the only person who'll ever read it at all.

Besides him, you, and D. Garnett, Mrs Shaw has seen some of it. I sent her two batches of the third draft which is very like your text: only a little rougher. My re-working was no more than planning. . . . Every sentence of the original was used: and very little was added: no significant addition, certainly.

'I hope *The Mint* will not make Trenchard hate me,' Lawrence wrote to Charlotte Shaw at this time. 'He is so very kind and large: but it offends against the tradition of loyalty, and perhaps he will think me a scab for betraying my service. I wish you knew Trenchard. It would explain a good deal to you. Now D.G. H[ogarth] has gone, he's the man whose opinion I shall be sorriest to lose. Of course he is not civilised like D.G.H., but he is larger.'[36] In fact Charlotte thought *The Mint* a masterpiece when she read it and she regarded the conversational obscenities as merely incidental to the main theme. G.B.S. took the work which he 'sampled' rather more primly, but he only suggested two excisions, one of which was the account of Queen Alexandra's funeral parade (which even Charlotte thought 'cruel') and the other the retelling of a military policeman's story of a London adventure in which a woman of easy virtue concealed her dead infant in her bed while entertaining the visiting corporal on a couch, too 'purple patchy' in its descriptive passages for Bernard Shaw's taste. Since *The Mint* was not destined to be published in Lawrence's lifetime, there is no knowing whether Bernard Shaw's suggestions would have been carried out, had Lawrence revised the work for publication.[37]

However, the news about *The Mint* made Trenchard sad when he learned of it from Lawrence, and he wrote telling him so on 10 April before he had seen the manuscript.

I feel rather that what you have written is what is quite comprehensible to you and to me as we both understand the position, but it would be seized upon immediately by the Press *if they got hold of it*, and they would say what a hopeless Air Force it was – how badly it was run – what hopeless officers we had, etc., when I know that is not what you mean at all, though *I have not seen* what you have written. I am certain you will believe that this is the sort of thing the Press will do *if what* you have written is ever published.

And the Air Force is still young. It cannot go on being continually abused by everybody, and I have enough of it as it is regarding accidents and one thing and another.

I do not feel a bit annoyed with you. I feel I always thought you would do it, though I hoped you would not. Anyhow I am going to see Garnett when I can, and I hope he will not publish it or let it be published, though when I have read it maybe I shall like it?[38]

As soon as he received this letter, Lawrence sent off a wire to the C.A.S. to reassure him that, since the copyright remained his, it was therefore impossible for anyone to publish *The Mint* 'without my permission which will never be granted'. He followed this up with a letter in which he told Trenchard that in addition to himself the only people who would see the text were Garnett and his son, Bernard Shaw and his wife, and E. M. Forster: 'a novelist I like'. There was 'no harm in any of those'. Meanwhile Lawrence told his brother Arnold, his literary executor, that no part of the work was to appear before 1950, or, if Trenchard preferred it, before 1970. 'You'll realise that even then it can't appear textually,' he explained. 'The language is too obscene, the thought too outspoken. I hope you will not write me off as dirty-minded for the filth in the book. We are all dirty, in the ranks: dirty of body, and dirty-mouthed: but underneath lies a courage and loyalty and humble cheerfulness, and honesty which make me proud to belong.'

Lawrence continued in the same letter:

Please make no mistake here. I've enlisted twice in the British Army, and twice in the Air Force. I've seen from the inside the Turkish and Arab armies, and something of the Navy. The R.A.F. is streets finer, in morale and brains and eagerness. Agreed it is not perfect. It never will be. We grumble – over trifles, mainly customs of dress which you've inherited from the older services. If I were C.A.S. or influential with him, this could be put right in one issue of A[ir] M[inistry] orders costing two-pence. These silly details (regular Royal Oakapples) agitate our leisures . . . hours: but the actual *work* 99% of the fellows enjoy. You have given us something worth doing.

Of course you have enlisted some duds. There are dud Englishmen: but the average of the R.A.F. is magnificent. As you know, I think the present other-ranks relatively good but for the officers. You must have some technical mastery to hold the respect of tradesmen indefinitely. It's no use, or very little use, being just a gentleman, today. But the officers have seen that, and are getting down to it. They are better taught than we are, and will soon beat us, when they try.

Do please credit your most experienced A/C, who has, in his time, been a man of action, and even made a tiny fighting service out of nothing, when he assures you that the R.A.F. is the finest individual effort in British history. As this is a private letter, I'm going to let myself go and tell you (what I'll never say in print, unless I survive you and write your life, which God forbid!) that the R.A.F. is your single work: that every one of us, in so far as he is moulded to type, is moulded after your image: and that it's thanks to your being head and shoulders greater in character than ordinary men, that your force, even in its childhood surpasses the immemorial Army and Navy. No other man in the three or four continents I know could have done what you've done.

South Hill, the home of Thomas Tighe Chapman, heir to an Irish baronetcy, near Delvin, County Westmeath, Ireland. From here Sarah Madden, governess to the Chapman daughters, eloped with their father, who changed his name to Lawrence. Thomas and Sarah Lawrence afterwards had five children, but since Mrs Chapman could not divorce her husband under Irish law, all the Lawrence children were consequently illegitimate.

Thomas Edward ('Ned') Lawrence was born in this house at Tremadoc, Carnarvonshire, on 16 August 1888, although his birth certificate (below) records his birth as having taken place a day earlier.

REGISTRATION DISTRICT DOSBARTH COFRESTRU				Festiniog					
1888 BIRTH in the Sub-district of GENEDIGAETH yn Is-ddosbarth				Tremadoc	in the *countiefther ineho batnat son* yn				
mus:— *nau:—*	When and where born Pryd a lle y ganwyd	Name if any Enw os oes un	Sex Rhyw	Name and surname of father Enw a chyfenw'r tad	Name, surname, and maiden surname of mother Enw, cyfenw a chyfenw morwynol y fam	Occupation of father Gwaith y tad	Signature, description and residence of informant Llofnod, disgrifiad a chyfeiriad yr hysbysydd	When registered Pryd y Cofrestrwyd	Signature of registrar Llofnod y cofrestrydd	Name entered after registration Enw a gofnod-wyd wedi'r cofrestru
	Fifteenth August 1888 Gorphennaf Tremadoc Carnarvon 1888	Thomas Edward	Boy	Thomas Lawrence	Sarah Lawrence formerly Madden	Gentleman	Thomas Lawrence Father Gorphwysfa Tremadoc	Twenty Seventh August 1888	Richard Parry Registrar	

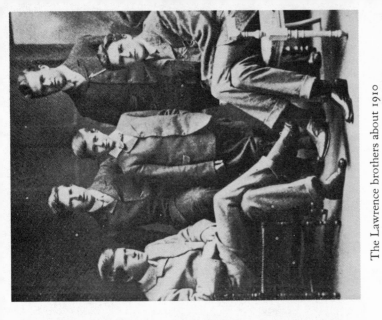

The Lawrence brothers about 1910
Left to right: Ned (T.E.), Frank, Arnold,
Bob, and Will.

Mrs Sarah Lawrence whom
her son Ned described as
'a very dominant person.'

This cottage, behind the house at 2, Polstead
Road, where the family lived in Oxford, was
built for T. E. Lawrence by his father so
that he could work undisturbed.

Major-General Sir Hugh Trenchard attended the Cairo Conference as an Air Marshal and Chief of the Air Staff, but for some reason does not appear in the large group picture. He met Lawrence there for the first time and offered him a commission in the Royal Air Force, which Lawrence refused, saying he would prefer to join the ranks. Trenchard later arranged to enlist him secretly as an aircraftman under the name of John Hume Ross.

Sir Ronald Storrs, Governor of Jerusalem and close friend of Lawrence. He was to act as chief pall-bearer at his funeral and to write the article on him in the *Dictionary of National Biography*.

Air Marshal Sir Geoffrey Salmond (left) and Air Vice-Marshal Sir John Salmond (right) with their father Major-General Sir William Salmond at a levée in 1925. Both the Salmond brothers, each of whom became Chief of the Air Staff, supported Lawrence, particularly Sir Geoffrey, who was Air Officer Commanding India when Lawrence was serving there as an aircraftman.

This was a typical recruiting poster at the time Lawrence joined the R.A.F. as an aircraftman in 1922. The oriental background reflected the responsibilities for air control and policing in the Middle East recently assumed by the air force.

The first part of the world which the recruits saw was the depot at Uxbridge, where a great part of their time was taken up with drilling and the discipline was harsh, as later described by Lawrence in *The Mint*. The photograph (below) was taken of a parade outside the airmen's huts.

When it was noticed that Lawrence, who had enlisted as J. H. Ross, was missing from the parade, the sergeant sent A. G. Turner, the recruit marked with a cross, to fetch Ross from his hut. But Ross refused to come on the ground that it was not an official photograph and he was excused.

Air Chief Marshal Sir Hugh Trenchard, Chief of the Air Staff, inspecting a passing-out parade of cadets at Cranwell in 1926. The officer on the extreme right of the picture is Wing Commander Sydney Smith, Chief Staff Officer at the College and later Lawrence's Commanding Officer at Mount Batten (Cattewater).

Letter from Lawrence written in the summer of 1926 to the editor of *The Journal of the Royal Air Force College* when Lawrence was serving as A/c Shaw at Cranwell, giving permission to quote from *Revolt in the Desert*, the forthcoming abridgement of *The Seven Pillars of Wisdom*, and also pointing out that he was never 'Prince of Mecca.' From the original in the library of the R.A.F. College at Cranwell.

Lawrence (A/c Shaw) and his commanding officer Wing-Commander Sydney Smith off duty at Thurlestone.

Lawrence called this picture 'The Judgment of Paris'. Clare Sydney Smith is on the right and her dog Banner is holding the 'apple' in the form of a tennis ball in his mouth at Thurlestone.

(Above left) The Air Minister Lord Thomson and the Prime Minister Mr Ramsay MacDonald at Calshot for the Schneider Trophy seaplane race in September 1929. (Above right) A/c Shaw talking to officers during the trials for the race.

The Supermarine S6B in which F/L J. N. Boothman won the Schneider Trophy outright for Britain in 1931 with an average speed of 340 m.p.h. It was from this aircraft that the famous Spitfire fighter was evolved.

Leaving Clouds Hill on Boanerges on one of his last rides on the machine from which he was thrown and fatally injured.

(Right) Some of the pall bearers wheeling Lawrence's coffin into Moreton Church for the funeral service.

The grave at Moreton.

The R.A.F. is 30,000 strong, too huge for you to have personal contact with many of us: but there is hardly a barrack room in which your trumpet does not regularly sound: and these thousands of your champions find no opponents. We grouse and grumble at everything and everybody, except you: and all but that one per cent of ignorant airmen know you as our exemplar and creator, and try (does it frighten you? it would me) to be better copies.[39]

Trenchard replied on 6 July after he had finally read *The Mint* which he had 'several times started to and always stopped'.

I know I shall not hurt your feelings; it was what I expected to read. I feel I understand everything you put down at the time and your feelings, but I feel it would be unfair to let this loose on a world that likes to blind itself to the ordinary facts that go on day after day. Everything you have written – I can see it happening – the way you have written it as if it was happening, but the majority of people will only say 'How awful! how horrible! how terrible! how *bad*!'

There are many things you have written which I do feel we know goes on and we know should not go on, though what you have written does not hurt me one bit – far from it, and yet, if I saw it in print, if I saw it being published and mis-understood by the public, I should hate it, and I should feel my particular work of trying to make this force would be irre-trievably damaged and that through my own fault. . . . But as the Air Force gets more and more of the spirit I want it to get, so a lot of what you have written will automatically leave the Air Force without there seemingly being any alteration in the eyes of the public. . . .

Last time I wrote to you I was sad. I am still a little sad and tired. I sometimes think people do not realize that I do not want to use the Air Force for killing only: the fact of an Air Force being about should in time ensure that we may not continually go on the warpath with as many casualties as we did in the past.

The C.A.S. went on to describe what he had been trying to do in the past three or four years on 'how to improve the careers of the men and the officers without it costing too much money', and that he had got the Treasury to agree, after arguing with the officials there for two-and-a-half hours, to a scheme for making promotion quicker for both branches of the force. 'We are getting a very good type of man to join the Air Force now, even with the career we have had to offer them up to the present,' he wrote. 'It will not bring about a splendid career tomorrow, but in another ten or fourteen years' time the scheme will begin to make its effect felt, provided nobody pulls the whole structure down. It is sufficiently flexible to improve, but who will interpret it? I hope it will be understood and extended and improved as the years go on.' He concluded his letter with these words:

There have been a certain number of letters recently – letters to the papers and sent to me anonymously – saying that I only care for drill. If they only knew how I hate drill and everything connected with rigidity! But it is awfully hard to get one's real intentions interpreted as one wishes. People will not understand that the regulation is only made for the fool to keep, but for the wise man to break.

When are you coming home? I have made up my mind to leave the Air Service at the end of next year. It is unfair to the Air Service to go on stopping, and I am not sure that I have not outstayed my usefulness ...

I am perfectly certain I am not really uneasy about *The Mint*, so don't think any more that I am. Your letter reassured me and I am certain you will understand my views, so I am pleased at having read it, and shall not probably remember it again in my life and time, though it will interest many people in many years to come.[40]

By the time Trenchard had dispatched this letter, Aircraftman Shaw had applied to the A.O.C. for a posting up-country and was on his way to Peshawar and Waziristan. It was the old story. 'It's not our Section Officers who are concerned,' he wrote at the time. 'I like the puzzled honesty of F/Lt Angell, my immediate C.O., and he is very decent to me. But higher up they panic, apparently, over my mere existence in their camp.'[41] He told Trenchard privately what was behind his move.

> ... A conversation between an officer and a civilian in a club after dinner was improperly repeated to me. The officer has never spoken to me. ... However this one is reported to have sworn he 'had me taped' and was 'laying to jump on me' when he got the chance. It was after dinner. They had all dined. I have no means, or wish, to check the story. But I'm pretty tired of fighting, and of risks: and my past makes my service character brittle. People easily believe of a man who has been an unconventional officer [unconventionality forced on him and also, I believe, exaggerated] and now prefers not to be an officer. So I'm going to run away to a squadron. They are small and officers mix with airmen, and aren't as likely to misjudge a fellow. I told Salmond I had private reasons.
>
> Don't think me a funk. At worst it's only overcaution. In September I apply to extend my active over the five years of my reserve service. You thought Records would consider the application if I passed the M.O. I'm as fit as any man here: never reported sick or missed an hour's duty. I want to keep my conduct sheet as clean as my medical one. Since you let me back into the R.A.F. I haven't been on a charge: but any officer who wants to get a man can find cause. Services only work by breaking half of King's Regulations daily. So I feel I'm not abusing Salmond's kindness in asking him to move me. Such prudence, far from making you apprehensive of my being in the ranks, should comfort you, as it is proof of my past carefulness. I had, you see, three Tank Corps years to teach me the cost of being cheerful.[42]

Lawrence's destination was Fort Miranshah in Waziristan, the most remote R.A.F. station in India, which he reached about the middle of August 1928. 'We are only 26 all told, with 5 officers, and we sit with 700 India Scouts (half-regulars) in a brick and earth fort behind barbed wire complete with searchlights and machine guns,' he wrote to his friend Ede at the Tate Gallery shortly after his arrival. 'We are not allowed beyond the barbed wire by day, or outside the fort walls at night. So the only temptations at Miranshah are boredom and idleness. I hope to escape the first and enjoy the second: for, between ourselves, I did a lot of work at Karachi, and am dead tired.'[43]

6

During the period of his service in India Lawrence's exchange of letters with Trenchard is particularly full and detailed. Indeed the whole correspondence, until Trenchard ceased to be Chief of the Air Staff, is unique as being between a man in the lowest rank of the service and the man at its head. Of course, Lawrence had an immense admiration for the man who had rebuilt the R.A.F. from scratch on a slender budget, while Trenchard developed an increasing affection for the wayward airman in the ranks. Since 1922 the policy of air control had been applied to Iraq, Faisal's kingdom which was under British protection. For a while things went well, but the situation began to deteriorate through the quarrel which broke out between King Faisal of Iraq and Ibn Saud, the King of Hejaz and Nejd (renamed Saudi Arabia in 1932), each side carrying out raids on each other's territory which it was the task of the R.A.F. to stop. Trenchard was worried and he asked Lawrence what he would do about it, if he were in his place.

> Iraq and the quarrel between Ibn Saud and Faisal worries me a lot. I do not want to kill either side, and I am not doing much in it, but people who live by raiding almost all their lives do not understand our feelings on the subject, and they dislike it when we try to stop them and think our methods are more brutal than theirs. Equally, the poor unfortunate officers and men who are in the desert trying to stop the raiding do not like it – it is unpleasant, and they always, I expect, feel that the faults are half on each side, like I do.
>
> However, I hope for the best through patience and the Air, if I can only get the Ibn Saud fanatics to believe in it and to go

up in it. If I can bring this about, I feel I may yet make peace between Ibn Saud and Faisal. Perhaps you will say this is impossible. Could you do it?

So many people get alarmed about these raids. There are rumours of 30,000 men moving, and rumours of all sorts of dangers – yells for reinforcements by political officers – some working one way and others another. It is hard to keep a firm hand on it all, and I am getting tired with having been 10 years in this office, and am beginning to wonder a little if I have done any good. Sometimes I feel I have done a lot, and at other times I wonder if I have done anything that will not collapse. Which is right?[44]

The Bedouin raiders, at least on Ibn Saud's side, were members of the Islamic Puritan Movement called Wahhabis or Brethren, who regarded as enemies all who did not purport to follow in detail the practice of the Prophet Mohammed, and every campaign waged against their enemies as a holy war in which death was a sure passport to Paradise. In his reply, Lawrence, after putting forward his ideas on the relative merits of the two chief antagonists, warned the C.A.S. against St John Philby, the Arabist and former British Representative in Trans-Jordan, who was now in Ibn Saud's confidence. He also gave some practical advice on how best to control the eastern salient of Trans-Jordan between Syria and Saudi Arabia.

The Wahhabi Business
I'm sorry for the Bedouin, high-spirited, ignorant animals, led astray by fanatics. Religious theories are the devil, when they are ridden too hard, and begin to dictate conduct.

An accommodation between Ibn Saud and Faisal could be arranged, but would not cure your trouble, at the moment. I don't think they are the main people, or the parties with the initiative. Ibn Saud is a fine company-commander, who's a bit out of his depth with a battalion. He's trying to bestride two worlds, the desert and the towns. It has never been done so far, except episodically. Faisal wanted to attempt it, in 1918: and I broke him away, then, from the nomads, roughly. I don't believe you can yet unite, or federate, or crush into one tyranny even, any two Arab-speaking districts: *yet*. Ibn Saud can only recover the Mteir and Ateiba by forgetting the towns, or by using the towns to crush them. By the first course he loses his revenue. He's too indebted to the tribes, and I hope too decent a fellow, to do the second. If you squeeze him he may try to do it; and will then, I think, break himself – to your loss, for he is our one real asset in his kingdom.

The fellow you need to influence is Feisal el Dueish, or whoever is the driving force behind the raiders. If I were at Ur, my instinct would be to walk without notice into his headquarters. He'd not likely kill an unarmed, solitary man (Arabs are very curious-minded) and in two days guesting I could give him horizons beyond the Brethren. He would make a wonderful border-warden, if he once got out of the ruck. Men of decision are rare in the Desert and in London.

I beg you not to order your Political Officer to execute this suggestion straight away: or Faisal may execute your P.O.s. Such performances require a manner to carry them off. I've done it four times, or is it five? A windy business. It's only my primary instinct. To change it into a plan would require local knowledge, of the situation's details, and the local casualties, and temper. In the East, if you have your ear right close to the ground, you hear everything that's happening, and a great deal more. The selective ear tunes out the false news, and that's the difference between good politics and bad. While I'm on that word 'bad' let me warn you against Philby. His 'red' complexion, in English affairs, is an index of his judgement. His politics are Corsican: that is they include blood feuds and personalities: and these small things exclude the principles, which alone, I fancy, distinguish the statesman from the mere politician. I am afraid of Philby, sometimes, lest he go wrong, wilfully.

Of course there's no danger in the Shamiya situation: it's a nuisance only. It should not be expensive unless you try to meet like with like. Bedouin on camels will make a meal of any civilised camel-corps: or of infantry in the open: or of cavalry anyhow. Nor does a static defence of a line avail. You need an elastic defence, in depth of at least 100 miles. Explored tracks for cars, threading this belt, approved landing-grounds, sited pill-boxes or blockhouses, occupied occasionally and then fed and linked by armoured cars, and supervised from the air. Care will open almost the whole desert to motor traffic, and petrol is the tactical key to the situation. I could defend all E. Trans-Jordan with a fist-full of armoured cars, and trained crews.[45]

Lawrence wrote again to Trenchard when he had settled down in Miranshah:

5.8.28. I was very glad to get your letter, and learn that *The Mint* had not decided you to cast me out of the R.A.F. again. Also to see that you do not think it a dreadful work. I do not think it is, any more than you do: – though the fools of the public (numerous creatures these are) would howl and say 'How DREADFUL' if it was published.

Your earlier alarm to Garnett did not do me enough credit. *The Mint* had been five years in my possession, and I had not hawked it about ... nor had I ever dreamed of publishing it. For one thing 'they' would feel let down; I had been in the hut with them for months, until they had learned to take me as one of themselves: and to go and blow the whole truth in print would have seemed to them a betrayal. 'All the characters in this book are real and every event actually happened' ... no, I'm not that sort of fellow.

For another thing, the R.A.F., about which I feel as keenly as yourself (you see, I'm in it, whereas you are only over it) would suffer if I printed it. If I printed it I would get £10,000 and a reputation as a writer. Do please count my not doing so to me, as a bit of righteousness.

After which I must hasten to say that if you dismiss me the force tomorrow in circumstances of the utmost barbarity, even then I shall not publish it. It will only come out before 1950 if I am made to hate the Air Force, somehow. ... and as I have survived spells of Bonham Carter and Guilfoyle, and still like the Service, that will be very hard to make come about.[46]

11 September 1928 ... I've not quite gone to Afghanistan:
Miranshah is ten miles or so short of its edge. This is the
smallest station in India. There are four permanent people (a
Stores Corporal, a W/T Corporal, an armourer, and a clerk:
I leave you to guess who the A.C.H. clerk is!) and a detached
Flight from one or other of the five neighbouring Squadrons
comes up every two months. I went to 20 Squadron, by Sir
Geoffrey's kind offices, to get on to the strength here: for I
knew that so tiny and so remote and so shut-in a place was
exactly what I needed to be quiet in. We are behind barbed
wire, and walls with towers, and sentried and searchlit every
night. It is like having fallen over the edge of the world. A
peace and hush which can be felt. Lovely. I hope to stay here
for the rest of my overseas spell.

At Peshawar I stayed only one night. So I cannot tell you
of it. Nor of the Khyber, nor of Waziristan. While I am in
India I will not (except under orders) pass outside the lines of
the camp I am attached to. I am always extremely fit.

And fitness is the main reason of my writing to you, so soon
after the last letter. You said, as I left England, that my application to extend my active service over my five years' reserve
period would or might be favourably considered, if I could
pass the doctor when the time came. The time comes tomorrow:
and I could pass all the M.O.s in the R.A.F. There is no hurry:
and no need for you to answer this. I shall take a silence from
you as meaning that your consideration continues: and shall
send in my application to 20 Squadron on November 5th next.
The rule is that we must apply within the last eighteen months
of our seven years' term: and that begins, as I said, tomorrow.

I greatly hope that your consideration does still hold. The
only thing, since 1925, that has happened to make you feel
sorry I am in the R.A.F. is, possibly, the Uxbridge Notes. But
they existed in 1922–1923: and my continued service will not
change or increase them. For better or worse (the Garnetts,
the Shaws, and E. M. Forster who have read them, call them
good) they exist. A very subtle C.A.S. would prolong my
service indefinitely, so that he could court-martial me if I published them! However I have told you that I will not publish

them, whatever happens to me, in the R.A.F. or out of it. So this is not blackmail.

You have never been reconciled to my serving, as I am quite aware. The senior officers all hate it. My immediate C.O.s (perhaps I've been fortunate) have all been exceedingly good to me, and have defended my harmlessness, when I have been absently discussed. I think, if you were the F/Lieut. Commanding Miranshah that you would lose your nervousness regarding me. I am nearly always cheerful; and work quite hard, and – amazingly – distract the other fellows in camp. For them I am almost an education, for I have done and read so much, and seen so many people and places, that they use me as a reference library. And I think that the spectacle of a semi-public character contented in their ranks does tend to increase their self-respect and contentment.[47]

Trenchard replied on 30 November.

I did not answer your letter on the subject of your re-engagement, because you said if I did not reply you would assume I agreed. I do agree to your extension for 5 years. I have also agreed that if you want to stop there until 1930 or 1931 you may do so. At the same time, I am quite ready to bring you home of course, if you are at all seedy, and station you again at a place like Cranwell or somewhere similar.

I have cabled to Sir Geoffrey Salmond telling him I agree to your extension, and to tell you, so you will probably be told before you receive this. Let me know how you are and how things are going.

Now let me tell you this. Various people at home have been to see me, rather to implore me not to allow you to re-engage, but to bring you back to England. I have said that when you like to write to me or my successor and say you are tired of the Royal Air Force, I will agree to your going, but I will not take it from any of your friends that you really want to go out. This much I know you will do, (and you owe it to me) – you will tell me when you want to leave us.

Anyhow, the question of keeping open a permanent job for

you for 5 years is, I fear, impossible, but when your time comes to clear out there is not the slightest doubt there will be lots of jobs you can get. I am not going to make plans for you 5 years ahead. But do you agree with what I have done – told them you are not available for any job as you have extended your service till 1935?

I should much like to see you and talk over things. My little boy is growing up fast. There is one thing you will hear by the time you get this letter, or very soon after, and that is that my resignation has been definitely accepted, and I leave at the end of December 1929. It is not, of course, decided who will succeed me, but I shall have done nearly 12 years by that time, and I think it is time for the good of the Air Force that I should clear out. You will probably agree, but may think it necessary, to write and say you don't agree. Do not do this, because you must not get dishonest by stopping in the Air Force. It is supposed to be an honest Service, and I think it is.[48]

By the time he received this letter Lawrence had already heard the news of Trenchard's impending resignation over the station radio.

Miranshah. 11/XII/28. This morning I was in the cabin at broadcasting time, and the message came through that you had resigned. So it's all over, and I can't tell you how sorry I am. Of course, I know it's your wisest move, and you have finished, and all that: but here I've just been able to take on for five more, as you go out. You'll feel it hard: for you have never really been in the R.A.F. at all. You've made it; and that means that you are not in it. People can't make things bigger than themselves: not bigger enough to get into. I'm sorry, because it feels nice, to be in it, like I am.

I think you have finished the job. A man would be slow, who couldn't exhaust all of himself into a thing in ten years. You were lucky to have the chance for ten years. No other man has been given a blank sheet and told to make a Service, from the ground up. Neither the Army, nor the Navy have a father in the sense of the R.A.F. Now you'll see the child tumbling down and hurting its knees, and getting up again. Don't worry, more than you need. It's a very healthy, and tolerably happy child. A C.A.S. with leisure would make it happier: only your successor will be pretty hard-worked, I expect, like yourself. However your resignation means that the child is on its own, and sooner or later it'll make itself happier.

You'll feel exceedingly lonely and tired for a long time: and I wonder what you'll do: for you aren't old enough to settle down. Perhaps you'll go and govern somewhere. That will be only the shadow of power, after what you've had: but shadows are comfortable, after too fierce a light. So possibly you will be contented.

You'll be rather shocked to find that three weeks after you're gone (about the time you're reading this) your past services haven't any interest or value in the Government's eyes. It's what we can do, yet, which makes us regarded.

I've said to you before, that in my eyes (very experienced eyes and judgmatical eyes) you have done the biggest and best thing of our generation: and I'd take off my hat to you, only at Miranshah I do not wear one. There'll never be another King like you in the R.A.F., and I'll feel smaller under whoever it is takes your place. Allenby, Winston, and you: that's my gallery of chiefs, to date. Now there'll be a come down.

You know that. I'm at your disposal (except in disposing of my body) at all times and circumstances.[49]

When Trenchard's letter reached him, Lawrence wrote again, two days after Christmas.

Hard luck: only last week I wrote to you: and today there comes your letter of November 30th, asking me a specific question, which my letter probably answered, by implication.

Sir Herbert Baker, it probably was, who suggested to you my coming straight back, to a job he had found for me as night-porter in the Bank of England. If the R.A.F. had refused my extension, that would have done, but I'd rather have the shortest R.A.F. extension than the best civil permanency. I have become curiously at home in the ranks, and wouldn't leave them for anything, so long as I am fit.

So you answered whoever it was quite rightly. I am booked surely and gladly till 1935. The only exception would be if my real age (and my past excesses) broke out on me suddenly. Then I couldn't well stick the comparative hardness of an airman's life, and would have, in decency, to go. I do not want to use the service as a sort of almshouse. Fortunately there are no signs of that yet. I'm a species of evergreen, apparently.

Incidentally, a Wing-Commander (Medical) once was rash enough to ask why I was in the R.A.F. My answer, on the spur of the moment, was that if a fellow wasn't mad enough for a lunatic asylum, or rotten enough for an almshouse, he must do *something*. Answer not well received.

Back to business. It is exceedingly good of you to let the show go on being bothered by an odd airman. Do explain to your successor what his chief liability is: & that I'm less trouble to the C.A.S. when I'm inside the service, than when outside it: but a trouble anyhow. It is like having a unicorn in a racing stable. Beast doesn't fit.

As for the friends and enemies who try to steer a course for me: – neglect them. They seem to disbelieve in my capacity to lay out a good course for myself: and refuse to understand that I prefer my course (however peculiar) to all their offers. Being in the R.A.F. for instance, though some people didn't want me there, has paid *me* excellently. Today I'm healthy, and sane, and happy at odd times. If you hadn't let me back in 1925, I shouldn't be alive now. Perhaps, though, that is a bit of bad.

I hope that letter of mine doesn't say that you are wrong to leave. I am very sorry you are going: it ends an epoch: and I had a personal pride in seeing you make the service, and helping you make it, from the bottom, and in being made by it, too. But I'm a believer in the parent birds getting out, when the chick's done his first solo. You may remember my getting right out of the Arab business, so soon as it seemed a going concern. Arab Nationality was as much my creation as the R.A.F. is yours.

A careless parent does no harm to the grown-up child: but

the more one has cared, the more one tends to keep excessive hold of the leading strings: and the only way a kid can learn to walk is by falling down & struggling up again. Your chicken is so fit, that a bit of tumbling will do it good.

As for my coming home, the obstacle is a Collingwood Hughes, who bought from the owners (I'm not one) of *Revolt in the Desert* the right to film it. Not that events are copyright. But he can now quote bits of the book, & use my former name on it.

I gather he hasn't yet begun to make his film. Short of cash. I am, too. Films involve much publicity and I fear to return to a home station till it is over: – either shown & forgotten, or abandoned. Therefore I say April 1930 for my return date. By the way, an army ship; from Bombay; & me the only R.A.F. detail on board! By so coming I shall avoid seeing the fellows I care for degraded in that horrible troop ship experience.[50]

'We have had an idyllic two and a half months here, under the best and kindest C.O. of my experience,' Lawrence wrote at the same time to E. M. Forster. 'When Miranshah is good it is very good.'[51]

At the Armistice Day parade on 11 November 1928, a bizarre incident occurred which Lawrence described briefly to Charlotte Shaw in a letter written the same afternoon and which he later liked to recall in more detail when reminiscing with his friends. It was arranged that, when the white and native troops had been drawn up in two straight lines on either side of the wall which divided the camp, while at the same time the native servants paraded in front of the Mess, the Armourer Corporal should fire two rockets on the stroke of eleven, since it was important that everyone should stand to attention at the same moment and finish standing in silence precisely two minutes later. As a precaution the Armourer Corporal brought a third rocket as a spare in case one of the others failed to go off and he laid it on the ground beside him. They were powerful rockets used for signalling to aircraft in foggy weather.

All went well until the hour of eleven began to strike and the Armourer Corporal let off the first rocket. Unfortunately the sparks from this rocket accidentally ignited the spare rocket on the ground which happened to be pointing in the direction of the Mess. According to Lawrence, this rocket gave a *wumph* and shot off like an angry cannon ball, scattering the native servants who howled loudly and leaped into the air like scared rats, while the rocket hit the Mess building whence it was deflected at a tangent, skimming down the side of the white troops, hitting the wall and eventually crossing a tennis court and ending up in the Officers' Mess front door, which it smashed through, setting it and a rug inside alight. Meanwhile within there were heard shrieks, crashes and thuds, mingled with the smoke and fire. A/c Shaw and his fellow airmen thereupon promptly seized fire extinguishers and buckets of water and eventually brought the conflagration under control.

A few minutes later Lawrence and his companions were having a breather in the mess, when a little brown man with a smiling face and a red turban, who was one of the native servants, popped round the corner and said: 'Please, Sar, Colonel Sahib say is Two Minutes Silence finish?'[52]

The C.O. for his part was quick to appreciate what 'an excellent orderly room clerk' Lawrence was – 'because he never produced a letter or a signal without the appropriate answer already typed and ready for signature.' He also had 'a steadying influence – magnetic – unseen and unheard. On the station he was not a hero – he was just "a jolly good scout".' Incidentally Lawrence was the first serviceman to show that there was no medical necessity for wearing solar topees or pith helmets as a protection against sunstroke, and he went about bareheaded.[53]

The airmen's mess there was extremely comfortable and had been furnished with curtains, easy chairs, cushions and a good library. A Wing-Commander who came up on a visit of inspection remarked: 'Mess? Why it is more like a Piccadilly lounge. Don't they smash it up?'

Lawrence, who was present in his capacity of librarian, replied: 'Why should they, sir? These men were not born in a barrack room. This is what they are accustomed to in their homes.'[54]

They had occasional visits from army units who did not behave as they should. 'Four army signallers, from the

Cameronians, were here to practise signalling from the air,' he
described their behaviour to Charlotte Shaw.

> They got roaring, fighting drunk. As it died out of them near
> midnight, they were very sick and there were no basins in the
> barrack room. Today they were to be flown for half an hour
> each. Air experience. We told the officers of the night we had
> had with them. Wild beasts at Ephesus: – it was more like pigs
> in clover, or a runaway sewer. Mr Smetham [the C.O.] said
> 'We will show them how to be sick.' He rolled them all over
> the sky. They came down all green and white, with all their
> insides churning like a millrace. We had to wash the machines
> with a hose. They went back to their camp today. I do not
> think the next instalment (if they can be forced to come) will
> get drunk.

'The great relief it is to me that Trenchard took me in for those
five extra years,' he wrote to the Shaws on Christmas Day. 'I am
like Charles II, too old to go on my travels again. Alas, I shall be
older yet in 1935 when the inevitable may happen. If only we
could stay able-bodied till we died. Death I like the sound of: but
decay is humiliating.'

On Boxing Day 1928, Lawrence wrote what was to be his last
recorded letter from India. It was addressed to John Buchan and
was primarily intended to inform him that his application to
extend his service had been agreed. He went on:

> I wanted you to know that I'm making the best use I can of the
> gift you led Mr Baldwin into giving me in 1925. Will you tell
> him, if you ever see him at leisure, that I'm still thanking him,
> whenever I think of it? The R.A.F. still suits me all over, as a
> home: quaint, that is, for it's probably not everybody's pre-
> scription. . . .
>   The R.A.F. hasn't yet found the way out between the rocks
> of discipline and individual technical intelligence – but it goes
> forward, and is very hopeful. Its salvation lies in its own heads,
> to work out internally. It's something new, in services: and I
> find it fascinating to watch its infant years.[55]

Unfortunately, through no fault of his own, Lawrence's idyllic existence in the little R.A.F. station in the Himalayan foothills was to be rudely shattered. This was indirectly due to the dramatic events which were taking place a short distance from Miranshah, across the border with Afghanistan.

7

Towards the middle of November 1928, while Lawrence was at Miranshah, the Shinwaris, one of the principal tribes in the eastern part of the country, rose in rebellion against King Amanullah, whose reforming zeal in the matter, for example, of the emancipation of women, following the example of Kemal Atatürk in Turkey and Shah Reza in Persia, gave offence to his more orthodox Moslem subjects, of whom the Shinwaris were prominent. At all events they occupied the main road from Kabul to the Khyber pass, cutting road and telegraph communications along this route. The rising quickly spread to the southern provinces and communications between Kabul and Quetta through Kandahar were likewise disrupted. The rebel leader, the son of a water-carrier, who called himself Habibullah Khan, was to succeed in rallying considerable support and in the event to force the King to abdicate, installing himself as ruler in the Royal Palace. Faced with the prospect of civil war, or at least a prolonged period of disorder, since the royalists could be expected to strike back, the British Minister in Kabul, Sir Francis Humphreys, who was called upon to exercise considerable courage and ingenuity, appealed to the British Government to evacuate the British civilians by air. This was agreed to after Trenchard had told the Foreign Secretary, Sir Austen Chamberlain, that the operation was feasible in spite of difficult weather conditions which were bound to be encountered by aircraft being obliged to fly over the snow-capped mountains of the Hindu Kush. The airlift began on 23 December and with a few temporary interruptions due to bad weather and grounded planes, was successfully completed over the next two months and included other foreign nationals, making a grand total of 586 individuals, to evacuate whom the R.A.F. flew more than 28,000 miles between Kabul and India.[56]

But this is to anticipate. On 5 December 1928, a paragraph appeared in the London *Daily News* to the effect that Colonel T. E. Lawrence was busy learning Pushtu, from which it was inferred that 'he intends to move into Afghanistan'. Eleven days later, the *Empire News*, a popular Sunday paper, came out with an article by a Dr Francis Havelock, described as a well-known medical missionary who had just returned to London from Afghanistan. According to the article, Lawrence had arrived in the country about three weeks previously and had interviews with the King, the Chief of Police and the War Minister, and then disappeared into 'the wild hills of Afghanistan' disguised as a 'holy man' or 'pilgrim'. The story, which the *Empire News* retracted shortly afterwards, was wholly fictitious and as likely as not had been concocted in a Fleet Street bar. Unfortunately it was to cause irreparable damage both to various individuals, not least Lawrence himself, since an agency had relayed the story to India where it was widely published in all the national newspapers and most of the local ones. One result of this unwelcome publicity was that a genuine 'holy man' named Karam Shah, who had joined a funeral procession in Lahore, was attacked and seriously injured by a mob which was fully convinced that he was Lawrence of Arabia in disguise. The wretched Karam Shah promptly issued a strong denial that he was Colonel Lawrence or that he was: 'in any way connected with any State or Government'.

'If I had gone to Kabul,' Lawrence wrote to the Shaws on Christmas Day after he had seen the original *Daily News* story, 'some Soviet agent would have made the mistake of murdering me lately. A mistake, for I think the Soviet is a really Russian thing, and should fit that distressful country, when it has ceased being afraid of everybody. It has persecution mania. If it is real Russian, then we may expect good things out of Russia after all. Yet as a Government system it won't export, any more than Parliaments export well. Look at the Dail, even! Let alone the French Parliament, or the Cortes. Kings are the only international constitution – because they aren't a constitution. Enough of this, I won't talk more of Kings till I've read the history of King Bernard the 1st. I hope it goes with a swing.'

A more serious development occurred on 3 January 1929 when Humphreys, in the Kabul Legation, telegraphed Sir Denis Bray, Foreign Secretary to the Government of India in Delhi, stating that the rumours about Lawrence, added to the fact that he was serving as an airman clerk under the name of Shaw at a station near the Afghan border, 'creates ineradicable suspicion in the mind of the Afghan Government that he is scheming against them in some mysterious way'. The British Minister went on to point out that these rumours were being encouraged by the Turkish, Russian and French missions. Since contradicting the stories would have no effect, Humphreys suggested that the R.A.F. be requested to remove Lawrence a long way from the frontier. Sir Geoffrey Salmond, A.O.C. India, was accordingly informed. In fact Salmond was already aware that the vernacular press in India, inspired in some cases by Soviet propaganda, had stated that Lawrence was behind the rebellion of the Shinwaris, not to mention recent outrages in Lahore, and that he had for this reason been stationed at Miranshah.

At first, Salmond, with whom Bray had discussed the matter, refused to have Lawrence transferred, or sent home. 'This was clearly stupid,' he reported by cable to Trenchard, 'as Lawrence had every right to expect an asylum in the Royal Air Force.' However, after seeing Humphreys' telegram to Delhi, which had been repeated to the Foreign Office in London, and learning that the Foreign Secretary considered that: 'Lawrence's presence anywhere in India under present conditions is very inconvenient', Salmond asked Trenchard for his views, adding that in his opinion the 'canard' would persist, 'whatever we do'. The C.A.S. immediately replied concurring in Lawrence's transfer and asking the A.O.C. to find out from Lawrence whether he would like to go to Aden, or to a small detachment consisting of two or three men in Somaliland, or to Singapore for a year, or whether he would like to return to England. 'I want to help him as much as I can,' Trenchard added.[57]

Trenchard's telegram to Salmond was dispatched on 5 January. He was anxious to let the Permanent Under-Secretary at the India Office, Sir Arthur Hirtzel, know what had been arranged, but he was unable to do this until next morning, which was a Saturday when he spoke to Hirtzel on the telephone, afterwards confirming what he said in writing. 'Both ourselves and Lawrence are anxious that there should be as little publicity as possible and I hope that it will not be necessary for the India Office to issue a statement to the Press that Lawrence is being sent away from India.' Hirtzel agreed and sent a private telegram to the Viceroy Lord Irwin, asking that there should be the least possible publicity. At the same time he sent the Foreign Secretary in Delhi a telegram marked 'Secret' which suggested on the face of it that Hirtzel thought there might be something after all in the stories circulating about Lawrence. 'It might be well that Government of India should have him closely watched lest confronted with departure from India he should bolt.' Hirtzel added that if Lawrence 'disappeared', it would be 'very awkward'.

When Trenchard heard of this latter telegram he was justifiably incensed and berated Hirtzel accordingly, pointing out that he (Trenchard) was co-operating with the India Office in removing Lawrence from India and here was the India Office behaving as if the rumours might be true. 'I am amazed,' he told the Under-Secretary on 8 January, 'to see this morning while the question of Lawrence was being discussed with me on the telephone on Saturday morning, you sent a wire to Bray lending colour to the rumours that are circulating without even consulting us on it.'[58]

That same day, Lawrence, who had been given only a night's notice that he was leaving Miranshah – 'wasn't fair on me', he complained – was flown down to Lahore where he was handed a letter from Salmond explaining the reasons for his hurried movement order, and asking him what he would like to do in accordance with Trenchard's suggestions. Lawrence then flew on to Karachi where he saw a senior officer and told him that he would prefer to return to England.

He had hoped to be able to go on to Delhi and see Salmond, but this was not possible as there was a mail and passenger ship leaving Bombay for England in a few days and he was told that a passage had been secured for him on this vessel.[59]

[6]

Flying Boats and Others

Lawrence embarked on board the P. & O. liner *Rajputana* at Bombay on 8 January 1929, with instructions to proceed with the ship to Tilbury and to report to the Air Ministry on arrival, unless he received orders to the contrary. An aircraftman named Hayter and his wife, with whom he had become friendly at Miranshah, sent him a telegram wishing him *bon voyage* and Lawrence wrote from the ship thanking them for their kind thought, and giving the letter to a passenger getting off at Marseilles and travelling overland to London. He was still feeling indignant that he had been whisked away from Miranshah at such short notice and had had to leave behind his gramophone and records and most of his books. 'I hope it will be better, now,' he wrote while the ship was steaming through the Mediterranean: 'but at Port Said, last stop, they picketed the quayside to prevent my going ashore. I'd like to say something with a B in it about the India Government. In London I'll try to find out what really passed concerning me, and try to ensure that they do not serve anyone else so.'

The only blessing has been the dodging a return by trooper. This is a 16,000 ton ship, & we have had a smooth journey. Second-class is comfortable. I have a cabin to myself, as the ship is nearly empty: and pass the whole day in it, working at that Greek book. Since we left Bombay I have done three sections of it – just as much as I did at Miranshah, all the while I was there. So you see things have moved. They are not finished, these sections: they will need fair-copying and typing out in London, during my month's leave: but they represent a good two months of Miranshah production, done in two weeks.

Voyages are binding things, & I'm lucky to have had this job to keep me busy.

At Karachi an irk lent me a civvy suit: so I sort of pass muster in the crowd. They stare at me too much for comfort. However, there it is. I shall be stared at, goodness knows, a lot more in England.[1]

At Port Said, where the ship anchored for several hours to bunker coal, Lawrence got his own back for being unable to go ashore when he raided the ship's pantry and came away with a trayful of soup cups, with which he proceeded to bombard the bargees and dockers and anyone else around who tried to catch them in their hands, much to the amusement of the rest of the passengers. One of these was a girl who joined in the operation and to whom he said with a smile: 'I'm sure dear old Inchcape* can well afford to pay the cost of the fun provided for the passengers and the coal trimmers.'

One of the passengers, an army major whose name was Stewart Humphries, has recalled that when the ship reached Malta and was in Valetta Harbour, he was on deck watching the scene ashore when he noticed Lawrence standing beside him and spoke to him, under the impression that the fine aerobatic display which had taken place when the ship anchored had been specially staged in Lawrence's honour. Major Humphries asked him if he had seen it.

'Yes, I saw much of it but did not come on deck,' he replied, but laughingly denied that it had anything to do with him. 'Actually this form of reception takes place every week when the mail ship arrives,' he explained. 'They save petrol for this as it gives the pilots the opportunity to practise close flying and aerobatics. The larger aircraft [which had flown past at deck level within a few feet of the ship's side] are bombers and those that did aerobatics are scout planes, much easier to handle than the ones we have in India. There the aircraft are so old that play in the joystick, the stays and so on make it difficult to gauge their flight within forty feet.[2]

* 1st Earl of Inchcape, Chairman of the P. & O. line.

When the *Rajputana* dropped anchor in Plymouth Sound on the morning of 2 February, it was very foggy. But this did not deter the press reporters who did their best to track down Lawrence. But thanks to the foresight of the Royal Navy and the R.A.F. the effort was unsuccessful. Lawrence was surprised and pleased to be met by his old friend Wing-Commander Sydney Smith, who had been the Chief Staff Officer at Cranwell and was now in command of the flying boat station at nearby Cattewater, where Lawrence was told that he was being posted as soon as he had taken some leave.

The P. & O. tender which came out to the ship brought Lawrence a large bundle of mail. After looking cursorily at the envelopes as they were going ashore in the Guardship pinnace, Sydney Smith was astonished to see Lawrence throwing some of them into the sea. 'Why are you doing that?' he asked him.

'Well, it's mostly rubbish,' was the reply, 'and when it's addressed to Colonel Lawrence I know it's from complete strangers, or from people who won't respect my change of name.'

'But remember all the journalists who are prowling round the Sound – they'll be only too delighted to pick up some of your mail, especially if it's unopened!'

'Oh, I'll risk that,' Lawrence answered carelessly and threw in the rest.[3]

One letter which Lawrence did not dispose of in this manner was handed to him by his new C.O. It was from Trenchard enclosing £2 'in case you may want it.' He was, the C.A.S. wrote, 'out to help you all I can', and invited him to stay at his house in Hertfordshire. 'I don't want to see a lot of placards to the effect that the Air Ministry have spirited you away in fast motorboats and cars,' he added. Unfortunately this was more or less what Trenchard did see. After breakfast at Cattewater, Sydney Smith and Lawrence motored to Newton Abbot, in the hope of avoiding the crowd of reporters and others on the boat train, only to find when they got there that the ordinary train had been hitched on to the boat train. When they reached Paddington, Lawrence was the target of a crowd of reporters, to whom he unwisely replied on being asked if he was Colonel Lawrence: 'I am Mr Smith.' The result was that he was recognised by a *Daily*

Mirror reporter who had managed to get a picture of him as he was climbing down a rope ladder at the side of the *Rajputana*, a scoop for his paper. Also the *Daily News*, which had started the false rumours about his going to Afghanistan, came out with another picture of him and a full story of how he was taken off the ship at Plymouth. 'Great Mystery of Colonel Lawrence', the headlines blared. 'Simple Aircraftman – or What?'[4]

Lawrence was eventually smuggled out of the flat where the Sydney Smiths were staying and taken to his old quarters above Sir Herbert Baker's office in Barton Street. Next day a summons came from the C.A.S., and Clare Sydney Smith drove Lawrence and her husband on the Sunday to Dancer's Hill House, near Barnet, where they gave him their version of the mishaps and adventures since leaving the *Rajputana*. According to Mrs Sydney Smith, the C.A.S. 'quite understood that they had been unavoidable and only regretted that there had been so much publicity'.[5] But there was worse to come.

Lawrence spent the night at Dancer's Hill and Trenchard drove him back to London in the morning, dropping him at Victoria. A few hours later, an agitated Sir Samuel Hoare rang up the C.A.S. and inquired pointedly whether Trenchard realised that Lawrence was in the House of Commons, wearing R.A.F. uniform and 'holding court' with a group of Labour M.P.s.

'I think you'll find he's instructing them in the error of their ways,' Trenchard answered curtly. 'But I'll find out.'[6]

'Indeed I am back: and not too quietly as your letter remarked,' Lawrence told T. B. Marson who had written to him about the publicity he was getting. 'Nearly got the sack again, I think, what a life.... For the moment I wander about London with my eyes on the pavement, like a man who's dropped sixpence, and can't remember in which street it was. Also it is more cold than I ever thought possible.'[7] Indeed it was one of the coldest winters in England there had been for many years.

On 30 January 1929, while Lawrence was still homeward bound, the Secretary of State was questioned about Lawrence by Mr Ernest Thurtle, the Labour M.P. for Shoreditch, who had been a junior minister in the first Labour Government in 1924, and as a prominent ex-serviceman was deeply interested in questions of military discipline. Mr Thurtle wished to know why Lawrence was permitted to enlist in the R.A.F. under an assumed name. Hoare replied that Lawrence preferred to be known by the name of Shaw and 'no objection was seen to his being accepted by the service for it'.[8] The Air Minister's reply did not satisfy Mr Thurtle, who now gave notice that in conjunction with his colleague James Maxton he intended to pursue the question of Lawrence using a 'false' name in the service. Hence Lawrence's visit to Westminster, where he met Thurtle and Maxton, and begged them to drop the matter.

What particularly concerned Lawrence was not the suggestion that he was using a different name because he was a spy in the British Secret Service, but that the fact of his illegitimate birth might come out, which would embarrass his brothers who were likewise illegitimate, as well as his mother who had now returned with Bob from China and was staying near Oxford. 'I have explained to Mr Thurtle, privately, the marriage tangles of my father,' Lawrence wrote to Trenchard as soon as he had got back to Barton Street from the House of Commons: '(*You* probably know of them: he didn't, and is asking questions which might have dragged the whole story into the light, and I hope that he will respect my confidence, and stop asking questions in the House). Probably an airman shouldn't discuss his family with an M.P., but I can hardly ask the Secretary of State to intervene and save me from curiosity.'[9]

Three days later he wrote again to Trenchard who had asked him to call and see him at the Air Ministry.

14 Barton Street, Westminster S.W.1 8/2/29. I will come in about Wednesday next [14 February] if you do not want me early, for any reason. Tomorrow I hope to go out into the country for four days, to stay with my mother.

As for the House of Commons raid, I think I was right. Mr Thurtle was enquiring into what was very much my private business. In explaining this I explained practically the whole affair, and probably the Labour Group will ask you no more questions on my account. In that case, I shall expect you to feel sorry that I did not go sooner to the House!

As for Blumenfeld,* whom I tried to see, and for whom I left a message, he is a very old friend of mine, who never publishes any account of my vagaries. What advice he gave as to ending newspaper talk was therefore disinterested, and he knows more of Fleet Street than we do. He can hardly have told you that I was meaning to make a statement: I would not do so without your very specific order: – and perhaps not even then without an argument.

However I have finished Thurtle, and will not visit Blumenfeld (or any other newspaper office) without your future leave.

Will you please shut up the *Daily News*? It goes on chattering, and a word from you to Sir Herbert Samuel, saying that it was my wish, would end the business. A silly rag of a paper.

Many thanks for the leave arrangements, and for the Cattewater posting. I shall breathe quieter when I get into camp again. Am still in uniform and have not once been recognised in the street, though I walk about all day.

As he had typed this letter, Lawrence added a postscript in his own hand.

I'm afraid the above reads too stiffly. That is the worst of type. I am very sorry to have annoyed you by my slight activity, and will be very patient henceforward. The trouble is that I know too much of the Government Offices to have proper confidence in them. They are manned by people just the same as myself, or rather less so: and anything outside their files scares them! However you know this too.

Perhaps I should report that Sir P. Sassoon has asked to me lunch on Thursday next and that I'll go unless you say no, meanwhile.

TES[10]

When they met at the Air Ministry on the following Wednesday, Trenchard asked Lawrence gruffly: 'Why must you be more of a damned nuisance than you need be?'

---

* R. D. Blumenfeld, Editor of the *Daily Express*.

'To stop Thurtle and his friends from asking any more foolish questions about me,' replied Lawrence. 'I'm sorry if I upset the Minister. But I think I succeeded.'[11]

This seemed to satisfy Trenchard. As events turned out, not only did Ernest Thurtle respect Lawrence's confidence but he and Maxton stopped putting down questions. Both also became friends of Lawrence, and he lent them *Seven Pillars* and *The Mint*, while enjoining them 'to be uncommonly discreet' over the latter, adding that he had 'been told by the Powers that my visit to the House was not approved: told very distinctly, I'm afraid'. Incidentally Lawrence's visit to the House of Commons gave rise to the unfounded report that he had been 'received into the Independent Labour Party by Mr Maxton'. Lawrence approved of Thurtle's reforming zeal in service matters, and he was later to take up with Trenchard some of his proposed reforms which, in so far as they were concerned with the R.A.F., ranged from the abolition of the death penalty for cowardice to unbuttoning great-coats and dispensing with wearing bayonets on church parades. The result was satisfactory. 'The C.A.S. has already done two or three of the reforms I urged on him, and repeated to you,' Lawrence was to tell his future biographer Basil Liddell Hart after he had settled in at Cattewater, 'so the job is lightened.'[12]

2

While he was on leave in London, Lawrence received from an anonymous source the gift of a new motor-cycle: 'A very new and large and apolaustic Brough,' so he described the gift to E. M. Forster. 'So large a present (valued at three years of my pay) pauperises me a bit, in my own sight, for accepting it.' The donor, or rather donors, turned out to be the Bernard Shaws. Clare Sydney Smith, the C.O.'s wife, recalls his arrival one cold March afternoon when the shining and powerful machine roared to a standstill outside the station gates. 'On it was a small blue-clad figure, very neat and smart, with peaked cap, goggles, gauntlet gloves and small despatch-case slung on his back.' After letting his mother know his new address ('I like the little camp'), Lawrence wrote to Charlotte Shaw:

13/3/29. R.A.F. Cattewater. It is a tiny station on a rocky peninsula, projecting into the Sound. From my bed the sea lies 30 yards to the South (at high tide: – beach all rock) and 60 yards to the North. The whole peninsula, with its quays and breakwater is R.A.F. There are about 100 of us living on the rock, in six huts. Today I had a hot bath. The airmen all praise the camp and its conditions, but complain that it is hard and slow to reach the town of Plymouth from it. This will not distress me.

My job? Not settled. For a fortnight I 'mark time' in the Headquarters Office: and they give me to the Workshops' Officer to employ clerically or on his motor boats. It seems to me that there are very few disagreeables here. The food is excellent: the place is comfortable: restrictions very slight, and those sensible. The Commanding Officer, of course, I know and like.

The bicycle is a heavenly machine. My ride down here was a golden occasion.[13]

From the beginning Lawrence got on well with the Sydney Smiths, their twelve-year-old daughter Maureen, nicknamed 'Squeak' and their two golden retrievers, Banner and Leo, and their cocker spaniel Billy. Soon he was being treated very much as one of the family, by whom, since his initials were T.E.S., he was familiarly called Tes. The C.O. consulted him on all matters affecting the airmen's comfort and efficiency, and Lawrence, who lived with the airmen, was able to tell the C.O. of little things that made for unnecessary irritation or fatigue and which the C.O. could then put right. 'You can see better at the bottom of the ladder than at the top,' Lawrence used to say. One thing they both disliked was the name Cattewater. 'Why,' said Lawrence jokingly one evening when he was in 'The Fishermen's Arms', as he called the C.O.'s quarters, 'if you instructed the laundry to deliver your clean clothes to Cattewater the vanman would be justified in throwing them into the sea.' Consequently, they concocted a letter to the Air Ministry requesting that it should be renamed Mount Batten after a nearby castle of that name. As Lawrence told Trenchard at the time: 'Nobody but the R.A.F. has heard of Cattewater. Everybody says – "How queer! Did they call it after Lady Astor?" '[14] The change was officially agreed to shortly afterwards.

In fact, Lawrence allowed more than a month to pass before writing to the C.A.S., taking the opportunity to congratulate him on a lecture he had given on the war object of an air force to a large group of officers at Uxbridge, of whom Lawrence's C.O. was one.

16.iv.29. I hope you realised that my not writing meant that all was well. Cattewater is in a lovely place, and will be perfection if the weather and water get hot. The camp is a good one: comfortably laid-out, compact and small, and we are a happy family, or two families: one of H.Q. the other of 104 Squadron. Mine is H.Q.: we are *quite* happy. The Squadron will be happier when it has machines, as you remark. It is hard for its technical people to sit here without jobs or tools. For the H.Q. people this lull before work is a god-send: it means that routine can be got running before the strain begins. Routine matters quite a lot in sections like Stores and Transport and Workshops. Now I am workshops. They put me into a bare room, in an empty shop (no machinery or benches!) and said 'Start a workshop routine.' I *did* reply that I was an A.C.H.

There are other things to do also. Too much paper work & too few clerks. So for a while I typed D.R.O.s. Then someone (everyone, almost) felt that there must be Station Standing Orders. So I was put on to compile the 'general' parts of those. God be praised that the technical orders didn't come my way!

John Bull (a weekly paper) has just announced that I do no duties. Hard, very hard. Nine of my first twenty days here I was on fire-picquet.

The bike is magnificent. It has taken me twice to London (fastest time 4 hrs 44 minutes). The Cornish Riviera train is 13 minutes better than that: but it does not start at Hyde Park Corner & finish at Cattewater.

I heard about your lecture. My officer, who is of the sporting type, a fine pilot, and lover of fast cars, liked what you said. He called it the most *severely* practical speech he ever heard. So if you'd tried to be Winstonianly eloquent, you didn't succeed! Winston's speaking is never severe. To collect all the officers was a great idea. Twice, I think, you've done that. Uxbridge must have been blue from end to end. I wish everybody could meet you. The R.A.F. would be happier as it knew your aims better. It is supremely hard, in a big show, to get through to the rank and file a clear knowledge of where they are going. You've got a lot through: but not enough to satisfy me, your very particular subordinate.

I enclose a separate sheet, of pure pearls. If you find them too pure and pearly for your Deportment Department, then put them in the fire. They are trifles. It is the trifles that irritate and do most harm.

I hope you will come down. The more abruptly the better, for then our agony of preparing for you will be short. Sharp it must be, but make it short. Choose a fine day. Today the world is weeping, and Cattewater feels as dismal as the sky and the sea.

Wing-Commander is a trump.

Yours

T. E. Shaw

This, as you said, is 'only for you'! A/Cs shouldn't have opinions upon Wing-Commanders.[15]

Some of the 'pure pearls', like the abolition of bayonets, particularly at church parades, have already been mentioned. 'A bayonet in a pew or church chair is as bad as a wooden leg,' Lawrence told the C.A.S. bluntly. 'The total abolition of bayonets will save money and time, and be a mercy to all airmen. Admittedly it will involve you in personal effort. But what is one more effort? Bayonets cannot in any conceivable circumstances be legitimately used by the R.A.F. so why lumber us up? It is the same as Officers' spurs.' Lawrence went on to suggest that Trenchard should also explore the possibility of abolishing 'the silly little stick we have to carry when we walk out. Our great-great-greats carried swords, and sticks were invented to comfort them when deprived of the honour of swords. Now we don't want even swords!' In the event all these reforms were put into effect.

Although Lawrence seldom went into Plymouth, his presence at the camp soon became known. 'The Plymouth papers are yapping about me,' he told Charlotte Shaw early in April. 'The C.O. here is making a scrap-book of their cuttings. He laughs, only.'[16] A few weeks later, when Lawrence happened to be in Plymouth, on one of his rare visits to the town: 'A pea-hen voice screamed "Aircraftman" from a car.' It was Lady Astor. Next day she rang up the Wing-Commander, and invited herself over to Mount Batten, a proposal which, since she was a local Member of Parliament, the C.O. could not turn down. 'We sparred verbally at each other,' Lawrence told Charlotte Shaw. 'She got on my motor-cycle: I drove with her and Michael [her son] to her housing estate, to her house (supper), to a children's club she runs in Plymouth. It has since been in the papers. Serves me right for walking about with a talkie sky-sign. She was very nice: at her swiftest and kindest: one of the most naturally impulsive and impulsively natural people. Like G.B.S., more a cocktail than a welcome diet.' He went on:

> . . . Life is fairly good. The flaw is that *John Bull* has announced that I do not work in camp, but tinker with my motor-bike and translate the *Odyssey*, and since that note appeared I've not been able to touch the *Odyssey*. I must think out what to do about it now. The sensible thing would be to give it up; the next best thing is to sign it T. E. Shaw. I will ask Bruce Rogers, and see what he thinks.
>
> Nancy's seat in Plymouth should be pretty safe. She seems to hold the town in her fingers – they are all friends and enemies, and none neutral. The R.A.F. is wholly hers, of course.[17]

It was common knowledge that a General Election was in the offing, since Baldwin's second term as Prime Minister was coming to an end. A fortnight later Parliament was dissolved and voting took place at the end of May, which resulted in Labour returning to office. In the event, Lady Astor only just managed to scrape home by a couple of hundred votes in the Sutton Division of Plymouth, where there was a three-cornered fight; indeed but for the intervention of a Liberal, who split the anti-Conservative vote, she would almost certainly have lost her seat. Lawrence wrote her a note congratulating her on her victory at the polls and she replied inviting him to visit her at Cliveden, her husband's famous Thames-side house near Maidenhead, and also to make any use he wished of her house in Elliot Terrace on Plymouth Hoe. But he considered it prudent to decline these invitations, fearing perhaps he might be 'lionised' at her parties. 'Alas! I can't come to Cliveden,' he wrote to her. 'Nor will I use Elliot Terrace. Thank you all the same. The best way to be content in the service is to stick to it, taking only such reliefs as one's own pocket affords. The helplessness of money: that's a very often forgotten point. Some day, if you revisit Plymouth quietly, ring up 1634, and we'll brighten the life of the Exchange girls again.'[18]

Nevertheless they continued to exchange letters. 'I do not know when, or with whom, I have ever maintained for so long so hot a correspondence,' he wrote to her after Labour had come back to office for the second time under Ramsay MacDonald. 'Clearly we are soul-mates. Incidentally an American dealer pays £20 for interesting letters from me: so heaven knows the prices which infatuated collectors will give for yours. Are we worth it? I mean, aren't we rather wasting our sweetness on the already sweet?'[19]

3

The famous international seaplane race known as the Schneider Trophy, founded a quarter of a century previously by the French armaments manufacturer Jacques Schneider, was due to take place at Calshot in the first week of September 1929, the course being round the Solent.[20] Wing-Commander Sydney Smith was in charge of the arrangements for the British team, since the race had become much more professional than hitherto and now had government backing. Sydney Smith used Lawrence as his secretary-clerk and took him along to all the preparatory meetings in London and elsewhere where it was Lawrence's duty to take notes of the proceedings. At one of these, attended by Mr C. P. Robertson of the Air Ministry press section and also by a representative of the Treasury, A.C. Shaw was recognised after a while by the Air Ministry man, but not so by his colleague from the Treasury, who proved unexpectedly unco-operative at this particular meeting.

'Why on earth did you adopt that sticky attitude?' Robertson asked the Treasury man after the meeting. 'I should have thought in front of the famous Colonel Lawrence you might have done better.'

'Colonel Lawrence! Where was he?'

'The little airman in the background taking notes.'

'Good heavens!' exclaimed the man from the Treasury. 'If I'd known that, they could have had what they liked – I'd have been so engrossed in watching him!'[21]

'This Schneider business,' Lawrence wrote to Trenchard on 20 June: 'I hope you will come down before the end of July. I've a suggestion to make, probably; more work for you, but only an hour or so. And one should get everything possible out of you in your last year. When you go I shall not like the R.A.F. so much. I hope the new Ministers are modest souls. "Modester" in the case of one of them.' Here Lawrence was referring to Hoare's successor at the Air Ministry in the new Labour Government, Lord Thomson, who had been Minister in 1924 and now returned to his former post.

Cattewater is a happy station. It would be an ungrateful station if it wasn't. They do their best for us here. Thank God it is warmer now. I hope to start bathing any moment.

Is this letter dull? I nearly fall asleep every now and then. Today's Thursday, and I was in bed on Monday night. Mostly Schneider since.

Tomorrow we get a Wapiti* to which I look forward. By the way, I'm workshop clerk, as well, and Motor Boat crew in my spare time. Isn't it odd how C.O.s tend to give me odd jobs

---

* A reconnaissance aircraft.

to do? There is something about my shape which suggests the square peg to them all.

By the way, when you come down enquire for Mount Batten, not for Cattewater. The Cattewater is a pool of sewerage inland from us, but Mount Batten is the old castle in whose shadow we live.

Don't rest on your laurels yet. Have a bayonet put in your IN tray every morning: and say to yourself 'I must get rid of that today'. Lay out all your shirts and socks nightly on your bed: and say 'My God, what a bore this is.' Meanwhile it is very good of you to have done so much.[22]

Lawrence had just returned from London, where he had spent a night in the Union Jack Club for other ranks. Where he heard that one of the minor reforms which he had been pressing on the C.A.S., leaving the top two buttons on airmen's greatcoats undone when they walked out, had been imqlemented.

In the dark corridors of the Union Jack (do you know them?) airmen were stopping their likes in uniform and saying eagerly 'Do you know?' 'Have you heard?' 'Did you see?' and they looked so pleased that I felt very grateful to you. Only I couldn't help blaming myself a little for not having tried to do it five years ago. Out of my hut of 19, six have been on the peg for undone overcoats.[23]

At the same time Lawrence urged the C.A.S. to keep up the good work with the Air Council by introducing further changes to make the airman's life easier.

Apparently Trenchard had no plans to visit the Mount Batten station in the immediate future, so Lawrence put down on paper the suggestion he had hoped to put to him orally. Two airships, the R100 and the R101, which had been under construction for the past five years, were now nearing completion and would soon be ready for their trials. The latter was a government project and was being built at Cardington, while the former was being undertaken by private enterprise at Howden by the Airship Guarantee Co., a subsidiary of Vickers, in which the moving spirit was

Commander Sir Dennistoun Burney, the inventor of the para-vane. One or other was certain to make a trial trip easterly, since mooring masts had been put in Egypt and India, and Lawrence thought this would provide an excellent opportunity for survey-ing an hitherto inaccessible and unexplored part of Arabia. Accordingly he wrote to Trenchard in this sense.

R.A.F. Cattewater Plymouth   12/vii/29. This is immensely important, quite different from last time. I have been saving it up for you for years: – not that you are the right person to go to, at all: but you are more likely to display imagination upon the matter than any other person of greatness in the Air Ministry.

These Airships: – one or two of them are to have trial trips soon. Some say to the States, others say to Karachi. I have seen the shed at Karachi, and the Mast at Ismailia, and think it likely that sooner or later one of them will go that way.

Well, by going just a few miles out of their course to the southward they can pass over the Ruba el Khali, the so-called 'Empty Quarter' of Arabia. This is a huge area of many hun-dred thousand square miles. No European has ever crossed it, nor any Arab any of us has actually questioned. All the Geographers refer to it annually as the great unsolved question of Geography.

Now, I want the trial ship of the airships to settle the Ruba el Khali. On every later trip they will be running to schedule, unless some American millionaire hires them for a million a second to go over the desert for him. On the first trip they will be inhabited mainly by their crew, and it will be easy to deflect them. To go over the empty quarter will also be an enormous advertisement for them: it will mark an era in exploration. It will finish our knowledge of the earth. Nothing but an airship can do it, and I want it to be one of ours which gets the plum.

If you consult the map you will see that it is a very slight diversion from their course between Karachi and Ismailia. I would like it to be an unheralded diversion. Not a newspaper stunt exhausted by superlatives before it begins. Take the geographical world by surprise.

The Navigator of the airship will be getting his W/T bearings and time signals all the way, and will plot his course exactly. I do not think there will be anything much to see – sand, sand and hills, perhaps – but the comfort of having finished, in twelve hours, what man has been projecting for 50 years. . . .

Do think it out, properly, and say yes. I do not ask to be let go, myself. I'd love it, of course: but the important thing is to get it done, without talk: and I think you have enough weight with the Civil side and with Burney's company to get it done.

Yours
T. E. Shaw

Push me on to them, as advocate, if they are constipated.[24]

At the same time Lawrence asked Bernard Shaw, who knew Thomson well as a fellow Fabian Socialist, to see the Minister and urge the idea upon him. However, G.B.S. was busy with rehearsals for one of his plays which was being put on at the Malvern Festival, so he wrote instead, suggesting that if the R101 was going to head east Lawrence with his expert knowledge of the Arabian terrain would be a good man to have along. The Minister's reply was not exactly encouraging.

Air Ministry 24 July 1929. Yours of the 19th July. I do not think it will be possible to act on your suggestion during the first trial flight of the airship to India, but I will certainly bear the suggestion in mind when subsequent experimental flights are being made. I am especially keen on this aspect of aviation and regard surveys of this sort as one of the principal uses of airships.

As regards including Lawrence, or Private Shaw, as you have yourself described him, I will consider the matter. His passion for obscurity makes him an awkward man to place and would not improve his relations with the less subtle members of the crew. However, as a friend of yours he will be remembered.[25]

Trenchard proved more sympathetic to the idea, although the Air Staff had never particularly liked airships on account of their vulnerability. Anyhow Lawrence wrote to him again, presumably after Bernard Shaw had let him know the Minister's view.

29.vii.29. I knew you'd consider the Empty Desert idea: I hope it will be in your time. Philip Sassoon would have helped it, with his imagination. I don't know your present team.

I spoke about it to G.B.S. and said if he met Lord T. would he urge it on him? Unfortunately, he wrote to him, instead. Writing isn't so supple an appeal. Also he seems to have mentioned me, which of course disquiets the civilians. I wanted the job considered on scientific grounds. It is the last piece of exploration on earth. Doing it completes our knowledge of the globe. It can only be done safely, cheaply and quietly by an airship. I want the doing it to be an Air Ministry deed, without press warning or pressure, beforehand. Let us get the credit: and for the Lord's sake do it quietly. If I am of the crew, I'll get the credit: the press loves that sort of cheap personal touch. It would be much better if your maps staff officer went, and your best navigator, and a draughtsman and an intelligence man, to write something plainly official.

> Yours sincerely,
> T. E. Shaw

Us is the R.A.F., in case you don't know![26]

Trenchard's former aide T. B. Marson had recently transferred his farming activities from Scotland to Gloucestershire and had asked Lawrence to visit him at his new farm near Northleach whenever he could get leave. For the final fortnight or so before the Schneider Trophy race, Sydney Smith and the other ground staff at Mount Batten moved to Calshot, at the entrance to Southampton Water, which was to be the seaplane base for the race. Just before they left Mount Batten, the C.A.S. came down to inspect them, as Lawrence wrote to Marson:

23.viii.29. I saw Boom today: he inspected Cattewater and spoke to me: gently telling me off as usual.

Do you know he is looking old? His moustache is going white, and he looks nearly his real age. I am sorry. You know he is finally resigning at the end of the year, and John Salmond comes in. It's the end of an epoch, in my life and judgement. I shan't feel as I do about the R.A.F. after he has gone. One takes a pride in being under Boom.

You've been very nice asking me to see you at your place this autumn. I'm of the Schneider Cup party, and tomorrow we move to Calshot, for three weeks at that worst of stations. Alas.

After the Cup (the Italians are asking tonight to have it postponed: alas again,) perhaps they will give me leave: and then I shall try to persuade my bike of bikes into Gloucestershire. Time is so short: people I want to see, would like to see, so many. Alas again. Life just fizzes past, and after it perhaps things do not greatly matter. I should have written to you before. Desperate venture, farming now-a-days. I hope you show up all the others at it. The big men make money. I am told: but you aren't rich, yet, probably.[27]

4

'The Schneider show ran like clockwork: a great relief, after all the months everybody spent on it,' Lawrence wrote to Trenchard when it was over. 'It tired me out, anyway.'[28]

The race took place on 7 September 1929 and for the second occasion in succession it was won by the British team led by Squadron-Leader A. H. Orlebar, the legendary 'Orly' of the R.A.F. The winning pilot was Flying-Officer H. R. D. Waghorn in a Supermarine Rolls-Royce S6 at an average speed of 328·63 m.p.h., which considerably surpassed the previous British record. The race was witnessed by a distinguished gathering, including the Prime Minister Ramsay MacDonald, the Air Minister Lord Thomson, the former Foreign Secretary Sir Austen Chamberlain, the Chief of the Air Staff Sir Hugh Trenchard and the A.O.C. Coastal Area Air Vice-Marshal Sir Charles Lamb. The latter made his headquarters on a luxurious motor yacht the *Karen* (in which incidentally Lawrence crewed), lent for the occasion by a rich friend of Sydney Smith's, Major Colin Cooper. Thus it became the air chief's Flagship, being the first and only time, according to Clare Sydney Smith, on which the flag of the C.A.S. has been flown aboard a private yacht along with the R.A.F. ensign. The winning Supermarine S6, it should be added, was designed by Messrs R. J. Mitchell and Henry Royce, and from it evolved the famous Spitfire fighter. As an appreciation of A/c Shaw's work Major Colin Cooper presented him and the Sydney Smiths with a two-seater baby speedboat with a 100 h.p. Scripps engine, which had formerly belonged to the famous speedboat racing driver Sir Henry Segrave. It was soon christened *Biscuit* and it was to give Lawrence and the Smiths immense pleasure.[29]

During the preliminary trials the American team dropped out, which besides the British left only the Italians, who had been having trouble with their engines and requested a postponement. But this was not possible under the rules, so the Italians, led by Marshal Balbo carried on under considerable difficulties. Nevertheless they gained second place with a Macchi-Fiat 52 piloted by Warrant-Officer Dal Molin. Another British pilot F/Lt D'Arcy Greig came third in another Supermarine. Incidentally Trenchard happened to be talking to Greig at Calshot before the race when he spotted Lawrence engaged in conversation with Lady Astor. 'Keep your eye on that damned fellow!' he told Greig, pointing in their direction.

Although, to do him justice, while he was at Calshot, Lawrence did not deliberately court publicity, his more or less unconscious habit of treading backwards into the limelight sometimes secured it for him. On one occasion Balbo, who knew Lawrence and recognised him, complained that the slipway allotted to the Italian team was covered with green scum. Lawrence undertook to see to it. Shortly afterwards F/Lt Breaky, who was responsible for the seaplanes, came down to the slipway with Mr Robertson of the Air Ministry press section, and there they found a corporal transmitting some orders about a boat.

'Who gave you those orders?' asked the Flight-Lieutenant.

'Mr Shaw, sir,' answered the corporal.

'Who is Mr Shaw?'

'Well, sir, Aircraftman Shaw.'

'And why should you, a corporal, take orders from an aircraftman?'

'Well, sir,' said the corporal with a certain logic: 'it seems perfectly natural to take orders from Mr Shaw!'[30]

Lord Thomson happened to appear about the same time and the fact that a British airman was observed to be cleaning the slipway of the shed where the Italian planes were housed prompted him to ask Aircraftman Shaw why this should happen. The encounter was too good for the press photographers to miss and the resulting picture of the Air Minister and an aircraftman in conversation made good newspaper copy, appearing as it did all over the world. Thomson was understandably annoyed; he became distinctly angry when Trenchard told him that Lawrence had applied for permission to crew in a Moth seaplane to be piloted by his friend Major A. A. Nathan on a European tour, in which it was planned to visit France, Italy, Switzerland, Germany and Holland. The C.A.S. had already given his permission for Lawrence to make the trip subject to the Minister having no objection; but Thomson positively vetoed it. 'You must come and see me as soon as you get your leave as I want to speak to you,' wrote Trenchard in a note forbidding Lawrence to go. When they met a fortnight later, the C.A.S. told the errant aircraftman that he had come very close to being kicked out of the R.A.F. again. Henceforth he was to 'stop leading from the ranks and confine himself to the duties of an aircraftman.' He was not to leave the country, he was not to visit or even speak to any 'great men' or women, such as Churchill, Birkenhead, Austen Chamberlain, Philip Sassoon and Lady Astor, though somewhat surprisingly his namesake Bernard Shaw was not included in the list.[31] Incidentally Lawrence told Liddell Hart that Bernard Shaw was rather 'piqued' when he learned that he had not been included in the prohibited category.[32] Nor was Ernest Thurtle, the Labour M.P., with whom Lawrence continued to correspond, but then no doubt the authorities were afraid to forbid any member of their service, even such a maverick as Aircraftman Shaw from writing to a Labour Member of Parliament. Furthermore Lawrence was expressly forbidden by the Minister to fly in any government aircraft, and this order was repeated by Trenchard.

The prohibition about leaving the country also extended to Ireland.

'Life here goes smoothly,' he wrote to his friend A.C. Hayter in India a little later. 'In November I had a tiff with Lord Thomson our present boss. He tried to sling me out: I double-crossed him. So am airmanning on. Our C.O. here is a treat. Grub is better than our Miranshah grub. Plymouth is a rotten hole; the sea is lovely in summer and hell in winter: and it's work, work, work. I wish Greek had never been invented.'[33] It was to take him another year before the *Odyssey* was in final shape for delivery to the publisher.

Trenchard's time as Chief of the Air Staff was drawing to a close, and in spite of occasional differences over disciplinary and similar matters they parted the best of friends in the service. Indeed the retiring C.A.S. found time to send his wayward aircraftman a valedictory note, to which Lawrence replied in character and also with a real sense of loss.

R.A.F. Mount Batten. 18.xii.29. It was very good of you to think of me in all your business of going away. I've been very sorry for you, as the time has shortened. You see, there is a fellow feeling. I shall be as sorry as I can be, in proportion, when I have to go.

I'm sure, all the same, that you are right in this move. The fact that we are all sorry you are going shows your rightness in going. The R.A.F. should be (and I feel it is) now big enough to stand on its feet. You are too big to be the father of a grown-up child. Let the beast go and make his own mistakes. It's going to be a very splendid service, and will always be proud of you. When you have been away from it, a while, you'll be very proud of it.

I'm all right: I do my eight hours a day of R.A.F. work (heavier lately, as my officer has been drafted to Singapore, and the new one isn't technical . . . they have no 'E' officers in Coastal Area to spare for here) and sit up all the other hours in camp translating Homer for an American rich man. I have not been out of camp twice since my leave: no bike-riding: no flying: no visits or letters or books. That's, I think, what your S[ecretary] of S[tate] wanted of me. Rough luck, in some ways: but at least it renders me harmless! And camp life is smooth and comfortable here. Our C.O. is like a father and a mother.

After you are 'out', may I come and see you, if you stay in England?[34]

Perhaps this is the most convenient point in the narrative to mention a literary experience which left an indelible impression upon Lawrence's mind. In January 1930, Peter Davies, an enterprising young publisher, who was J. M. Barrie's godson and reputedly the original of Peter Pan, published a remarkable novel about the First World War entitled *Her Privates We* under the pseudonym Private 19022. (Incidentally the anonymous author dedicated the book to Peter Davies who, he said, 'made me write it'.) *Her Privates We* was generally acclaimed as a masterpiece of its kind by the critics of this period, who included Arnold Bennett, J. C. Squire, St John Ervine, and Ralph Straus. 'Whoever he is,' wrote one newspaper, 'this Private 19022, about whose identity so many are speculating, he can write. He "can get it over". The whole atmosphere, rhythm and whiff of the Front comes at you from every page.' Lawrence immediately obtained a copy and when he had read it he had no difficulty in recognising the author as the Australian writer Frederic Manning from his earlier work *Scenes and Portraits*, which he had read some years previously. 'The preface gives it away,' he wrote to Manning afterwards. 'It is pure *Scenes and Portraits*. How long, I wonder, before everybody knows. You need not worry about their knowing. It is a book everybody would have been proud and happy to have written.'

As soon as he had finished reading it, Lawrence went to the nearest telephone and put through a call to Peter Davies, whom he had never met, at the publisher's London Office. According to Mr Davies, the following conversation ensued:

Lawrence: I want to congratulate you as strongly as possible on *Her Privates We*. It's magnificent, a book in a thousand. You've published a masterpiece. But tell

	me this. How did you get Frederic Manning to write it?
Davies:	Thank you very much, and I'm delighted to hear you like it, but –
Lawrence:	Like it! It's not a question of like! The book's a classic. And it *is* by Frederic Manning, isn't it?
Davies:	The author of *Her Privates We* prefers to be known only as Private 19022. I've said so to dozens of literary detectives, and I've said so on the jacket of the book. So how can I answer your question. Besides I don't even know whom I am speaking to.
Lawrence:	Oh, Shaw's my name, you probably won't know who I am, but I once wrote a book myself, called *Revolt in the Desert*.
Davies:	(*An ejaculation indicative of impressed astonishment.*)
Lawrence:	But about Private 19022. You see, I've read *Scenes and Portraits* at least fifty times; that's a masterpiece, too, and the man who wrote it is the only man who could possibly have written *Her Privates We*.
Davies:	(*After a pregnant pause.*) You know, I'm not supposed ... When he went abroad, I promised him ... He can't have foreseen this, though ... Oh well, here goes. You, Sir, and your method of attack combined, are too much for me and must surely justify my surrender in the eyes of Private 19022. Yes, of course you're right. Only do please keep the secret, or I'm lost.
Lawrence:	I won't tell a soul, though it's bound to come out before long. Meanwhile, will you let him know how enormously I admire and love his book? If people don't run to it in thousands, it'll be because they don't care to see themselves in a glass, magnificently. .... I can't say half of what I feel on the telephone. Look here, I'll write to you now, and you can pass on my letter, or the substance of it to him.

'No praise could be too sheer for this book,' wrote Lawrence to the publisher in the letter that followed. 'I am sure it is the book of books so far as the British Army-in-the-War is concerned. . . . Anyone would be proud to have written it. It justifies every heat of praise. Its virtues will be recognised more and more as times goes on.'

With Lawrence's permission the publisher produced a pamphlet to help sales. This contained parts of their telephone conversation and Lawrence's letter together with extracts from the reviews. 'Reader,' wrote Peter Davies, 'the object of this pamphlet is to persuade you to buy *Her Privates We*, to read it yourself, and to leave it on your shelves to be read by your children and your grand-children.' It ran to 450 pages octavo, and cost 7s. 6d.

'Peter Davies is trying to use my dregs of reputation as one more lever in the sales,' Lawrence wrote to Manning from Mount Batten on 25 February 1930. 'Do not let that worry you.'

Adventitious sales and adventitious advertisements are very soon forgotten: but the cash will remain with you, and your book be famous for as long as the war is cared for – and perhaps longer, for there is more than soldiering in it. You have been exactly fair to everyone, of all ranks: and all your people are alive.

This is not a very sensible letter. I am very tired, and this weather gets me down: only I owed it to you to thank you for the best book I have read for a very long time. I shall hope to meet you and say more – and bore you by saying it – for what is so dead as a book one has written?

They did meet eventually, being introduced by Peter Davies, and although they cannot have met very often, they continued to correspond intermittently until Manning's death fifteen years later, which upset Lawrence greatly. In 1933, Lawrence told Robert Graves that since D. G. Hogarth died Frederic Manning was one of the three writers he most cared for. The other two were E. M. Forster and the Armenian poet Ernest Altounyan, whom he had known since 1911 and who was to write a touching poetic lament for Lawrence after his death, which he called 'Ornament of Honour'.

5

There was not much love lost between Lawrence and Lord Thomson, who years before had offered Lawrence a place in the crew of the R101, an offer which Lawrence had turned down. 'I'm afraid Thomson is cheap,' he had written to Charlotte Shaw before the Schneider trophy race. 'His book and his peerage were both cheap things.* I must try and meet Lord Thomson [again] one day and see if it is as I suspect. Probably if I saw him I should like him: that's the worst of meeting people.' But on the only two occasions they did meet they did not take to each other.

There is no evidence, apart from their chance encounter at Calshot, and their confrontation at the Peace Conference, that Lawrence and Thomson ever met again. Nor was there any possibility of Lawrence being included in the crew of the R101, even if it had been intended that the ill-fated airship should traverse the Arabian 'Empty Quarter'. It was in the early hours of the morning of 5 October 1930 that the R101 crashed on a hillside near Beauvais with the loss of forty-eight lives, including those of Sir Sefton Brancker, Director-General of Civil Aviation, and of Lord Thomson himself, who had insisted on pressing on with the flight in the face of adverse weather reports.

Rumours of the crash came through to Mount Batten later the same day when Lawrence happened to be writing to the Shaws. 'Last night was an awful night,' he wrote. 'I tried to do the *Odyssey* and then to read: but the wind and the rain (I was duty crew and was partly responsible for the craft at moorings in the Cattewater) prevented any hope of quietness. We never dreamed

---

* Lawrence is being rather severe on Thomson here. His book *Air Facts and Problems* (1928) was merely a collection of topical articles he had previously contributed to newspapers. Ramsay MacDonald was anxious to have him in his first Government as Air Minister and as he had unsuccessfully contested several seats in an attempt to get into the House of Commons, MacDonald had him made a peer so that he could answer for the Government in the House of Lords.

the airship would leave. I knew so many people in her. I wonder who was saved.' In fact there were only six survivors. 'All the same it was a horrid smash, and an unnecessary one. No need for it at all.'[35]

Four months later there was another nasty air accident, this time in Plymouth Sound, where it was witnessed by Lawrence. High up overlooking the Sound and below a Martello tower was a sheltered spot frequently visited at off-duty times by Lawrence, and in the mornings also by Clare Sydney Smith, who used to bring a thermos jug of coffee and share her 'elevenses' with Tes, as she called Aircraftman Shaw. Wednesday 4 February 1931 was such a morning, warm and spring-like with the sun shining. Several flying-boats were circling the Sound as usual practising firing at targets at sea. Presently one of them began to descend, but on nearing the water made no attempt to 'flatten out'. Lawrence immediately spotted it, remarking to his C.O.'s wife: 'That boat looks queer.' A minute or two later she nose-dived straight into the sea with hardly a splash and when she surfaced a few moments afterwards there was no sign of human life in her. For a brief but ghastly period they thought that the C.O. might be aboard, but when they ran down the hill they found Sydney Smith safely standing on the slipway, not knowing what had happened. Lawrence immediately took control of the situation, Smith following his suggestions and letting him dive into the sea with the other rescuers. Of the twelve on board, six were rescued, but the remainder, including the officer who was at the controls at the time of the crash was drowned. The accident seemed in-explicable, since the machine, an Iris III, was powered by three Rolls-Royce engines capable of developing 2000 h.p., with a cruising speed of 80 knots, and it was only quite recently that Sir Philip Sassoon, when Under-Secretary for Air, had flown to India and back without mishap in this type of flying boat.[36]

'You will have seen the news of our crash here in the papers,' Lawrence wrote to Charlotte Shaw two days later.

It was due to bad piloting, on the part of a man who (as we all knew) should never have flown with passengers. He would not be convinced of that. Fortunately he died with the rest.

It was horrible to see a huge Flying Boat so cast away by incompetence. I happened to be standing by the sea watching it come in to alight. So that is going to involve me in Enquiries and Inquests. At the Enquiry (which is an R.A.F. affair not open to the Press) I propose to say just what I saw, and what it meant, in the endeavour to bring the responsibility home upon an Air-Marshal Webb-Bowen at the Air Ministry, who refused to listen to reports made to him on 3 separate occasions, regarding this officer's unfitness to fly.* I shall try to do it without getting myself into trouble, if I can. If not – well, I think such a case had better not happen again, and I have facts enough to prevent it happening again if I publish them.[37]

A public inquest was inevitable and Lawrence was told that he would be required to give evidence. This meant publicity for him which in the circumstances was far from welcome. When he heard about it, Bernard Shaw wrote to him.

As to the crash, you seem to be in the position of the sentinel in Macbeth who, having seen Birnam Wood start to walk, could say only 'I should report that which I say I saw, but know not how to do it.' You are a simple aircraftman: nothing but an eye-witness's police report can be extorted from you. However, as you will probably insist on conducting the enquiry, and as you will want to save your ambitious commander from being sacrificed, the future, to my vision, is on the knees of the gods. Pray heaven they sack you![38]

'I was made clerk for the Air Ministry Court of Inquiry,' he wrote again to Charlotte Shaw ten days later, and was able to approve and agree with its findings. 'G.B.S. will laugh at that. Please thank him for his letter. When all is over I shall be so relieved.'[39]

At the inquest the Coroner began by asking Lawrence to

---

* Air Vice-Marshal T. I. Webb-Bowen was Air Member for Personnel on the Air Council at this time. This incident had no immediate adverse effect upon his career, as he was appointed A.O.C. Wessex Bombing Area later in the same year and was made K.C.B. in 1932. But he received no further promotion and retired from the service in 1933, at the age of 54.

describe the accident as he saw it and Lawrence replied in the
sense that Bernard Shaw anticipated. 'About 11.30 a.m. on
Wednesday, February 4th, I was standing on the rocks at the
shore-end of Batten watching the flight of Iris III, which was
circling in the sun. It came out of the haze and circled over my
head. At the time she was flying normally and the engines
sounded absolutely all right. After watching her for less than five
minutes I saw her turn into what wind there was and approach,
throttle back her engines and glide steeply as though to alight on
the water.'

'Did she seem to glide down under perfect control?'

'Perfect.'

'But very fast?' the coroner queried.

'Yes, very fast,' Lawrence replied. 'She struck the water just
under the pilot's seat, forward near the bows.'

'You saw the waves crash over her?'

'Yes, the wave she made herself,' said Lawrence, and went on
to explain what happened then. 'The tail of the machine came up,
her main planes crashed into the water and folded back together.
The hull dived straight to the bottom, and the tail swung very
slowly towards Batten breakwater, until it rested upside down only
a few feet above the water. The crash occurred about six hundred
yards south of Batten breakwater in about twenty-six feet of
water.'[40]

With the help mainly of Lady Astor working behind the
scenes, Lawrence made a gallant and successful attempt to protect
his commander, thus pointing the way to much needed reforms
in the methods of air–sea rescue. In the result the Air Ministry
was very worried, particularly Air Vice-Marshal Webb-Bowen.
'I *think* the battle is won,' Lawrence wrote to Lady Astor after
the inquest. He went on:

The Coroner was a perfect pet. He asked all the nibbly, difficult,
hurtful questions, so innocently and so smoothly that everything came out. The poor officers did nobly (Wing-Commander
Smith at the head of them, adjuring all of us to tell the truth)
and the press followed up, saying nothing mean or spiteful,
but scaring the Air Ministry almost to death.

The best results are coming, although slowly. They have set
the reforms afoot, and I think they may be trusted to push
them through. I am watching very closely and will move
another little lever or two when or if it is necessary. There has
been no reflection upon me, and no threat to end my happy
days. Good.

I need hardly say how grateful I am to you for your help.
It is such a pleasure to get a thing done cleanly and naturally,
without fuss. Nobody knows that anything has been done, and
yet, I fancy, there will not be another case of this sort in our
memories.[41]

'The consequences of that crash have been all we wanted: the
lesson rubbed in and precautions taken,' he wrote to Charlotte
Shaw on 8 March. 'I think that particular difficulty is checked for
good. There will be no harm to myself, I think. Nor, apparently,
is anyone but the Air Ministry to touch the Schneider Cup this
year. That is an easement for me: they will not enjoy their task,
I grimly think.'[42]

The scrapping of the Government airship programme after the
tragedy of the R101 put an end to Lawrence's hopes that the
Arabian Empty Quarter might be discovered by this type of
aircraft. To his surprise the discovery was made not by air but by
camel by the British Political Agent for Muscat, the Persian Gulf
sheikhdom, who did it at his own expense. The Agent's name
was Bertram Thomas, and Lawrence wrote to Edward Marsh,
then the Colonial Minister J. H. Thomas's Private Secretary,
suggesting that his namesake's achievement should be suitably
recognised. 'Every explorer for generations has dreamed of it.
Its difficulty can best be put by saying that no Arab, so far as we
know, has ever crossed it.'

Now something good must be done for this most quiet and
decent fellow, in the Birthday Honours, if not sooner. It may
be all arranged; but if not I beg you to see to it. Do not let the
swag be all carried off by the Rositas and Lawrences of the
vulgar Press. Here is one of your own men doing a marvel.

Give him a K. will you? Well, it's a mouldy sort of thing,

but as a civil servant he cannot refuse. So it would do: but your sense of fitness, which o-emmed Henry James (now I address E.M. not J.H.T.) might prefer a C.H., or some other honour of which I know nothing.

Properly he should be India Office; but his success decorates England. K.C.S. eyes or ees would be unfitting. Better a Michael George.

I trust the imagination of J.H.T. to understand your enthusiasm & mine for what is the finest geographical feat since Shackleton and to persuade his colleagues into action and unanimity. It will be a welcome change for them all.[43]

Indeed, nothing was done for this brilliant Political Officer and intrepid explorer, for which learned societies recognised his achievement by awarding him a number of gold medals. But apparently the Foreign Office for some reason disapproved of his activities and the fact that he was supported by 'Lawrence of Arabia' may have been officially frowned upon as a recommendation. Later Lawrence wrote a foreword to his book *Arabia Felix*. Nevertheless Bertram Thomas had to wait for eighteen years for his 'Michael and George', a C.M.G. which was tardily given him in 1949, barely a year before his death at the age of 58.

During the earlier part of 1931 Lawrence was temporarily seconded to Hythe on Southampton Water to test the R.A.F. 200 class motor-boat, whose design had interested him greatly and which he had long thought should be developed by private contractors for the Air Ministry. Here he worked closely and harmoniously with F/Lt W. E. G. Beauforte-Greenwood, head of the Marine Equipment Branch of the Air Ministry. On 13 April 1931 he wrote to Liddell Hart: 'My two-year war with the Air Ministry over the type of motor-boats suited to attend seaplanes is bearing results now, and experimental boats are being offered by contractors. I've become a marine expert, and test the things for them, acquiring incidentally and by degrees quite a knowledge of the S.W. coast of England! A minor consequence is extensive absence from home, and a major (secondary and indirect) consequence is the paralysis of my *Odyssey* translation. It is stuck at Book XXI, and I begin to despair of finishing it. Motor-boat testing is an all-time job, and leaves one too exhausted to write.'[44]

Consequently Beauforte-Greenwood ordered eight boats which were to be ready by the end of July in time for the tests preparatory to the Schneider Trophy race. Lawrence returned to Mount Batten in May, and in the letter of thanks which he wrote to Sydney Smith for lending Lawrence for testing the new speedboat, Beauforte-Greenwood was able to state that they were now at least four to five years ahead of the Admiralty in this type of marine small craft.[45] On his return to Mount Batten Lawrence wrote up his notes on the R.A.F. 200 and sent them to Beauforte-Greenwood. 'I see that in all I have written you almost a book on the boat and her engines,' he wrote in a covering letter. 'It has been interesting and difficult, and therefore I am grateful to you for giving me the chance of doing it.'[46] Edward Garnett described it as 'a masterpiece of technology', and even the author prided himself to Robert Graves that 'every sentence in it is understandable, to a fitter.'[47]

The manual, which in fact Lawrence had written and which he called his 'parvenu opus', was entitled *The 200 Class Royal Air Force Seaplane Tender*. 'It comes to about 15,000 words, and has not an unbusinesslike moment,' he told Charlotte Shaw. 'If they print it as it stands as an official publication, then it will be a curiosity. Of course official publications are never signed, except by the Secretary of the Air Ministry, who has least to do with them. If I can get a copy, you shall have it as a Christmas card.'[48] In the event copies were duplicated for the use of crews and mechanics employed on the new R.A.F. Speedboat. In addition to the mechanics of the boat, the directions given on the proper manner to carry out air–sea rescue operations are a model of their kind.

There was no Schneider Trophy Race in 1930 and the one held in 1931 was something of an anti-climax, since the French and Italians withdrew, pleading for a year's postponement; but this was not possible under the rules. Thus the English team were left as solitary competitors, which meant that they were the automatic victors, and therefore won the trophy outright, since it was the third time they had won in five years. The race was flown over the same course as in 1929 – seven laps of 50 kilometres each –

the winner being F/Lt J. N. Boothman in a Supermarine S6B, powered by Rolls-Royce 2350 h.p. engines, at a record speed of 340·08 m.p.h.

'I have been tasting leisure – a new and good feeling,' Lawrence wrote to Charlotte Shaw. 'During the Schneider Cup time all R.A.F. coastal stations go slow, and there is not even Homer to do. So I have been reading all my neglected books, and riding a little and boating very little.'[49]

6

'It seems to me that the *Arab Revolt*, of activities of the body: and the *Seven Pillars* and *The Mint*, of activities of the mind, may be all my tissues can do,' Lawrence had written to Charlotte Shaw from India in 1928. 'Certainly for the moment, it is all.'[50] Then came the offer from Bruce Rogers in America to do a new prose translation of the *Odyssey*, a project which went much more slowly than he first thought, owing to the demands of his R.A.F. duties at Mount Batten, though when it was finished the £800 he received for it paid for all the repairs that had to be done at Clouds Hill. After that, when he had written his foreword to Bertram Thomas's *Arabia Felix* and the technical manual on the R.A.F. speedboat, he used to say the manual would be his last literary effort, but some other idea used to come along to catch his fancy. For instance, he was greatly attracted by the story of the Irish patriot Sir Roger Casement, for whom Bernard Shaw had offered to write a speech in his defence at his trial for treason in 1916 'which will thunder down the ages', an offer which Casement refused, preferring to make his own speech from the dock.

After a distinguished career in the British consular service, in which he had exposed atrocities committed against the natives of the Belgian Congo and the Putamayo region of Peru, Casement resigned from the service on the eve of the Great War and went to Germany to recruit an Irish Brigade from Irish prisoners-of-war, to fight for Irish independence alongside the German army. He was later landed on the Irish coast by a German submarine shortly before the Easter Week rising, and immediately captured and brought to London to stand trial. An unpleasant feature of the case was the surreptitious circulation of Casement's homosexual diaries to divert sympathy for a reprieve after he had been condemned to death. In the event Asquith's Government decided to let the law take its course and Casement was executed. However, in spite of persistent prodding by Bernard Shaw, the Government refused to let him or anyone else have a sight of the diaries: indeed they would neither confirm nor deny that they were in their possession. Lawrence latterly often thought of doing a book about him.

'Yes, I still hanker after the thought of writing a short book on him,' he told Charlotte Shaw in one of his last letters to her. 'As I see it he was a heroic nature. I should like to write upon him subtly, so that his enemies would think I was with them till I finished my book and rose from reading it to call him a hero. He had the appeal of a broken archangel. But unless the P.M. will release the "diary" material, nobody can write of him. Do you know who the next Labour P.M. might be? In advance he might pledge himself, and I am only 46, able, probably, to wait for years: and very determined to make England ashamed of itself, if I can.'[51]

This was one of Lawrence's literary ambitions which was destined never to be realised. Indeed it was not until a quarter of a century had passed and both Lawrence and Bernard Shaw were dead that the authorities eventually capitulated, and as a result of a sustained campaign by the present writer in Parliament made the diaries available to approved historians and other responsible students of Casement's life.[52]

Lawrence was a prolific letter writer and he in turn was the recipient of large numbers of letters from friends and strangers alike. However, although he once jokingly told Lady Astor that his letters were fetching quite a lot of money on the market, he was annoyed when a letter or other document of which he was either the author or the recipient was dealt with commercially. For instance, he was rather put out when his faithful literary agent Raymond Savage proposed to sell for his benefit a draft contract for the publication of *Revolt in the Desert* with manuscript annotations by himself and Bernard Shaw. 'However, I bear him no grudge,' he wrote to Shaw, letting him know that he had told Savage that he must be guided by Shaw's advice and if there was to be a deal Shaw must agree and the transaction must be assured of absolute privacy. In informing Shaw of the matter, he added, by the way, that he had no intention of selling the copy of *The Intelligent Woman's Guide to Socialism* which Shaw had given him. He went on:

> Swinburne's sin lay in writing his name and his friend's name in a copy of William Morris's *Love is Enough*, the supremely lovely Kelmscott version of that splendid poem. There is no harm in that for him and his friend: but it is a sorrowful thing to my mind when these kindnesses become merchandise, as happens in the inevitable march of time. I have five or six inscribed books which make me proud and happy: – but I use them, and read them in the hope that they will last no longer than myself. I do not like seeing personal things in the market – not even if they are unbeautiful things, like worn clothes, they are exposures.[53]

He was also considerably upset by the action of J. G. Wilson, the manager of Bumpus's bookshop and an enthusiastic collector of Lawrence manuscripts and memorabilia. He complained about it to Charlotte Shaw.

> By the way, Dunn, an airman, tells me that the Oxford edition of the *Seven Pillars* was on show at Bumpus's, lately, together with a letter from G.B.S. to me. I cannot understand how Wilson can do these things: I wonder how I'm to get out of it. Do you think I can write and ask him to put them away? I didn't know that any of my G.B.S. letters had gone astray.
>
> Nor do I like the Oxford printing being shown. I let him keep it in his little room, because I could see how he enjoyed showing it to his private customers: but that's a long way from public exhibition: and I'd never show a letter to anyone.[54]

He was also embarrassed by a rumour that he had 'lost his heart' to a woman aged sixty whom he had recently met for the

first time at Sir Philip Sassoon's house at Lympne, who had subsequently invited him to lunch and upon whom he had afterwards
called to apologise for not lunching with her. Then there were
the people of both sexes who imagined they were in love with
him. 'Probably it would be wholesome for me to lose my heart,'
he wrote to Lady Astor; ' – if that monstrous piece of machinery
is capable of losing itself, for till now it has never cared for anyone, though much for places and things.'

> People seem to my judgement to lose their heads rather than
> their hearts. Over the Christmas season two men and four
> women have sent me fervent messages of love. Love carnal,
> not love rarified, you know: and I am uncomfortable towards
> six more of the people I meet, therefore. It's a form of lunacy,
> I believe, to fancy that all-comers are one's lovers: but what
> am I to make of it when they write it in black and white? If
> only one might come nearer to people than in the street. Miss
> Garbo sounds a really sympathetic woman! The poor woman.
> I feel for her.[55]

Nevertheless he could and did care for people, particularly if
he knew them and they were down on their luck. An example
was Trenchard's former aide who had taken up farming and
lacking the capital necessary to make such a venture pay in those
days had got into financial difficulties. He had also written a book
of his experiences, *Khaki and Scarlet*, which Lawrence criticised
helpfully and advised him how to promote it when it was published. In 1930, when Marson was farming in Gloucestershire,
Lawrence wrote to him:

> Saw Boom last week: said 'Marson's written a book.' 'Good
> Lord,' said he. 'Indeed yes,' said I, 'a good book, though it says
> too little about you. 'Good Lord', said he. Shaken, I assure you,
> to the core.[56]

Eighteen months later Marson was forced to give up farming
and move to a small house. 'I am sorry,' wrote Lawrence. 'That
place of yours was a good part of the earth, Claybrooke sounds

less exciting. Yet you had no alternative I suppose. You are fortunate among many farmers in being able to get out. So large a proportion of the unfortunates cannot afford even that. The farmer near me in Dorsetshire told me a month ago that he had laid by £1000 last year, more than usual because times were lean. He drives a rackety Morris and looks worthless. I wonder what the truth is.'[57]

An old friend faced bankruptcy and a receiver was appointed. When he heard about this Lawrence immediately arranged to let him have £200 to stave off the threatened bankruptcy. 'Treat it as your own,' he told him, 'and shove it back on me as and when you can with convenience.' Lawrence was able to do this since his translation of the *Odyssey* was going well in America; so he arranged the matter with his banker Buxton. 'A very decent friend of mine lost his cash and is broke,' he told Buxton. 'They were going to bankrupt him, but I said I could manage £200 directly; and that has saved the situation. . . . Will you please get me an overdraft to meet this, pro tem? I will arrange to satisfy the account very soon: but must overdraw first. . . . *Odyssey* selling well in U.S.A. Four printings gone, to date. Looks like netting me £300 by next settling day. Good to plunder the Yanks.'[58]

Over the years Lawrence had turned down offers which might have led to high honours. But one mark of distinction which he did accept at this time, though at first with some misgivings, was an invitation from the Irish poet W. B. Yeats to join the new Irish Academy of Letters, by virtue of his being an Irishman, or at least the son of an Irishman. 'You know it staggers me that I should seriously be considered in such company,' he confessed to Charlotte Shaw. 'All the best Irish, except A.E. I fancy: and many of the not-so-good too. I don't think any other country of the size would produce such a list. I would like it, because it is a gesture on my part, that I am Irish: and I would like to think that. My work, from the *Seven Pillars* onward, probably does not justify joining that company. My reputation probably does. So on the whole I ought to say yes to W.B., and to thank him for such an unexpected and extraordinary compliment. Will you write for me?'[59]

Charlotte Shaw did so, conveying Lawrence's acceptance to the man whom, as he told her, he had always regarded as 'an exquisite and unattainable poet'. Yeats immediately replied to Lawrence whom he addressed as 'Mr Shaw': 'Your acceptance of our nomination has given me great pleasure, for you are among my chief of men, being one of the few charming and gallant figures of our time, and as considerable in intellect as in gallantry and charm. I thank you.'[60]

Lawrence, who had never met Yeats but had once seen him many years before in the street in Oxford which made him want 'to call the street to attention', replied in character.

I am Irish, and it has been a chance to admit it publicly – but it touches me very deeply that you should think anything I have done or been to justify this honour. I'm afraid the truth – if people could look inside – would destroy the flattering picture of myself that I have put about.

... I never expected this. It is very good of you, and touches me particularly, for I have been reading your work for years. You got your compliment in first, so I will not try to butter back in praise from one who has almost a lifetime of growing work behind his judgement.... I hope that you are going further yet, in poetry, for our benefit. That sounds greedy; but you never repeat yourself, and so everything matters.

'Thanks again,' he concluded. 'It's not my fault, wholly, if I am not more Irish: family, political, even money obstacles will hold me in England always.'[61]

7

What Clare Sydney Smith called 'the Golden Reign' at Mount Batten came to an end in the autumn of 1931, when her husband, who had been promoted to Group-Captain, was posted to Manston, a large station near Ramsgate. 'We are all dreading the arrival of some dud to succeed him,' Lawrence wrote to Charlotte Shaw when he heard the news. 'The R.A.F. is full of dud C.O.s.'[62] Lawrence drove over with the C.O.'s wife to Manston in her car and saw her and his former C.O. into their new quarters. Shortly before leaving Mount Batten Lawrence suddenly appeared in the drawing room of the C.O.'s house at Mount Batten where Clare Sydney Smith was arranging the flowers. He was carrying a large book which he laid on the table. 'I put down the flowers I was holding,' Clare has recalled. 'It was *The Seven Pillars of Wisdom* in the beautifully bound and very precious limited edition – a truly royal gift!', particularly as it was a complete copy with all the illustrations. When Clare opened it, she read the following inscription on the fly-leaf: 'From T.E.S. to W.S.S. on dissolution of partnership.' Clare immediately telephoned her husband in his office and he came over to the house 'simply delighted, but sad too, that parting was the reason for the gift'.[63]*

'I think it is going to be all right,' wrote Lawrence on getting back to Mount Batten from Manston. 'The routine has stiffened with the going of G/C Smith, and I, at least, feel less secure: but the new C.O. (W/C Burling) shapes well. He will do, I fancy. I'm going to keep myself more to myself this time, as with the last C.O. I had too much to do.'[64]

It was at this time, in the autumn of 1931, that Trenchard, who had been made a peer on his retirement as C.A.S., was appointed Commissioner of Metropolitan Police, and Lawrence wrote to him from Mount Batten 'saying how delighted we all are that the Government has found a new job big enough for you. The Police are fortunate.'

When the news came out all the airmen walked about and said 'I reckon that's all right about Hugh.' (Boom has been extinct for years. They say Hugh, now.) Personally, as I have not to go to the rotten places, I hope we shall have bigger and better night-clubs.

Mount Batten is under Wing-Commander Burling, and is all right, still. I haven't so much work as when Group-Captain

* Sydney Smith retired with the rank of Air Commodore in 1941 and died in 1972. The copy had previously been sold by Mrs Sydney Smith to J. G. Wilson of Bumpus's for £150 and subsequently changed hands at least once, since it appeared with another owner's bookplate in Sale Catalogue No. 261 of the rare book dealers Dawsons of Pall Mall in August 1975, priced at £3600.

Smith was the C.O.: and am proportionately contented. This is an excellent life.[65]

Of course things were not quite the same with the new C.O. and Mount Batten did not seem quite such a cheerful place as in Sydney Smith's time. Nevertheless Wing-Commander Burling turned out more or less as Lawrence had anticipated during the fourteen months he was the station commander, before he was moved elsewhere. 'He has been a very quiet and uninterfering C.O. and we are all very sorry he is going,' Lawrence wrote to Clare Sydney Smith on 16 December 1932. 'Mount Batten is not very cheerful at the moment. It is to be upgraded on April 1st and so there's yet another change in prospect. All very unsettling.'[66]

The year 1933 opened tragically at Mount Batten with another Iris flying-boat crash. This time only one life was lost and the air–sea rescue operations were seen to have improved enormously since the previous tragedy. 'The power boat did well,' Lawrence wrote in his account to his old C.O.'s wife. 'From our breakwater she reached the crash ($\frac{7}{8}$ of a mile) in 1 minute 58 seconds. This is a 400 per cent improvement on the 238 crash, when 700 yards took 4 minutes. As usual, having arrived, there was nothing to be done. I am putting in another moan about salvage equipment.'[67]

Early in March 1933 Lawrence formally applied to be released from further service in the R.A.F. with effect from 6 April. 'The discharge of this airman will cause no manning difficulty,' the new C.O. reported unimaginatively. But the news was somehow leaked and it got into the newspapers. 'Are you leaving the Air Force, or have you been kicked out?' Trenchard wrote to him when he read about it. 'Let me know some time. I would like to have a talk with you. You will hear of my iniquities if you come anywhere near London.'[68]

Trenchard had been getting some unfavourable publicity in the press for his activities in cracking down on night-clubs. Hence Lawrence's reply:

Indeed you do make a great noise in the papers. It is good you are not an aircraftman, or the Ministry would sack you!

I'm not being turned out. Coastal Area are very obstruc-
tionist, and won't let us do anything from Batten, in the way
of boat-testing or experiment. The savour of living
here in barracks is not what it was. So I put in to go, as from
April 6 – unless my services are for any purpose specially
required.

Last week I saw Sir Geoffrey Salmond, who will sit in your
chair (not ignobly, too, I think: he has brains and skill and
knowledge) and explained myself fully: so I must leave it at
that. Unlike you, I grow older and my temper hardens with my
arteries, making me less fit to deal with folly.

Plymouth is 200 miles away, and week-ends do not let me
reach England and return – even though my present bike
averages 43 m.p.h. But I shall try to find you on my next visit,
at an as yet unfixed date. Scotland Yard or Dancer's Hill? The
Yard would be shocked, probably, by your low taste in
visitors! Also you would probably be raiding a night-club,
and would miss me.

Whether I go or stay, I shall look back upon the years
1922–1933 as the best decade I have tasted. The R.A.F. has me
deeply in debt.[69]

Meanwhile Lawrence's application had reached the desk of the
Air Member for Personnel, Sir Edward Ellington, who had
succeeded the ill-fated Sir John Webb-Bowen, and he wrote to
W/C Andrews, the new C.O. at Mount Batten, asking him to see
Aircraftman Shaw and find out if he had a grievance, as the
Secretary of State Lord Londonderry was concerned to know
why he wished to leave the Service. However, Lawrence suspected
that Londonderry's curiosity had been prompted by Sir Philip
Sassoon, who was Under-Secretary with a seat in the House of
Commons and a friend of Lawrence.

I replied that I had no grievance, and was only too sorry to be
leaving – but that I could no longer be content to do station
duty at Mount Batten. My present job is looking after the boats
and their engines here, and that is purely routine and not a
day's work, even for my hands. I am a reasonably-skilled

mechanic, after all these years, but without ambitions to excel in it.

My feeling was that I should do something more, if I was to justify my staying on in the R.A.F. At Karachi, for instance, they let me revise the procedure of engine-overhaul in the Depot. At Batten Sydney Smith gave me the Schneider Cup ground organisation. Then the D[irector] of E[quipment] gave me the R.A.F. fleet to put on new lines, and I did eighteen months on that and got half-way in it.

So I told the C.O., for Ellington, that if there was any special job in which the C.A.S. thought I could be particularly useful, then I was at his service: but if not I would prefer my discharge. That meant, I am sure, that they would discharge me: many people would be glad to see me go, and I am not fond of pushing in where I am not wanted. The only thing that troubles me is that there is much I could yet do. In these eleven years I have learned every square inch of the R.A.F. and it seems a pity to leave so much knowledge unused.[70]

After a delay of several weeks it was eventually decided by mutual agreement that A.C. Shaw should be posted to Felixstowe for employment in work which was done there in the Marine Craft Section, and to avoid publicity he should wear plain clothes. In a confidential report in his personal files the writer stated that he could very advantageously be employed watching the Air Ministry's interests at contractors' yards, in compilation of trial reports, and notes on running and maintenance. 'He has ideas on high-speed craft worth considering.' At the same time the Secretary of the Air Ministry, Sir Christopher Bullock, sent Trenchard a note for his information.

Lawrence of Arabia has decided to stay on in the Air Force. As he knows a good deal about motor boats he has been given a fairly free hand to go round various motor boat firms in the country, Ellington's people can send on a letter at any time or find out where he is now if you wish.[71]

Thereafter the official correspondence in A.C. Shaw's personal file was confined to when he should wear plain clothes, what travelling expenses he should be allowed and whether he could 'live decently' on thirty shillings a week plus his pay, if he went to Messrs White's yard at Cowes in the summer for a month. Thus Lawrence was free to get on with the kind of job he really cared about, instead of being kept to dull station routine duties which was the lot of the average airman. For this purpose he was based at Southampton where he found a room in a house in Birmingham Street, No. 13, now commemorated by a plaque on the outside wall recording the fact that 'T. E. Shaw, Lawrence of Arabia' lived there between July 1933 and November 1934. 'I am so nailed into Southampton Water by these jobs,' he wrote to the Sydney Smiths, who were shortly going to Singapore, and he was anxious to spend a night with them at Manston before they left. 'Up and down all day and all week: that's me.' Or, as he put it to Liddell Hart: 'I have web feet now and live on the water.'[72]

He did manage to get to Manston for a night and he also met Clare and her husband just before they sailed in London where he went to see the Motor-Cycle Show at Olympia. Afterwards Clare wrote of this meeting.

> He looked older . . . tired . . . worn. The air of nervous strain he had lost so completely in the Golden Reign hung about him. His impending discharge and what he would do with his leisure weighed on his mind. We had little to say; he disliked an emotional atmosphere and so I strove to hide what I felt. . . .
>
> I drove him to Addison Road Tube Station and he got out of the car and stood watching me for a few moments before he disappeared into the station. He was standing in the shadow of immense Olympia, and as I turned and looked at him, he had his hat in his hand, as on the first day in 1921 I met him in Cairo. In this eyes was a wistful far-away look and his figure appeared small and a shade dispirited. I never saw him again.[73]

Meanwhile Liddell Hart had completed his biography of Lawrence. 'I hate it,' its subject told his mother after he had been through it. 'These people all exaggerate so, and make me more of a mountain than a man. I read his proofs and knocked out a good deal of stuff that wouldn't do. Unhappily I had to put in something, each time to replace what I knocked out.'[74] However, he left in at least one or two good stories. One was to the effect that when he recently reported for duty at a new station and was asked in stereotyped form for the name and address of his next of kin in case of accident, he replied: 'Oh, report it to the Editor, *Daily Mail* – and mind you get a special rate!' Again, when King Faisal of Iraq, with whom Lawrence had lunched at the Hyde Park Hotel in London in August 1933, died two months later, Lawrence was warned that several reporters were on their way from London to Southampton by train to interview him. He promptly jumped on a train for London, passing theirs in the opposite direction, as the most effective way of evasion. To add zest to their pursuit, however, he left behind a false trail which led them to embark on an undesired, if short, sea-trip to the Isle of Wight.[75]

In fact he did come temporarily to rest at Cowes during that summer after going via Felixstowe, Manchester and Hythe, as he wrote to Marson, who had apparently recovered from his financial troubles, thanks largely to Lawrence's help, and now had a job as Civil Adjutant at R.A.F. Donibristle. 'So Batten is a pleasant memory,' he mused in his letter to Marson; 'as of a tiny rock-peninsula, sea-battered and held only by airmen: so private, so away, so clean.'

At Cowes I watch a yard building five stupid pinnaces of Admiralty design. By God, we do pay the price of Admiralty! Thousands are thrown away on them ...

How are you? Does Civil Adjutanting at Donibristle irk you? I hope not. The R.A.F. is a thing worth serving, I always think, and if the pay is small, that's why. You never get much for being pleased.

Rumour that Donibristle is going over to Coast Defence. I suppose they lost too many torpedoes. Give Inverkeithing my affection if you ever visit it. A quiet spot, but not clean and flyless, like Batten.

Mrs Marson? Scotland? Hum. The villages are so grim, and the leaves too green.[76]

His journeys sometimes took him further afield than the Solent. On one of his journeys he met H. G. Wells in the train and he retailed their conversation to Charlotte Shaw.

'Yes,' I said rashly, 'you probably want to write no more stories now.' He replied: 'I dare not: my reputation is too great to risk a failure: and one writes a good story only by writing three or four bad ones, and till the public has read them the good ones do not appear from the bad. So I can only afford to write histories and things.'

'There is something behind that,' was Lawrence's comment: 'Probably an excuse for growing up.'[77]

When he was in Wolverhampton early in 1934 overseeing the testing of a new group of motor-boat engines in a factory, it was working two shifts and this gave him little time to write. However, he did manage to let his mother know what he was doing – she and Bob had recently returned to their old missionary work in China – and as with Clare Sydney Smith he dwelt uncomfortably upon the future.

The Air Ministry still allow me a reasonably free hand with boats and engines, and so they get the boats and engines that I want, and not always what they want. I have just over a year of my time to serve, and shall then fall quietly into Clouds Hill and stay quiet for a while, to see what it feels like. I have a queer sense that it is all over – all the active part of my life, I mean; and that retirement from the R.A.F. is also retirement from the stream. I shall be 46; which is neither young nor old; too young to be happy doing nothing, but too old for a fresh start. However there is nothing that I want to do, and nothing particularly that I am glad to have done. So I am unlikely to live either in the past or in the future. Man is not an animal in which intelligence can take much pride. The cottage is finished, so far as its main lines go. The tinkering with details will be distraction for my leisure. You see, since I grew up I have never been at leisure at all. It will be a radical and not very enjoyable change.[78]

On Sunday, 25 February 1934, he visited Chartwell, Churchill's country home in Kent, where one of the guests, a cousin of Mrs Churchill's, Sylvia Henley, afterwards recalled Churchill putting a question 'rather out of the blue at luncheon' to Lawrence. 'In the event of an air attack what would be our best defence?' Lawrence immediately replied: 'Multiple air force defence stations to intercept.' 'Churchill,' she added, 'seemed satisfied' with this reply.[79]

'May 1934 be a decent year for you: and for me!' he had written to Marson, with whom he continued to keep in touch, as with many others of his old friends. 'It is my last in the R.A.F. and I am glad and sad, both.' Then, as an afterthought, he added a few lines about their old Chief, who was having trouble with corruption in the Metropolitan Police force: 'What a time Boom is having! I do hope he finds somebody honest to help him through. Those police *smell* dirty.'[80]

He wrote again to Marson after the Government had announced the first of its expansion schemes for the Air Force in the 1930s, which envisaged a greater proportionate increase in fighter over bomber squadrons as compared with what Trenchard had insisted on when he was C.A.S., and an expansion which might well lead to an accumulation of obsolete and obsolescent planes.

It is bad when a new and uncertainly led service is suddenly expanded. I fear we are going to waste money, for no object. The international horizon is quite clear for the near future, and we might with gain to ourselves have breathed peacefully and built up our efficiency. I wish Trenchard was ten years younger and due for another term of office. Chiefs like that arise once or twice in a century.[81]

One trouble for Lawrence in 1934 was the discovery that he was being impersonated. He first heard about it from Liddell Hart who had been told that there was a man going round calling himself 'Aircraftman Shaw, formerly Colonel Lawrence'. He also signed a letter in the name of Lawrence, which convinced Liddell Hart when he saw it that an impersonation was being attempted. 'Do you feel I ought to do something?' he wrote to

Hart. 'It is rather hard to catch him by post. However, there is Eliot: the Hon. E[dward] Eliot . . . He is a very balanced solicitor, who looks after the legal interests of *Revolt in the Desert*. My trouble is that I cannot well risk legal expenses: but Eliot might feel able to assume that a "T. E. Lawrence" in being today was an infringement of his trust property, for the *Revolt* Trust owns the property in that name. If so he could ask the bloke to stop his games, and charge his trouble to the fund. I'd pay a small bill, up to 3 or 4 pounds, but couldn't risk the promising of more. Will you send on the suggestion (or perhaps this note) to Eliot and see if he can square his conscience to the idea?'[82]

Mr Eliot was a partner in the firm of Kennedy, Ponsonby and Prideaux, besides being a brother of Lord St Germans. Liddell Hart went to see him and Eliot promised to take up the matter, which he did most effectively. Lawrence and Eliot, accompanied by two detectives from Bow Street, went along to a certain office where the man was waiting by invitation. Eliot went up first and was introduced to 'Colonel Lawrence', who interposed 'now Aircraftman Shaw.' 'That's curious,' said Eliot, 'because he is just coming up the stairs.' According to Liddell Hart, who got the account from Lawrence himself, 'the man recovered himself well, and said this was the proudest honour of his life: and frankly said he was a complete fraud'. Lawrence afterwards remarked to Liddell Hart that 'he was glad the man did not stick to his claim, or he [Lawrence] would have begun to doubt himself'.

The man said he had done it to get himself a position. He had been to the Zoo, and condemned the camels as mangy. He'd tried to float a company and to get Ward Locke to publish two of his poems. He had also been six months in a mental home – T.E. remarked that this was the unkindest cut of all!

T.E. said he was about the same build, but a little rat of a man, with no forehead and thin on top. Not very flattering. As no money had actually passed, they let him off after making him write letters of apology to various people.[83]

As the date for his retirement from the R.A.F. drew nearer, Lawrence became increasingly worried and despondent over what he would do when he had retired to Clouds Hill. 'Do you know Gissing's *Private Papers of Henry Rycroft*?' he asked Charlotte Shaw in a letter summing up his feelings. 'I have been lately reading them again, my memory having been that it was the only written product of contentment. So I thought it, while I was active and afoot: but now I cannot face its words. What Gissing says and feels is so exactly what I know is coming to pass when I leave the R.A.F. and fall into quietness at Clouds Hill; and in the light of knowledge I see clearly that what I once took for contentment is resignation: and what I thought was happiness is sense of failure.'[84]

L'Envoi

I

In November 1934 Lawrence was posted to the Marine Craft Detachment at Bridlington on the east coast of Yorkshire. When he arrived he was met by a marine contractor named Ian Deheer. At this time there were ten boats lying in different garages in the town, five armoured boats and five seaplane tenders, most of them waiting for their engines which were being overhauled at Scott Paine's Yard at Hythe. Near by at Catfoss there was an armament training camp, which with Bridlington was responsible to the Air Armament School at Eastchurch, Kent, a difficult line of communication which somehow seemed to work. When a boat had been fitted out with its engine, it was towed on a large trolley through the streets of Bridlington to the harbour where it was launched by the civilian contractors and tied up in the harbour. Gradually more airmen arrived as more boats were commissioned, the airmen's postings being regarded as permanent since it had been agreed at the Air Ministry that Bridlington would have to serve the expanded and expanding air force throughout the year instead of during the summer only as had been the practice hitherto.

The officer in charge of the Marine Craft Detachment at Bridlington was an ex-Lieutenant-Commander, R.N., H. E. E. Weblin, who had been attached to the Air Ministry after retiring from the Navy. He formed a high opinion of A.C. Shaw from the beginning, being favourably impressed by his general correctness and smartness and the respect he showed to officers and N.C.O.s. 'I feel it my duty to point out to you, sir,' Lawrence told him on the day he reported for duty, 'that I am only an aircraft hand and therefore not eligible to take any of your boats to sea, and I make a point of never doing so unless there is a qualified coxswain on board.' After he had been in Bridlington for a few weeks and several more airmen had arrived, Lawrence told Weblin with a smile: 'They are all doing exactly as I tell them already. I suppose some day some N.C.O. will tell me to mind my own business – but I doubt it.' Indeed his influence extended to others on the station, whether civilians or serving officers. At conferences or discussions which he attended he would listen quietly until everyone had had his say and then respectfully intervene: 'If I might be allowed to suggest, sir . . .', and he would then present what was obviously the best solution of the problem under discussion. Needless to add his suggestion was invariably adopted.[1]

Weblin particularly appreciated his sense of humour and in his brief recollections of Lawrence at Bridlington he has given several examples of it. One will suffice. Weblin had occasion to write telling him that on running the trials of an engine, a part was found to be missing and that the corporal in charge had put the blame on him. 'I am sorry about the manifold washer, sir,' replied A/c Shaw. Then he went on by way of explanation: 'Two great Oxford scholars, called Liddell and Scott, worked for twenty-five years and produced what is still the world's standard Greek dictionary. Then Scott died. As time passed and the users of the book now and then drew the University's attention to a misprint or error in the book, Liddell used to sigh and shake his head, "Ah yes – poor Scott, still it may have been mine".'[2]

Soon after Lawrence got settled in at Bridlington, a new deputy C.O. arrived to whom the airman was nominally responsible. This was Pilot-Officer (later Air Commodore) F. J. Manning, then a young officer of 23. He had travelled up from London on an overnight train and as soon as he had had a bath and change of clothes, Ian Deheer brought him along to the hangar at the harbour, where he was introduced to A/c Shaw. The latter, according to Manning's recollection, was dressed in a blue jersey, a scarf, a kind of sports jacket, a very creased pair of flannel trousers, with no hat. 'How do you do,' he welcomed his new C.O. politely. He then suggested that there was no point in Manning remaining at Bridlington for the immediate future, since there were no other airmen there besides himself and most of the boats were still under repair, and he thought that the best thing Manning could do would be to go home on leave. In fact, he added, he had already been in touch with Eastchurch and his suggestion had been approved. He added that there was a train back to London in two hours' time. P/O Manning did not need much persuading and he accordingly went off for another week's leave.

After Manning's return more boats were launched, so that by the middle of January 1935 all ten were in the water, complemented by thirty airmen and ten hangar tradesmen. The crew of each boat would be a coxswain, a deck hand and a wireless operator. Whenever any boat went out on trials Lawrence always insisted on the presence of a cox in accordance with the regulations, although in effect he was in charge of the boat throughout her exercises. He and the other airmen were accommodated in a private hotel overlooking the harbour, appropriately called the Hotel Ozone. It was kept by a certain Mrs Barchard, 'a portly woman of Amazon appearance who ruled the airmen with a rod of iron', according to Manning. 'There was never any need for me to do inspections because she did her own,' Manning has also recalled. 'I remember with her "grace and favour" being allowed to go over the Ozone Hotel in my early days there and when Shaw was living there, to see how and where the airmen lived. In fact they had greater comfort than in a barrack room of course. I remember Mrs Barchard opening the door of a room and saying, "This is where Mr Shaw lives. He is such a gentleman." '3

'The name of the Hotel is real,' Lawrence wrote to his fellow Arabist Sir Ronald Storrs. 'So I think is the ozone, or is it the fish market that smells?' He added that the place was empty, cold and rather nice.4

'My room is a tower room, over the harbour wall,' he told his friend Henry Williamson, author of *Tarka the Otter* and other tales, 'and the waves roll all day like green swiss rolls over the yellow sand, till they hit the wall and run back like spinning rope. I want to walk out in the wind and the wet, like at Clouds Hill, and can't, for my landlady's sake.'5 And to H. S. Ede he also wrote from the Ozone Hotel: 'No, the address is not a spoof. . . . A summer seaside resort is an uncanny place in mid-winter.'

The refit is due to be completed by the end of February; and early in March I 'get my ticket'. It's like a blank wall beyond which I cannot even imagine. Exactly what leisure is like, whether it will madden me or suit me, what it means to wake up every day and know there is no compulsion to get out of bed . . . it's no good. When it comes, I shall try to deal with it; but now, beforehand, I can only say that I wish it had not to be.[6]

The Equipment Officer and Civil Adjutant at Catfoss was a retired Flight-Lieutenant, R. G. Sims, who had served in Iraq where he had struck up a correspondence with Lawrence on the subject of insects, which he had photographed and described meticulously. Naturally he was delighted when he heard of Lawrence's posting to Bridlington. Afterwards he wrote of him.

One memorable day he came to Catfoss, and I saw and heard him speak at a conference. He was a small, slight man, singularly well developed, wearing no medal ribbons, but otherwise in smart airman's walking-out dress. He spoke in a very low distinct voice – I have never heard him speak otherwise – but there was no question that any officer could speak to him, or get him to speak, except on the business for which he had appeared.

Several times after this I spoke about Service matters to him on the telephone, and I loved to hear that beautifully quiet, distinct voice answering with 'Bridlington R.A.F. detachment, A.C. Shaw speaking'. Then he would answer very politely, giving the information required in the fullest manner, and the fewest possible words, calling me 'sir' most meticulously at every sentence. I never heard him address an officer otherwise.[7]

On one occasion, when Sims went over to Bridlington and discovered Lawrence engaged in reading a blue-print in the garage, he waited until Lawrence had completed his scrutiny of the document. Then, when Lawrence lowered the print and looked at Sims, his eyes blazed forth for a moment or two in what Sims took to be scorn or hate. Then there was a sudden half-smile of recognition. 'Oh, I am so sorry, sir,' A.C. Shaw murmured apologetically, 'but for a moment I took you for a reporter.'

Sims then asked Lawrence if he would come back to his living quarters in Hornsea. At first the airman begged to be excused; he was not dressed for the part; he felt dirty after clambering over boats for most of the morning, and there was the question of transport back, since he had to be in Bridlington again inside two hours. Sims then suggested the use of his bathroom and indicated the baby Ford outside the hangar. 'Then,' said Lawrence gravely, 'all that remains for me is to say thank you.'

When they arrived at Hornsea, Lawrence looked at the cottage appraisingly, with his closed fists and a finger pressed to his chin, a favourite attitude. 'Ah, yes,' he observed. 'Cobble built, repaired with brick facings, about sixteenth or early seventeenth century. Nice cottage.' When he went into the cottage, he set Mrs Sims, their child and dog at ease immediately. After lunch they ensconced him in a large chair from which he proceeded to hold forth about books, people, music and the R.A.F. until, very much against the grain, Sims reminded him it was 3.15 and perhaps it was time to be going. Whereupon, according to Sims, he pulled himself out of his chair like a steel spring unbending, and said that 'everything had conspired to make him forget there was such a thing as work'.[8]

Reggie Sims, and particularly his wife, were devoted to Lawrence and undoubtedly they were his closest friends during his time at Bridlington. They had him often to meals and once thought nothing of driving him thirty miles to Hull to a celebrity concert at which Sir Henry Wood was conducting and delivering him back to the Hotel Ozone after the concert was over. It was a good concert, Lawrence thought, except that the piece by Schubert was 'just one piece of sugar too much'. On another occasion, when Eric Kennington the artist appeared, the Sims's gave a dinner for him to which Lawrence and Manning came. At first Manning had some misgivings, as he wondered whether a C.O. should dine with one of his airmen. However, the evening went off very well without the slightest trace of embarrassment on anyone's part, particularly as Kennington got going on the illustrations he had done for the *Seven Pillars* and described how one of his Arab sitters had attacked him with a knife while he was engrossed in the drawing. Sims had given his son a book entitled *Heroes of Modern Adventure*, which contained a thumb-nail sketch of Lawrence. 'Not quite right,' was Lawrence's comment. 'Bad shot. Very inaccurate.' Then he said: 'Give me a pencil and let us make some notes.' And with the pencil he added some further fictionalised annotations in a spirit of fun.[9]

Another officer visiting the detachment, on being told that Shaw hoped to see him to put forward some suggestion, replied curtly: 'When I want the advice of an A.C.1 I will ask for it.' Next morning, Weblin happened to see the two of them together in the hangar, and after the other officer had gone Weblin asked Shaw if he was amenable. 'That is hardly the word for it,' he replied. 'He ate out of my hand; in fact, he is on the telephone to headquarters at the moment ordering everything we want.' 'This is quick work,' Weblin remarked, 'because only last night he said that when he wanted the advice of an A.C.1 he would ask for it.' At this the aircraftman smiled and said: 'He *has* asked for it, sir, and had it!' The following night they were seen dining together.

At Bridlington he generally managed to avoid publicity, but there was one occasion when he was recognised which Weblin cited as an example of his quick wit. He was in dirty overalls stripping an engine in the open hold of a vessel alongside the pier, when two sailors from ships of the Royal Navy visiting the port spotted him. One remarked to his friend: 'You see that chap down there with the fair hair? That's Lawrence of Arabia.' Lawrence looked up with annoyance and quick as a flash said: 'I thought you fellows belonged to the silent Service!'[10]

He still had time to write to his friends, including Trenchard. The publishers of a memoir of Sir Sefton Brancker, who had been killed in the tragedy of the R101, had sent him the proofs which, he told Trenchard, 'brought back you and the war and the beginning of the R.A.F. very distinctly to my mind. Not a good book, but interesting to those who know something and care something about the time and subject.'

Probably you are all buried in the Police, now-a-days, and seldom get away to things that matter. I suppose there is a small construction side, however, even in the Police – wireless and traffic development, and possibly other things. Otherwise you must sigh for the lively Service.

My time is almost out: two months to go. I have had over twelve years (thanks to that false start which ended at Farnborough) and only regret that I'm not young enough to do a second term. It has been very good, and I've given almost as much as I've received, and that's all. I shall feel like a lost dog outside.

Plans? Well, I have 25/o a week, and I plan to settle in my cottage (Clouds Hill, Moreton, Dorset) and live on it and in it till I no longer want to live in it! That is as good a plan as any, I think. Leisure is about the only experience I have never yet had and it will, I hope, suit me.

When the change has happened, and I get reconciled, I shall try to see you again . . . for no reason there being nothing I want . . . but it would please me. So I hope that will be agreed.

Please remember me to Hugh the Second. Poor kid! Not content with loading upon him the responsibility of having to follow you, you now add the House of Lords to his cargo-of-life. If I were him, I'd change my name and start again fair, from scratch.

Yours
T. E. Shaw

Scotland Yard has ceased being news: which means I take it that you have got your way. We all knew you would. What a clean-up they must have had![11]*

'I was delighted to get your letter,' Trenchard replied from Scotland Yard. 'I am immersed in Police work, but not sufficiently so as to prevent me still taking a great interest in my old Service and also in you. Come and talk to me some time. . . .

---

* The reference was to the various cases of bribery and corruption which had recently been brought to light in the Metropolitan Constabulary and which led to the Metropolitan Police Act, embodying important reforms, passed largely at Trenchard's instigation.

Little Hugh is very fit, and I am equally sorry that I saddled him with the name.'[12]*

So far as is known Lawrence and Trenchard never met again. But a few weeks afterwards Lawrence sent him a print of a drawing which Augustus John did of him when he was in what the sitter called 'a ripe and happy mood', and which Lawrence seemed to think flattered him. 'A fashion plate, I call it,' he wrote from Bridlington in a brief note accompanying the print. 'It is a very good fashion plate,' Trenchard replied, 'and I am very glad to have it.'[13]

2

Apart from week-end leave and a break of several days over the Christmas holidays, Lawrence did not ask for any special leave, which an A.C.1 would not normally be given. However, Manning remembered one leave week-end chit on which Lawrence had failed to put the initials in the top right hand corner W.P.T.W.C. ('With permission to wear plain clothes'), and Manning sent the chit back with the Flight-Sergeant. Shortly afterwards the Flight-Sergeant re-appeared in the C.O.'s office and said: 'He doesn't want it. He's going in uniform.' According to Manning A.C. Shaw's destination that particular week-end was the home of a member of the Air Council. This was almost certainly Lympne, the beautiful house of Sir Philip Sassoon, the Parliamentary Under-Secretary for Air. Sassoon was about to fly out on an official visit to Singapore. Lawrence found himself beside Lady Louis Mountbatten at lunch and seems to have enlisted her co-operation in getting their host to take out several new hats for Clare Sydney Smith to wear at official functions in the colony, and also some bathing costumes (Clare had something of a passion for bathing costumes and there was one embarrassing incident at Mount Batten when she walked across the parade ground clad in a particularly fetching model while the men were drilling). So far as the hats went, Lady Louis fitted them one into

* The Hon. Hugh Trenchard, who was commissioned in the Grenadier Guards in the Second World War, never succeeded to his father's peerage, since he was killed in action in 1943 while Lord Trenchard was still alive.

another like a nest of Chinese boxes until in effect they were really only one hat, after which Lady Louis overruled Sassoon's objections about excess luggage and handing the boxes to one of his servants instructed him 'to throw out some unimportant part of the Under-Secretary's kit and insert the hats'.[14]

During the Christmas leave Lawrence spent a night at Clouds Hill, where he discussed with his friend and neighbour Pat Knowles the possibility of setting up a small printing press in a structure over the hot water tank. ('A good place, for the atmosphere would always be damp and good for printing.') Here he intended to print a limited edition of *The Mint* by this means, to be followed by the work of 'some good but obscure poet'. He also collected one of Augustus John's drawings of him, and Knowles drove him to Wool station on his motor-bicycle, which he was leaving behind, while he rode pillion. As soon as he got back to Bridlington he wrote to Knowles.

I caught the train just after you went (it was a good idea, that pillion ride – though pretty awful pillioning with a suitcase and John's masterpiece in one's arms) and dumped the m-p in London on Emery Walker, to be photographed half size and collotyped 100 copies. That is my frontispiece – 'airman 1934 type' – if ever I put together my notes on the R.A.F.[15]

He was in London again in January when he had several further sessions with the artist. But first he and his solicitor had to meet Alexander Korda, who was anxious to make a film of *Revolt in the Desert*. 'I am confident of persuading him off it,' he wrote to Charlotte Shaw. He wrote to her again a few days later.

Last Monday Eliot and I lunched with Alexander Korda, the film king. He was quite unexpectedly sensitive, for a king; seemed to understand at once when I put to him the inconveniences his proposed film of *Revolt* would set in my path ... and ended the discussion by agreeing that it should not be attempted without my consent. He will not announce its abandonment, because while he has it on his list other producers will avoid thought of it. But it will not be done.

You can imagine how this gladdens me. Eliot took it like a
dear.

Thereafter I sat to John for two days, twice each day; and he
painted with great ease and surety (a new John, this) a little
head and shoulders of me in oil, R.A.F. uniform, with cap on
head. I think it much the best thing of me he has ever done. It
sparks with life, is gay, coloured and probably not unlike my
real face when thinking, so lively and clean. He himself agreed
that it had come off and was comforted as lately he has found
it hard to finish anything. In his pleasure he went on to do two
charcoal drawings of me, three-quarter length standing – and
he gave me the better of them.[16]

Lawrence loathed the notion of being 'celluloided', as he told
Robert Graves. 'The camera seems wholly in place as journalism:
but when it tries to recreate it boobs and sets my teeth on edge.
So there won't be a film of me. Korda is like an oil company
which has drilled often and found two or three gushers, and has
prudently invested some of its proceeds in buying options over
more sites. Some he may develop and others not. Oil is a transient
business.'[17]

In the latter part of January 1935 an amateur theatrical company played Bernard Shaw's *Too True to be Good* at the Spa
Pavilion in Bridlington. This play, which was first produced at
the Malvern Festival in 1932, was not a great success, though one
of the characters Private Meek was admittedly based on Lawrence. Before its first production the author read the play to
Lawrence, which as originally written included a passage where
the Colonel asks Private Meek why he is not at least a corporal,
to which Shaw made Meek reply that he was illiterate. This
wouldn't do, Lawrence explained, with the result that the private's
reply was changed to: 'Not educationally qualified, sir,' which
indeed was the reason A/c Shaw always gave for not seeking
any promotion higher than Aircraftman First Class.[18] Lawrence
wrote to Charlotte Shaw from Bridlington, explaining why he
had not seen its performance.

Too True made an awful lot of talk. Bridlington in winter is a large village only, and I'm a known character. So I funked going to see the play. They would have cheered, or jeered, probably: cheered, I'm afraid; so I funked it. Sorry. They also did it at Oxford! The London people don't worry, having full-sized affairs daily; but here in the provinces any reputation is rare: and *Too True* surprised them with its immediacy. 'It is not really entertainment at all,' said our foreman. 'It means something.'[19]

However, it would appear that Lawrence had second thoughts and went to another performance which was attended by a number of visiting R.A.F. officers, including Weblin, and Beauforte-Greenwood, who headed the marine craft headquarters at Felixstowe. They all came up to see the last of the ten boats safely out of the garages and into the water and they rounded off their visit by going to the theatre, where incidentally Ian Deheer played a leading role. Manning, in his account of the incident may not have appreciated the extent of A/c Shaw's interest, since he afterwards said, recalling the performance: 'Shaw watched the play very attentively, and seemed to comprehend more amusing passages than the rest of us, frequently chuckling to himself, when the rest of the party were silent and "po-faced". He sat right in the middle of us all, again with the scarf and the sports jacket. The wives of Ian Deheer and Weblin were there, and he was extremely sociable with them: he always seemed to be very much at ease in ladies' company. I remember him auto-graphing their programmes and behaving in an almost juvenile way in the vestibule at the interval; in great form, nothing to suggest he resented women's company. I think this is a skeleton that's now been well buried.'[20]

Lawrence was no misogynist, but at the same time he was acutely conscious of the fact that there was no place for women in his work in the R.A.F. 'You remember me writing to you when I first went into the R.A.F. that it was the nearest modern equivalent of going into a monastery in the Middle Ages,' he wrote to Robert Graves at this time. 'That was right in more than one sense. Being a mechanic cuts one off from all real com-munication with women. There are no women in the machines, in any machine. No woman, I believe, can understand a mechanic's happiness in serving his bits and pieces.'[21]

However, the existence of one woman did bother him and the matter came to a head in January 1935 when Lawrence had what he called a 'dust-up' with the Chief Constable of Birmingham over an obstreperous female who kept on writing him letters, calling him Jim, and begging him to go back to her and: 'all would be forgiven'. He answered the first letter telling her that he was not her Jim and didn't know her from Eve, but she went on writing about twice a week. Finally, after about two years of this nuisance, Lawrence wrote to the Chief Constable and asked 'if as a favour he'd send an officer to ask her to abate her nuisance'. The Chief Constable, who appears to have believed her story, replied in a letter addressed to the C.O. Bridlington R.A.F., which was not marked 'Confidential', to the effect that the lady had been interviewed, was 53, an eccentric widow, with two grown-up sons, that she had lived with T. E. Shaw while he was serving in an Anti-Aircraft Battery in Birmingham, and furthermore that she had no intention of ceasing to write to him.

'I sent him back a snorter,' Lawrence wrote to an airman friend in Birmingham, 'saying that I had written to him personally, and that he had no right to communicate with my supposed C.O. That in a big station his action would have led to much gossip, very unpleasant to myself: but that fortunately there was no C.O. at Bridlington, and so his letter had come direct to myself! Since then, complete silence from my abandoned widow *and* from the Chief Copper.'[22]

As already indicated, the local R.A.F. station was not at Bridlington, which merely had a Marine Craft Detachment under Commander Weblin, but at Catfoss, where there was an armament school which worked closely with the Bridlington boats. The C.O. at Catfoss was Pilot-Officer Manning, and many years later, Air Commodore Manning, as he had become, recorded his recollections of Lawrence during the last few weeks of his service.[23] A rapport was first established between them at the supper party given by Reggie Sims and his wife for the artist Eric Kennington. On this occasion Manning remarked to A.C. Shaw that for a young man it was quite a distinction in that presumably his first, certainly one of his early Commanding Officers, was General Allenby. Now he (Manning) was 'at the other end of the line', and in due course he would have something to say to his grandchildren about it. 'This actually drew a little titter of a laugh from Shaw,' Manning remarked, 'so he certainly didn't take objection to it.'

'When we were aware that his days in the Air Force were drawing to a close, I had one or two conversations with him about going,' Manning went on to recall. 'I asked him why, if he was so happy with the Service, he didn't continue. And he said that his twelve years were up; he didn't think he should take on for any more. At the time I thought of these engagements in orthodox terms; if you went beyond twelve years it would have to be either a pensionable one, or a very special and unusual extension – of a year or two. But I now know he was never on orthodox engagements. He was on a unique take-it-or-leave-it form of contract in which he could leave the Service at any time subject to a month's notice either way. But twelve years appeared to be the point at which *he* had decided to call it a day, although clearly, the man was rather upset about going. He'd finished his job at Bridlington. All boats were in the harbour and in running order. He displayed immense pride in their performance and, I am sure, also in the fact of their existence, because he had a considerable measure of influence over the development of these boats, particularly the armoured boats which were designed as high-speed targets simulating the characteristics of battleships under bombing attacks by aircraft.

'In another conversation I remember him saying that one of his problems after leaving the Service would be that of his income; he felt that if he was not careful he'd either be a pauper without an income at all, or so wealthy that he'd be worried about the use of it. He wanted to establish a balance, ensuring his independence – if not with comfort but certainly with a clear and calm mind – he felt that he could exist on for example, two pounds a week or something like that. He was trying to strike this rather austere balance between having nothing at all and letting his talents rip, so to speak, and bring him what would have been an income of gross inconvenience.

'I also, incidentally, by the time he left, started to talk to him fairly freely about his life in Arabia. We reached, during his last fortnight of service, a kind of chatting stage and I found him very patient with my ill-informed observations, and most helpful. But I was no exception in being able to quiz him about his Army life. Most of the officers I have mentioned knew very little about Arabia, and they too chanced their arms in speaking to him about it. I should say some of our questions must have been rather boring to the little chap; he once recommended that I should read Liddell Hart's book about the Arabian venture – the only one worth reading in his view. He advised me NOT to read Lowell Thomas's book *With Lawrence in Arabia.*'

Lawrence's decision to leave is confirmed in the fragmentary *Leaves in the Wind*, which he seems to have intended to form a continuation of *The Mint*, to the effect that he wrote to his parent unit at Felixstowe on 6 February 1935 that he must not try to sign on again in the R.A.F., because in twelve years' time he would be too old to be efficient. 'The wrench is this,' he added reflectively: 'I shall feel like a lost dog when I leave – or when it leaves me, rather, for the R.A.F. goes on. The strange attraction in the feel of the clothes, the work, the companionship. A direct touch with men, obtained no other way in my life.'[24]

'There is no doubt about it,' was Air Commodore J. F. Manning's considered conclusion that: 'of all the interests that Shaw had in his rather unusual life, his last six years in the Air Force represented a haven, represented an object of great devotion, gave him a technical challenge which he couldn't have believed would arise. It came by chance. And out of all the things that he did he took the opportunities made available to him at Mount Batten, and made the best out of them, and with distinction.'

Purely by chance, arising out of the rescue operations associated with a flying boat crash in Plymouth Sound in 1929, his long association with motor boats began. Once involved, entirely unprofessionally at first, he soon became deeply committed to a personal crusade of technical improvement of

R.A.F. safety launches. In retrospect we know that his contribution to the development of new boats of revolutionary design was immense. *My own view is that he was one of the prime architects of our Air Sea Rescue Service.* Although he did not live to see this service grow beyond its adolescence, I feel sure that had he lived to see the 64 foot launches in operation during the last war, and had known of the thousands of lives they helped to save, he would have felt both contentment and pride in his achievements; something that Lawrence appeared not to experience after his Arabian venture.

3

'Aircraftman Shaw, sir, interview before discharge,' said the Flight-Sergeant as he stamped into the C.O.'s office. Shaw then marched in and Manning noted that he was in uniform for the first and last time that he saw him. His discharge form and records lay on the table. They contained the statement presumably written by Manning or Weblin: 'He is an exceptional airman in every respect and his character and general conduct have at all times been "very good" '. They had a short delightfully informal conversation in which Manning asked him about his immediate plans. He intended to leave Bridlington on his bicycle, not the Brough but an ordinary push-bike, and go first to Bourne in Lincolnshire where he hoped to meet the Australian novelist Frederic Manning, with whom he had corresponded for some years and whose works he admired, and afterwards make his way to his cottage in Dorset. After he had been dismissed, he returned to the Ozone Hotel and there wrote the letter to the then Chief of the Air Staff Sir Edward Ellington, which has been quoted at the beginning of this book.[25]

Next day, Tuesday 26 February 1935, according to F. J. Manning, who was presumably present: 'A few of us saw him off from the harbourside at Bridlington, including Ian Deheer who took a snapshot of him just before he pedalled off. He was in his familiar rig – scarf, sports jacket, flannel trousers, sitting on his bicycle, and leaning against the harbour wall. This was the last photograph ever taken of him. He gave a half smile, and a half wave of the hand and he was on his way. We never saw him again.'

'On Tuesday I took my discharge from the R.A.F. and started southward by road, meaning to call at Bourne and see Manning,' Lawrence wrote two days later to Manning's publisher Peter Davies: 'but I turned eastward, instead, hearing that he was dead.... My losing the R.A.F. numbs me, so that I haven't much feeling to spare for a while. In fact I find myself wishing all the time that my own curtain would fall. It seems as if I had finished, now. Strange to think how poor Manning, sick, poor, fastidious, worked like a slave for year after year, not on the concrete and palpable boats of my ambition, but on stringing words together to shape his ideas and reasonings. That's what being a born writer means, I suppose. And today it is all over and nobody ever heard of him.... I suppose his being not really English, and so generally ill, barred him from his fellows. Only not in *Her Privates We* which is hot-blooded and familiar. It is puzzling. How I wish, for my own sake, that he hadn't slipped away in this fashion; but how like him. He was too shy to let anyone tell me how good he was.'[26]

At Cambridge Lawrence stopped to see his brother Arnold, then Reader in Classical Archaeology at the University. But if he had any premonition of any impending disaster, he did not show it, chatting away quite relaxed and contentedly of his plans for taking up printing at Clouds Hill and using it as a base for touring and exploring England, as the fancy took him. However, on his arrival at the cottage, he found to his dismay that it was besieged by reporters and press photographers, so he pedalled off again, this time heading for London where he stayed at youth hostels on the way. He saw various people in the Press Association and press photographic agencies and he presumed upon a slight acquaintance with Esmond Harmsworth, son of Lord Rothermere and chairman of the Newspaper Proprietors Association, to draft a letter appealing for his help. He remarked that he had returned to his cottage with the intention of settling quietly in retirement. 'Unfortunately the quietude has been a complete failure,' he went on. 'Reporters and press photographers have visited the place in some numbers, anxious to photograph it and me, or to ascertain my future intentions. . . . Their eagerness to find me drove me out: and after I had gone it led them to break the tiles on my roof, split the door and trample all over my patch of land in search of me. I have had to ask the local police to patrol the place in my absence.' He added that he had just enough money to keep himself 'in modest idleness', that he was not looking for employment, nor was he writing or intending to write any more books, and that it was unlikely that he would ever go abroad again. He concluded by saying that it would be a great comfort to him if editors could generally deny him space and not accept pictures of him supplied by staff or freelance photographers.[27]

Apparently Lawrence decided on second thoughts not to send this letter but try instead to arrange an interview with Harmsworth, after he had been back at Clouds Hill and was again beset by the Press. 'The most exigent of them I banged on the eye,' he told John Buchan, who had just been appointed Governor General of Canada as Lord Tweedsmuir, 'and while he sought a doctor I went off again on my wanderings,' seeing the same agencies as before and also Esmond Harmsworth, pleading to be left alone. 'They agree more or less, so long as I do nothing that earns a news paragraph: and on that rather unholy compact I am back here [Clouds Hill] again in precarious peace, and living a life that has no fixed point, no duty and no time to keep. . . . May you be happy in Canada. Perhaps you may make more out of it than I think: but to me these new countries are bitterly lacking in upholstery.'[28]

Among Lawrence's numerous correspondents was the novelist and short-story writer James Hanley, whose work Lawrence admired. One of his novels entitled *Boy* had been favourably reviewed on its first publication in 1931. It is a brutally frank tale of a working-class lad of thirteen who ran away to sea, of the hardships and sexual assaults he endured on board ship, of his introduction to the brothels of Alexandria by a shipmate, and of his murder by the captain of the vessel because he had contracted syphilis. Although the book shocks the reader as no doubt it is designed to do, it is not pornographic and it has a serious purpose. In 1934 it was reprinted in a cheap edition with certain words and phrases omitted or paraphrased. To the surprise both of Lawrence and the publishers, Boriswood Ltd, with whose directors he was friendly, the Lancashire police seized a copy of the reprint at a local lending library, and in the result Boriswood, the firm's two directors and the librarian of the library where it was seized, were prosecuted for indecent publication. All the defendants pleaded guilty on legal advice at Manchester Assizes, Boriswood being fined £250 and the others £50 each. Lawrence was considerably concerned by this case, as was his friend E. M. Forster.[29]

'It seems to me monstrous,' he wrote to one of the Boriswood directors, 'to say that every publisher is at the mercy of the discretion of any Police Chief, at any time – why, it makes publication almost an impossibility. This altogether apart from the personal question of penalties assessed upon your firm and yourselves. They seem wholly disproportionate to Boriswood, but would be a fleabite to Macmillan for example. What evidence had the Judge as to your means?' While the case was pending Lawrence had seen E. M. Forster, since he thought it would be more effective if he tackled Forster before rather than after judgement. ('A subtle mind, that one.') 'He is one of the few writers who might dare lead an attempt to help. Most of them are afraid of the word sodomy. I wonder why?'[30] Forster indeed did help by coming down to Clouds Hill at the beginning of May and by reading a paper entitled 'Liberty in England' to the International Congress of Authors in Paris a few weeks later, in which he deplored the use of the English law to crush the book, which he described as 'a novel of much literary merit'. The paper was delivered in June, but Lawrence was neither to hear nor to read it, nor was he to know that it was to be republished by Forster in his own book *Abinger Harvest* in the following year.*

Nor was he to welcome Forster again to Clouds Hill as he had hoped. 'Your arrival will be marked by the setting of a white stone into the new wall,' he wrote to Forster early in May. 'Wool station: taxi to here: any day after the 14th superb.'[31] Until a day or two before that he had another house guest, Jock Chambers,

---

* James Hanley's *Boy*, after its suppression in England, was subsequently published by the Obelisk Press in Paris.

an airman friend from Uxbridge days, now a sorter at the Post Office spending his annual fortnight's leave at the cottage.* Meanwhile Lawrence had enlisted Marson's help in Donibristle in obtaining a port-hole for one of the upstairs rooms, which had no natural light and was too small for an ordinary bed. So Lawrence had built a bunk of shipshape type with drawers beneath for his clothes. He thought perhaps Marson might find something suitable in a shipbreaker's yard at Inverkeithing or Rosyth. 'Finishing off, or rather fitting up the cottage is the only pursuit that interests me at the moment,' he wrote to Marson in the letter containing his request. 'I am grateful for its quiet and the loneliness: but lost, all the same.'[32]

Marson was able to produce exactly what was wanted and in due course the port-hole was dispatched by rail. Lawrence was delighted with it. At the same time Marson offered him a chair. On 5 May he wrote to Marson thanking him again for the port-hole.

It is cleaned up, trimmed and only waiting for a guest to go ... before building into the wall. It is a good port-hole. I have inscribed your initials on its brass rim, in memory. All here is very quiet, but I am still calling the R.A.F. 'we' in my talk. That is sad.

I thank you for the offer of the chair: but the cottage is too small. I go about all day happy to see something that can be thrown out. Otherwise I shall stifle in it.[33]

Beauforte-Greenwood and his colleague F/Lt H. Norrington in the Marine Craft Detachment at Bridlington persuaded him to accept a personal memento of their association in the form of a pair of stainless steel candlesticks, suitably inscribed. He told them that he would try to get over to Hythe on Wednesday 24 April 'and then collect the art-work which will be a very good reminder of our long spell together'.

*Chambers recalls Lawrence waving a sheaf of papers during this visit and saying, 'This is for Winnie [Churchill]. It'll help pay my debt to him. It's about the German Air Force,' adding *à propos* the next war: 'It will be aircraft and tanks.' (Communicated by A. E. Chambers.)

As times passes, I fancy that association will develop into one of the pleasantest recollections of my life – the best stage of the R.A.F. embodiment which I have so much enjoyed.

They met at Hythe as arranged and had lunch together when the presentation was made. 'They look lovely,' wrote Lawrence when he got back to Clouds Hill. 'In exact keeping with their upper room.'

By day they sit on a brown oak mantelshelf above a Stainless Steel fender. By night they move to my writing table (as at present) or to my reading chair. They clean easily; stand solidly and feel good. I only wish they had not been possible – in other words our association had not ended. I try to cure myself of the habit of saying 'we' when I mean the air.

Life here is quiet and good enough but a very second best. I advise you all to hang on as long as you feel the job is in your power. There's such a blank afterwards.

They also talked over old times. For instance, there was the occasion when Lawrence was spotted by a local newspaper reporter in an East Coast port. The reporter walked across the room and asked: 'Are you Colonel Lawrence?' 'No,' was the reply; 'I am better-looking than that officer.' On another occasion when they were visiting an engineering works and put up in a hotel where Lawrence signed the register as 'Smith', a name he often used, the hall porter, who happened to have served in the East, recognised him and inquired the reason for the pseudonymous signature. Lawrence replied: 'Only people who want a divorce sign their correct names in the hotel registers.'[34]

To the artist Sir William Rothenstein, who had written to him twice and sent him a note through Thomas Hardy's widow, since he was uncertain of his address, Lawrence wrote back on the same day: 'I am sorry to appear so remiss; but my discharge from the R.A.F. (which had to come) has rather done me in, so that I no longer have the mind or wish to do anything at all. I just sit here in this cottage and wonder about nothing in general. Comfort is a very poor state after busyness.'[35] A week later he wrote in similar terms to Sir Karl Parker, Keeper of the Department of Western Art in the Ashmolean Museum: 'At present I am sitting in my cottage and getting used to an empty life.'[36]

Various jobs were offered to him at this time, ranging from being a kind of secretary to the Bank of England to taking over Sir Maurice Hankey's job running the Committee of Imperial Defence. But for none of these had he any inclination, nor did he wish to take up Lady Astor's invitation to talk over one of them: 'You can't live alone like that,' she wrote to him on 7 May. 'I knew it.' She went on:

> If I wasn't heavily engaged I should swoop down and see you. Please join me Plymouth Friday until Monday. I have evening engagement on Friday, but not a lot to do. So why not come down? The room is ready. Philip [Lord] Lothian is right as usual. I believe when the Government reorganises you will be asked to reorganise the Defence Forces.
>
> If you will come to Cliveden Saturday, the last Saturday in May . . . you will never regret it. Please, please come. Lionel and Pat [Curtis], Philip [Lothian] and, far the most important, Stanley Baldwin.* Please think about this.[37]

'No,' Lawrence wrote to her firmly by return, 'wild mares will not at present take me away from Clouds Hill. It is an earthly paradise and I am staying here until I feel qualified for it. Also there is something broken in the works, as I told you: my will, I think. In this mood I would not take on any job at all. So do not commit yourself to advocating me, lest I prove a non-starter.'[38]

Old friends, whether servicemen or writers, he liked to see and they were always certain of a warm welcome at Clouds Hill, whether they dropped in on the chance of his being at home or wrote in advance. One of the latter was Henry Williamson, whose *Tarka the Otter* had won the Hawthornden Prize and so impressed Lawrence when he first read it. Williamson proposed a visit to Clouds Hill to discuss Anglo-German relations, which had recently taken an ominous turn when Hitler had openly breached

---

* Baldwin was about to succeed MacDonald as Prime Minister.

the Versailles Treaty and admitted that Germany now had an air force, which she had been secretly engaged in building for some years in violation of the Treaty. Williamson was a friend of Sir Oswald Mosley, the founder of the British Union of Fascists, and in his talks with Mosley, Williamson apparently expressed the view that although Lawrence had no sympathy with the German dictator or his government, Williamson might be able 'to send him along the proper track'.* Williamson's letter to Lawrence proposing himself for 14 May has not survived, but something of the substance of what it contained may be gained from what he wrote in a brief monograph after Lawrence's death:

> ... it was time something was done about the pacification of Europe through friendship and fearless common sense. The spirit of resurgent Europe must not be allowed to wither, to change to a thwarted rage of power. With Lawrence of Arabia's name to gather a meeting of ex-servicemen in the Albert Hall, with his presence and stimulation to cohere into unassailable logic the authentic mind of the war generation come to power of truth and amity, a whirlwind campaign which would end the old thought of Europe (usury-based) for ever. So that the sun should shine on free men!

He must therefore, Williamson felt, 'go at once to Egdon Heath and tell the only man who could bring it about'. Hence his letter proposing himself for Tuesday 14 May 'unless rainy day'.[39]

On the morning of the 13th Lawrence rode into Wool on his motor-cycle, posted some books to 'Jock' Chambers who had recently been staying at the cottage, and then sent the following telegram to Williamson at his home in north Devon from the local post office, stamped at 11.35 a.m. precisely:

Lunch Tuesday wet fine cottage 1 mile north Bovington Camp
SHAW[40]

---

* In this context it should be noted that in his autobiography Sir Oswald Mosley has expressly stated that he never met nor had he any communication whatever with T. E. Lawrence, 'despite many later rumours to the contrary': *My Life* (1968), p. 226.

It was on his way back to Clouds Hill that disaster struck.

4

According to George Brough, the motor-cycle manufacturer, T. E. Lawrence was one of the finest riders he had ever met. 'In the several runs I took with him,' Brough has written: 'I am able to state with conviction that T.E.L. was most considerate to every other road user. I never saw him take a single risk nor put any other rider or driver at the slightest inconvenience – but when the road was clear ahead, it required a very good and experienced driver to keep anywhere near T.E.L.'[41] Yet accidents can happen to the most careful rider through no fault of his own, and such an accident befell Lawrence on the short run home from Wool Post Office.

The distance by road between Wool, with its few shops and post office which served Bovington Camp, and Clouds Hill is about a mile and a half. The road, which crosses Egdon Heath, is fairly straight but has three undulations or dips at the Clouds Hill end. The first and deepest is about 600 yards from the cottage, the second less deep is 200 yards nearer and the third about 100 yards leading to the gate of the cottage itself. The first two are deep enough to hide approaching traffic from anyone at the bottom of them, while the visibility at the foot of the third is normally perceptible. Exactly what happened is by no means altogether clear, since no one actually witnessed it. According to a Corporal named Ernest Catchpole, who was walking his dog from the camp across the heath in the direction of Clouds Hill, a black car emerged from the third dip, i.e. that nearest the cottage, travelling in the opposite direction. He also saw two boys on push-bicycles on the crest of the road between the first and second dips. Then he saw Lawrence enter the middle dip and for a moment Lawrence, the car, and the boys were all lost to sight. Then the car emerged from the middle dip and went on towards Bovington. A moment later Corporal Catchpole heard the noise of a crash and then a riderless motor-cycle appeared turning over and over along the road. He ran to the scene and found the motor-cyclist lying in the road, his face covered with blood which he tried to wipe off with his handkerchief. It was Lawrence. The two boys whom he had seen were near their bicycles and one seemed dazed and badly shaken, though he was not seriously injured. At this moment an army lorry drove past and waving it down Catchpole stopped it and told the driver to take Lawrence and the injured boy to Bovington Camp hospital. He did so because it happened to be the hospital nearest to the scene of the accident, but once Lawrence was there and it was realised who he was, the Army took over. The War Office was informed, and all ranks at Bovington were reminded that they were all subject to the Official Secrets Act.[42]

Lawrence was unconscious when he arrived at the hospital and in fact he never recovered consciousness before he died six days later. Meanwhile four skilled doctors, including two of the royal physicians, were sent for, and as they struggled to save his life messages and telegrams of sympathy poured into the camp from all over the country and overseas once the news had been flashed round the world. Arnold Lawrence, who was on holiday with his wife in Majorca, was telephoned by the Cambridge police and arrived at Clouds Hill on the following day. According to Lawrence's latest biographer Desmond Stewart, officials of the Air Ministry, or some other Government department concerned with security, had already visited the cottage where they would have no difficulty in going through the contents, and they probably found Henry Williamson's letter which has disappeared. This version of events has been strongly refuted by the dead man's brother. 'We stayed in Clouds Hill till after the funeral, seeing and hearing nothing of the security services,' he recently told the present writer. 'If they had already searched the cottage they would not have left the two typescripts of *The Mint* and the hundreds of letters – some in very difficult handwriting – that I found there.'

The King himself telephoned and asked to be kept informed of the patient's condition. Unfortunately it continued to deteriorate as congestion of the lungs developed. The end came shortly after eight o'clock on the morning of Sunday, 19 May, when his heart stopped beating. The wildest rumours were current about foreign agents, that Lawrence was not really dead but had been spirited away by these agents since he had: 'the plans for the defence of England in his head'. But, as his brother Arnold put it, 'whatever secret service he may have done in the past is over'. The inquest was arranged for the morning of 21 May before the East Dorset Coroner and a jury, to be followed the same afternoon by the funeral in a new burial ground near the churchyard.

Corporal Catchpole was the principal witness. He estimated that Lawrence's speed at the time of the accident, judging from the sound of the machine, was between fifty and sixty miles an hour and that it had passed the black car safely. 'I heard the crash,' he said, 'and I saw a motor-bicycle twisting and turning over along the road.' On the other hand, Pat Knowles, who also gave evidence, swore that he heard the motor-cycle change down twice and as the gear was found to have jammed in second, it could not have been going faster than 38 m.p.h. which was the machine's maximum speed in that gear.

Frank Fletcher, one of the two boy cyclists – the other was a butcher's boy named Alfred Hargreaves – also gave evidence: he was the son of an army bandsman in the camp. When they heard the sound of a motor-cycle coming from the rear the boys who had been riding abreast changed to single file, and then Fletcher heard a crash, after which his companion's cycle hit him and he fell off. What probably happened was that Lawrence met the black car on the crown of the middle dip, coming out of it as he was about to go into it. The road was quite narrow at this point and as the two vehicles approached each other, Lawrence pulled over to the left-hand side of the road. On doing so, he saw the two boys directly in front of him and in swerving to avoid them his machine skidded colliding with Hargreaves's bicycle and he was thrown over the handlebars landing on his head. He was not wearing a crash helmet. According to young Fletcher, Lawrence hit the ground with his feet about five yards in front of his machine which in turn was about five yards from where Fletcher fell off his.

Fletcher was positive that there was no other car or other vehicle on the road at the time, so that the black car remains

something of a mystery. 'There were no cars on the road,' he
repeated in answer to a question from a police officer in court. 'I
did not pass a car from the time I left Bovington Camp to the
accident.' In reply to a question from the jury, he added: 'We did
not leave the road at all.' 'The road was clear,' he said. 'Bert or
I would have seen it if there had been one.' On the other hand,
Corporal Catchpole, who was recalled and re-examined about the
black car, insisted that he had seen it. 'It was a private car,' he
stated, 'and the motor-cycle passed that safely. I then saw the
motor-cyclist swerve across the road to avoid two pedal cyclists
going in the same direction. The motor-cyclist swerved immediately after he passed the car which was going in the opposite
direction.' Yet it is curious that no attempt seems to have been
made to locate the driver of this vehicle so that he could give his
version of the event. There was a story, current at the time, that
Lawrence and an airman had seen the black car being tested on a
lonely stretch of road about a fortnight before. On the other
hand, Pat Knowles stated that a small black delivery van went
past Clouds Hill at about this time every day except on Sundays,
and it is possible that seen from where Corporal Catchpole was
standing about a hundred yards from the road, the black van
could easily have been mistaken for a private car.

These are some of the unsatisfactory features of the inquest.
The coroner commented in this sense, observing that although it
did not mean that it necessarily had anything to do with the
accident, the question of the black car puzzled him. Nevertheless
he had no difficulty in his direction to the jury.

I do not think you will have any difficulty in arriving at your
verdict. The facts are only too clear and that the collision was
an accident there can be no doubt. What caused the deceased
to run into the pedal cyclist from the rear we shall never know,
but the evidence would lead one to think that Mr Shaw must
have been travelling at a very fast speed and possibly lost
control of his motor-cycle. I do not think there can be any
other conclusion on the evidence. Under the circumstances you
will doubtless consider the proper verdict to bring in will be
one of accidental death.

In the event the jury brought in a verdict that Lawrence had died from injuries received accidentally. 'Needless to say I entirely concur with your verdict,' the coroner commented, 'and I am sure you would wish me to convey your sympathy as well as my own to Mr Shaw's relatives in the loss they and our country have sustained through the untimely death of such a gallant Englishman.' The death certificate described him as Thomas Edward Shaw, retired aircraftman, and gave the cause of death as 'Congestion of the lungs and heart failure following a fracture of the skull and laceration of the brain sustained on being thrown from his motorcycle when colliding with a pedal cyclist'. According to Dr C. P. Allen, of the Camp hospital, who carried out the post-mortem examination, had Lawrence lived he would have lost his memory and power of speech and would have been paralysed. Such are the facts of Lawrence's death and its cause so far as they are known. Yet in spite of the findings of the coroner's jury, the story spread that he had been deliberately killed and the accident had been engineered by the black car which had run him down. Both Williamson and Bruce, for instance, suspected foul play. Stories were spread about that he had been assassinated by agents of a foreign power, French, German or Arab. It has also been suggested that he was killed by British agents because his next book would have exposed government secrets. But all these legends can be dismissed as fantasy. His death was the result of a pure accident.

On his arrival, the dead man's brother took charge of the funeral arrangements. Sir Ronald Storrs, deputed to be the chief pall-bearer, was allowed by Arnold Lawrence to photograph the body as it appeared in his coffin, and although his activities were interrupted by the coroner who came to view the body, one of Storrs's photographs came out reasonably well. Storrs, who had worked closely with Lawrence in Arabia and was later to write the admirable brief biography of him in the *Dictionary of National Biography*, has described the scene in the mortuary chapel.

I stood beside him swathed in fleecy wool; stayed until the plain oak coffin was screwed down. There was nothing else in the mortuary chamber but a little altar behind his head with

some lilies of the valley and red roses. I had come prepared to
be greatly shocked by what I saw, but his injuries had been at
the back of his head, and beyond some scarring and discoloura-
tion over the left eye, his countenance was not marred. His
nose was sharper and delicately curved, and his chin less
square. Seen thus, his face was the face of Dante with perhaps
the more relentless mouth of Savonarola; incredibly calm with
the faintest flicker of disdain. The rhythmic planes of his
features gradually became the symbolized impression of all
mankind, moulded by an inexorable destiny. Nothing of his
hair, nor of his hands was showing; only a powerful cowled
mask, dark-stained ivory alive against the dead chemical
sterility of the wrappings. It was somehow unreal to be watching beside him in these cerements, so strangely resembling the
aba, the *kuffiya* and the *aqal* of an Arab Chief, as he lay in his
last littlest room, very grave and strong and noble . . .

As we carried the coffin into and out of the little church the
clicking Kodaks and the whirring reels extracted from the dead
body their last 'personal' publicity.[43]

The funeral, which took place in Moreton church in the afternoon immediately following the inquest, was private and was
attended by only personal friends and relations. But some were
unavoidably absent, such as his mother and his brother Bob who
were in China, the Bernard Shaws who were in South Africa, and
Allenby and Trenchard, who for some reason were prevented
from coming. But Winston Churchill and his wife were there,
also Lord Lloyd, General Wavell, Alan Dawnay, Siegfried
Sassoon, Lord Winterton, Lionel Curtis, Mrs Thomas Hardy,
Lady Astor and Augustus John, among others who had known
him. The other pall-bearers besides Sir Ronald Storrs were Eric
Kennington, Corporal Bradbury of the R.A.F., Private Russell
of the R.T.C., Pat Knowles from Clouds Hill and Colonel
Stewart Newcombe. Other old comrades like Alec Dixon who
had served with him in the Tank Corps were also there. John
Bruce, who was familiar with the dark side of Lawrence's private
life, also claimed to have been present at the funeral, although on
the day of Lawrence's death he wrote to Arnold regretting his

inability to attend owing to financial reasons.[44]

After the ceremony in Moreton Church the six pall-bearers carried the coffin to an open grave which had been dug in a tree-lined annexe to the main churchyard. According to one observer the coffin bore the inscription 'T. E. Lawrence', but according to the newspaper reports there was no name-plate on the coffin. As the first earth fell into the grave, a little girl ran forward and threw in a little bunch of violets. Afterwards Henry Frampton, the local squire and former High Sheriff of Dorset, entertained the chief mourners in Moreton House. Curiously enough he was related to Lawrence through the Chapmans; Frampton had originally rented Clouds Hill to his kinsman and in 1929 had sold it to him for £450.[45]

At Moreton House, where Squire Frampton no doubt offered the mourners some refreshment as was customary on such occasions, Lady Astor, her eyes red from weeping, is said to have tried to cheer everyone up with a rather forced gaiety. To Canon Kinloch, who had taken the funeral service, she is said to have remarked: 'That was a bloody fine sermon, the first time I've heard you sound really sincere!' But when Winston Churchill, who had also wept during the service, took his leave and went back to his car, Lady Astor ran after him calling 'Winnie, Winnie', clasping his hands in hers.[46]

'Your brother's name will live in history,' King George V told the dead man's brother Arnold in a sincere tribute. A similar tribute came from Lord Trenchard, who recalled the remarkable grasp of flying Lawrence had when they first met in 1921 at the Cairo Conference, when: 'His helpful and friendly attitude throughout the discussions were of the greatest value to me.'

From that time forward I had the greatest admiration and liking for him and when he asked to join the Air Force in the lowest rank, though I tried to persuade him that he could achieve more in a more responsible position, he was so insistent that I eventually agreed. His influence in the Air Force was all for the good in spite of the fact that wherever he went impossible stories were circulated about him, I feel . . . that in him I have lost a real and close friend.[47]

5

Clare Sydney Smith was in Singapore with her husband when she heard the news, and in a letter to Charlotte Shaw she reacted as no doubt did many of his other friends at the time. But in her case there was a particular reason, because, as she told Mrs Shaw, 'our beloved Tes (as we call him)' once told her that he only had two women correspondents, Charlotte Shaw and herself. 'You Mrs Shaw will realize *how* we loved him, after 3 years of seeing him nearly every day. For myself I am heartbroken, for him I cannot feel sad, he wasn't a happy man, and he was lonely. But what a loss.... He would hate a fuss and I am trying not to grieve, but it is hard. I adored him.'[48]

Shortly afterwards a modest headstone was erected over the grave in Moreton with the following inscription:

To the dear memory of
T. E. Lawrence
Fellow of All Souls College
Oxford
Born 16 August 1888
Died 19 May 1935
The hour is coming & now is
When the dead shall hear
The voice of the
SON OF GOD
And they that hear shall live

A small carved stone at the foot of the grave embodied an open book, with the words in Latin from the 27th Psalm which form part of the arms of the University of Oxford: DOMINUS ILLUMINATIO MEA.

Later Lawrence's bust by Eric Kennington was placed in the Crypt of St Paul's Cathedral, followed by other memorials including a plaque on the wall of the house No. 13 Birmingham Street, in which he had lived in Southampton between July 1933 and November 1934. Eric Kennington also sculptured a striking recumbent effigy in St Martin's Church, Wareham. The effigy was from a piece of Portland stone weighing three tons and completed wholly by hand, no mechanical methods being used. It depicts Lawrence in Arab dress, wearing on his head an Arab chief's *kuffiya*. In 1938 Clouds Hill was presented to the National Trust by Professor A. W. Lawrence with its contents, and many more exhibits have since been added through the generosity of numbers of T. E. Lawrence's friends. The cottage is now open to the public during the summer months.

Touching as were the many tributes to T. E. Lawrence at this time, perhaps the one which would have touched and pleased him most came from Winston Churchill, one of Lawrence's three heroes, when Churchill unveiled the bronze plaque to Lawrence's memory at his old school, the Oxford High School for Boys in 1936. It is interesting to compare and contrast what they thought of each other. 'I know that he is a bogey-man for all the left wing of the House of Commons,' Lawrence had written to Charlotte Shaw when Churchill was Chancellor of the Exchequer in 1927: 'That's because he does not really ever make himself a party man. A Tory instinct, a Liberal intellect: give him time, and the atmosphere to think, and he takes as gently broad a view of subjects as ordinary human kind can expect. Don't forget that he stood, in good and bad seasons, for Irish Home Rule: and that his Colonial Administration did more solid good for our native clients than all the good wishes of their loudest advocates. Men in opposition promise everything. Winston in office does a great deal: and he is as fond of his friends as they are of him.'[49]

'Happily he found another task to his hands which cheered and comforted his soul,' said Churchill on the occasion of the unveiling of the plaque at Oxford nine years later.

> He saw as clearly as anyone the vision of Air power and all that it would mean in traffic and war. He found in the life of an aircraftman that balm of peace and equipoise which no great station or command could have bestowed upon him. He felt that in living the life of a private in the Royal Air Force he would dignify that honourable calling and help to attract all that is keenest in our youthful manhood to the sphere

where it is most urgently needed. For this service and example, to which he devoted the last twelve years, of his life, we owe him a separate debt. It was in itself a princely gift.[50]

In 1954, when Churchill was Prime Minister for the second time, he was asked by Mrs Sarah Lawrence if she might reprint the text of Churchill's address at the unveiling of the plaque for an edition of *The Home Letters of T. E. Lawrence and his Brothers.* In giving his consent, as he readily did, Churchill wrote from 10 Downing Street: 'Eighteen years have passed since those words were spoken, but now, pondering them again, I find not one to alter. The vast perils and catastrophes of the years between have not dimmed the splendour of his fame, nor blurred the impress of his personality upon the memory of his friends. It is the measure of his greatness that his multiple achievement has passed beyond opinion into history.'[51]

Sources and Notes

The following abbreviations are used:

Add MSS=Additional Manuscripts, British Library.

AHB=Air Historical Branch, Ministry of Defence, London.

Bodleian Tss=Transcripts of letters from Lawrence and others in the Bodleian Library, Oxford.

Friends=*T. E. Lawrence By His Friends*. Edited by A. W. Lawrence.

Home Letters=*The Home Letters of T. E. Lawrence and His Brothers*. Edited by M. R. Lawrence.

Letters=*The Letters of T. E. Lawrence*. Edited by David Garnett.

LHB=*T. E. Lawrence To His Biographers Robert Graves and Liddell Hart*.

Mack=*A Prince of Our Disorder: The Life of T. E. Lawrence* by John E. Mack.

Secret Lives=*The Secret Lives of Lawrence of Arabia* by Philip Knightley and Colin Simpson.

Trenchard Papers=Private papers and correspondence of Hugh Viscount Trenchard.

Chapter 1   The Background

1 AHB: Lawrence's personal files.
2 LHB I, p. 93.
3 *id*, I, pp. 106–7.
4 *id*, I, p. 79.
5 Lawrence to Charlotte Shaw 1 November 1926: Add MSS 45903.
6 *id*, 16 Feb 1927: Add MSS 45903.
7 *id*, 18 Oct 1927: Add MSS 45903.
8 *Letters*, p. 355.
9 *id*, p. 357.
10 A. W. Lawrence. *Letters to T. E. Lawrence*, p. 160. Stanley Weintraub. *Private Shaw and Public Shaw*, p. 8.
11 *Letters*, p. 362.

12 *id*, p. 363.
13 Lawrence to Edward Garnett 23/28 Dec 1927: Humanities Research Center, University of Texas.
14 LHB II, pp. 75–6.
15 Lawrence to Greenhill 20 March 1920: Humanities Research Center, University of Texas. Cp. Lawrence to F. N. Doubleday: *Letters*, p. 301.
16 *Letters*, p. 783.
17 LHB I, pp. 48, 60; pp. 55, 67, 78, Burke's *Peerage* 1914 ed. Personal knowledge.
18 Lawrence to Charlotte Shaw 18 March 1927: Add MSS 45903.
19 Lawrence to Edward Garnett 27 August 1924: Bodleian Tss.
20 Lawrence to Charlotte Shaw 24 August 1926: Add MSS 45903.
21 *Friends*, p. 32.
22 Thomas Jones. *A Diary with Letters*, p. 174. *Friends*, p. 29.
23 *Secret Lives*, p. 16.
24 LHB I, 60; II, 67.
25 Lawrence to Charlotte Shaw 14 April 1927: Add MSS 45903.
26 *id*.
27 *Friends*, p. 27.
28 LHB II, p. 209.
29 Lawrence to Charlotte Shaw 8 April 1928: Add MSS 45904.
30 *id*, 8 May, 18 Aug 1928: Add MSS 45904.
31 Mack, p. 33. Colin Simpson to Leonard Russell n.d. Imperial War Museum: Lawrence Papers.
32 LHB II, p. 51.
33 *Friends*, p. 30.
34 Victoria Ocampo, *338171 T.E.*, p. 32.
35 *Friends*, p. 31. See also on the Chapman–Lawrence family generally *A Passionate Prodigality. Letters to Alan Bird from Richard Aldington*. Edited by Miriam J. Benkovitz (1975).
36 Ronald Storrs in *Dictionary of National Biography 1931–1940 sub* T. E. Lawrence.
37 Mack, pp. 64–6 and references there cited.
38 Lawrence to Charlotte Shaw 10 June 1924: Add MSS 45903.
39 LHB I, p. 92. Aldington. *A Passionate Prodigality*, p. 15.
40 28 June 1919: Humanities Research Center, Texas.
41 Richard Meinertzhagen. *Middle East Diary*, p. 32.
42 Lawrence to Charlotte Shaw 26 March 1924: Add MSS 45903.
43 LHB I, p. 77.
44 *The Seven Pillars of Wisdom* (1935), p. 161.

Chapter 2   Uxbridge and Farnborough

1 LHB II, pp. 25, 131.
2 *Letters*, p. 719.
3 *id*, p. 279.
4 Trenchard Papers, cited Boyle. *Trenchard*, p. 384. See also Montgomery Hyde. *British Air Policy Between the Wars*, p. 92 *et seq* and authorities there cited.
5 Trenchard Papers.
6 Churchill, *Great Contemporaries*, p. 161.
7 Trenchard Papers, partly quoted by Boyle, p. 427.
8 A. W. Lawrence. *Letters to T. E. Lawrence*, p. 23.
9 Lawrence to Charlotte Shaw. 1 Nov 1926. Add MSS 45903.
10 Trenchard Papers.
11 AHB: Lawrence's personal files.
12 *Letters*, p. 363.
13 A. W. Lawrence. *Letters to T. E. Lawrence*, p. 187.
14 *The Mint*, p. 19.
15 *Sunday Times*, 8 April 1951 ('How Lawrence joined the RAF').
16 *The Mint*, p. 19. The statement in Desmond Stewart's recent biography *T. E. Lawrence* (1977), at p. 265, that 'when he came to bare his body at the Recruiting Depot it was to display the stigmata of recent flagellation', repeated in a letter from Mr Stewart to the *Sunday Times* (26 June 1977) to the effect that 'the weals were too fresh to derive from Lawrence's Arabian adventures', is quite untrue and unsupported by the medical evidence in Lawrence's personal file at the Air Ministry. Nor is there any truth in the story that Lawrence had previously attended flagellation parties in Chelsea conducted by an underworld German called Bluebeard. Lawrence is said to have written to the Home Secretary asking for the expulsion of Bluebeard and the banning of a German magazine which had described these alleged parties and hinted at Lawrence's connection with them: see p. 275. In a note at the top of p. 332, Mr Stewart states that he owes this information to 'one of the few students of Lawrence's life who have been given access to certain otherwise embargoed documents in the Bodleian Museum [*sic*]'. In the same issue of the *Sunday Times* mentioned above, Mr Colin Simpson, co-author of *The Secret Lives of Lawrence of Arabia* (1969), the first work to produce evidence of Lawrence's interest in flagellation, admitted that he (Simpson) was the individual who had supplied Mr Stewart with this information, adding that the letter to the Home Secretary, which he copied from the so-called

embargoed Lawrence papers in the Bodleian subsequently disappeared: at all events, according to him, it was not there when he was correcting the proofs of his book four months later. On the other hand, as one of the few individuals to have been given access to the Lawrence reserve material in the Bodleian – there have been only six in all besides the Bodleian library staff – I recently made a prolonged and thorough search of the many hundreds of letters comprising the material in question and failed to find any trace of the missing letter. Incidentally Bluebeard's real name was Hugo Baruch, but in England he called himself Jack Bilbo.

17 *Letters*, pp. 363–5.
18 *The Mint*, p. 27.
19 LHB I, p. 65.
20 *The Mint*, pp. 28–9.
21 *Letters*, p. 365.
22 *id*, p. 369.
23 *The Mint*, p. 107.
24 *id*, pp. 74–8. Douglas wrote in his autobiography: 'In the long run, many of us came to feel that T. E. Lawrence, so far as the R.A.F. was concerned, was scarcely more than a nuisance. To appreciate that one has only to imagine the difficulties that he created for the more junior officers under whom he served as an airman when they knew that he was writing personal letters direct to Air Vice-Marshal Sir Oliver Swann, the Air Member for Personnel, and to other senior and distinguished officers, and even to the Chief of the Air Staff, Trenchard himself.' Sholto Douglas. *Years of Command* (1966), pp. 144–5.
25 *id*, p. 106.
26 *id*, p. 109.
27 *id*, p. 73.
28 *id*.
29 *id*, pp. 108–9.
30 *id*, pp. 98–9.
31 *The Mint*, p. 161. *Daily Express*, 28 January 1955; *Illustrated*, 26 February 1955.
32 *The Mint*, pp. 161–2.
33 *id*, p. 163.
34 AHB: Lawrence's personal file; *Letters*, pp. 281–2.
35 C. Findlay. *The Listener*, 5 June 1958 ('The Amazing AC2').
36 *Letters*, p. 391.
37 AHB: Lawrence's personal files.

38 *id.*
39 Findlay, *op. cit.*
40 *id.*
41 Viscount Templewood (Sir Samuel Hoare). *Empire of the Air*, p. 40.
42 *Letters*, p. 425.
43 A. W. Lawrence. *Letters to T. E. Lawrence*, p. 196.
44 *Letters*, p. 394.
45 A. W. Lawrence. *Letters to T. E. Lawrence*, p. 197.
46 *Letters*, p. 398.

Chapter 3   Bovington
1 *Letters*, p. 396.
2 L. S. Amery. *My Political Life*, II, p. 249.
3 *Letters*, p. 401.
4 *id*, p. 410.
5 Bodleian Tss.
6 LHB I, p. 53.
7 Blanche Patch. *Thirty Years with GBS*, p. 86. Stanley Weintraub. *Private Shaw and Public Shaw*, pp. 31–6.
8 Bodleian Tss.
9 AHB: Lawrence's personal file. This letter is printed in *Letters* pp. 404–6, but there is no indication that it is to Trenchard, the addressee being simply described by the editor as 'a high official at the Air Ministry'.
10 *Friends*, p. 361.
11 Imperial War Museum: Lawrence Papers, cited *Secret Lives*, pp. 190–1.
12 *Letters*, p. 410.
13 *id*, p. 411.
14 *id*, pp. 414–15.
15 *id*, p. 416.
16 *id*, p. 425.
17 *Friends*, p. 366 et seq.
18 *Letters*, p. 407.
19 *Friends*, p. 341.
20 *Secret Lives*, pp. 169–71, 192.
21 *The Times*, 22 November 1969. Cp. a somewhat improbable story related to Robin Maugham at Bovington in the winter of 1939–40 by a sergeant-instructor who claimed to have whipped Lawrence there: Robin Maugham, *Escape from the Shadows* (1972), p. 116.

22 *Letters*, pp. 416, 417.
23 LHB I, p. 27.
24 Cited Mack, p. 347.
25 *Letters*, p. 435.
26 National Trust. *Clouds Hill* (1974), p. 16.
27 *Letters*, p. 528. The gold dagger was bought by Lionel Curtis and presented to All Souls College, Oxford.
28 *Letters*, p. 436.
29 *Friends*, p. 375.
30 *id*, p. 377.
31 *Letters*, pp. 435–6.
32 LHB I, p. 25.
33 *Letters*, p. 406.
34 *id*, pp. 423–4.
35 *id*, p. 427.
36 *Friends*, p. 490.
37 *Letters*, pp. 429–31.
38 *id*, p. 446.
39 *id*, p. 447.
40 Trenchard Papers.
41 *Friends*, p. 363.
42 *Letters*, p. 440.
43 *Friends*, p. 363.
44 *Letters to T. E. Lawrence*, p. 197.
45 Cited Mack, p. 349.
46 *Letters*, p. 448.
47 *Friends*, p. 244.
48 AHB: Lawrence's personal files.
49 *id*, *Letters*, p. 458.
50 Hyde. *British Air Policy between the Wars*, p. 197.
51 *Home Letters*, p. 357.
52 *Letters*, p. 28.
53 LHB I, p. 28.
54 *Letters*, pp. 444–6.
55 Bodleian Tss, cited Philip Knightley and Colin Simpson. *Secret Lives of Lawrence of Arabia*, p. 196.
56 Add MSS 45903.

Chapter 4   Cranwell

1 AHB: Lawrence's personal file.
2 Christopher Hassall. *Edward Marsh*, p. 530.

3 *Letters*, p. 477.
4 Andrew Boyle. *Trenchard*, p. 516.
5 *Secret Lives*, pp. 196–7.
6 *Letters*, p. 477.
7 *Letters*, p. 478.
8 AHB: Lawrence's personal files.
9 *Letters*, pp. 980–1.
10 *The Mint*, pp. 170–1.
11 *Letters*, p. 482.
12 *id*, p. 483.
13 *Secret Lives*, p. 225.
14 *The Mint*, p. 167.
15 *id*, pp. 175–7.
16 20 November 1926: Trenchard Papers.
17 *The Mint*, p. 206.
18 *id*, p. 181.
19 Robert Graves. *Lawrence and the Arabs*, p. 434.
20 *The Mint*, pp. 186–7.
21 *id*, pp. 184–5.
22 *Letters*, p. 493.
23 28 Sept 1925: Add MSS 45903.
24 Graves, p. 434.
25 Interview with Borton. Imperial War Museum: Lawrence Papers.
26 Clare Sydney Smith. *The Golden Reign*, p. 14.
27 Graves, pp. 433–4.
28 Add MSS 45903.
29 *id*, (12 Aug 1927).
30 Graves, p. 435.
31 10 May 1926: Add MSS 45903.
32 29 May 1926: Add MSS 45903.
33 22 Feb 1926: Add MSS 45903.
34 Graves, pp. 430–1.
35 18 March 1926: Add MSS 45903.
36 *Home Letters*, p. 361.
37 20 April 1926: Add MSS 45903.
38 Graves, pp. 435–6.
39 Michael Howard. *Jonathan Cape*, p. 90.
40 *Letters*, p. 494.
41 8 Feb 1926: Add MSS 45903.
42 *Home Letters*, p. 362.
43 20 Nov 1926: Trenchard Papers.

44 *Letters*, p. 468.
45 *id*, p. 497.
46 *id*, pp. 437–8.
47 *id*, p. 468.
48 *Letters*, pp. 295, 466.
49 *id*, p. 501.
50 9 Feb 1928: Add MSS 45903.
51 22 Nov 1926: Trenchard Papers.
52 A. W. Lawrence. *Letters to T. E. Lawrence*, p. 198.
53 29 Nov 1926: Trenchard Papers.
54 Florence Hardy. *The Later Years of Thomas Hardy* pp. 249–50.
55 *Letters*, p. 503.
56 Add MSS 45903.
57 Cited Mack, p. 360.
58 *Home Letters*, p. 363.
59 Cited Mack, p. 364.
60 26 Oct 1926. Bodleian: Lawrence Tss.

Chapter 5   *India*
1 16 Dec 1926: Add MSS 45903.
2 Mack, p. 29. *Letters*, pp. 299, 504.
3 *Letters*, p. 505.
4 *id*, p. 502.
5 Buchan. *Memory Hold the Door*, p. 228.
6 *Letters*, pp. 502–3.
7 *id*, p. 505.
8 *id*, p. 506.
9 Weintraub. *Private Shaw and Public Shaw*, pp. 112–15.
10 Michael Howard. *Jonathan Cape*, pp. 93–4.
11 *Letters*, pp. 513–14.
12 A. W. Lawrence. *Letters to T. E. Lawrence*, p. 199.
13 Trenchard Papers.
14 *Home Letters*, pp. 366–7.
15 29 June 1927: Bodleian Tss.
16 23 Dec 1927: Trenchard Papers.
17 19 May 1927: Add MSS 45903.
18 *Letters*, pp. 570–1. The 'two words omitted' from the text on p. 570 are 'The Wing-Commander'.
19 22 Dec 1929: Trenchard Papers.
20 Trenchard Papers.
21 *id*.

22 *Letters*, p. 566.

23 *id*, pp. 564–5.

24 9 Feb 1928; 17 Nov 1927: Add MSS 45903. The poems have been published with an excellent critical introduction by J. M. Wilson, *Minorities* (1971). The MS volume from which they were taken is now in the Bodleian Library.

25 *Friends*, p. 401 *et seq*.

26 Bodleian Tss, cited Mack, pp. 366–7.

27 *Friends*, p. 409.

28 *Letters*, p. 567.

29 *Friends*, pp. 411–16.

30 LHB I, p. 143.

31 *Letters*, p. 573.

32 *id*, pp. 579–80.

33 17 May 1928: Add MSS 45904.

34 Blanche Patch. *Thirty Years with GBS*, p. 80.

35 Trenchard Papers.

36 17 May 1928: Add MSS 45904.

37 Blanche Patch, p. 80.

38 A. W. Lawrence. *Letters to T. E. Lawrence*, p. 200.

39 1 May 1928: Trenchard Papers. *Letters*, p. 598.

40 A. W. Lawrence. *Letters to T. E. Lawrence*, pp. 202–5.

41 *Letters*, p. 607.

42 1 May 1928: Trenchard Papers.

43 *Letters*, p. 614.

44 A. W. Lawrence. *Letters to T. E. Lawrence*, pp. 201–6.

45 *Letters*, pp. 598–60; Trenchard Papers. The passage about Philby is omitted from the published version.

46 Trenchard Papers.

47 *id*.

48 *id*.

49 *id*.

50 *id*.

51 *Letters*, p. 625.

52 *T. E. Lawrence Studies*, edited by J. M. Wilson, Vol. 1 No. 1 (Spring 1976), pp. 37–9.

53 Mack, p. 374.

54 Stewart Humphries. 'At sea with T. E. Lawrence': *Observer Magazine*, 20 Feb 1977.

55 *Letters*, p. 626.

56 Montgomery Hyde. *British Air Policy*, p. 203 *et seq*.

57 Trenchard Papers.
58 *id.*
59 *Letters*, p. 633.

Chapter 6   *Flying Boats and Others*
1 *Letters*, p. 640.
2 Stewart Humphries. 'At sea with T. E. Lawrence': *Observer Magazine*, 20 Feb 1977.
3 Clare Sydney Smith. *The Golden Reign*, p. 23.
4 Montgomery Hyde. *British Air Policy*, p. 209.
5 Clare Sydney Smith, p. 29.
6 Andrew Boyle. *Trenchard*, p. 575.
7 22 February 1929: Bodleian Tss.
8 *Letters*, p. 635.
9 5 Feb 1929: Trenchard Papers.
10 Trenchard Papers; Boyle, p. 575.
11 *Letters*, p. 641; Montgomery Hyde. *British Air Policy*, p. 210.
12 *Letters*, p. 664.
13 Smith, p. 30; *Home Letters*, p. 375. Add MSS 45904.
14 20 June 1929: Trenchard Papers.
15 Trenchard Papers.
16 Lawrence to Charlotte Shaw 5 April 1929; Add MSS 45904.
17 *id*, 22 April 1929; Add MSS 45904.
18 Christopher Sykes. *Nancy: The Life of Lady Astor* (1972), p. 309.
19 *Letters*, p. 665.
20 On the Schneider Trophy generally see Ralph Barker. *The Schneider Trophy Races* (1971).
21 Smith, p. 47.
22 Lawrence to Trenchard 20 June 1929: Trenchard Papers.
23 *id.*
24 Lawrence to Trenchard 12 July 1929: Trenchard Papers.
25 Add MSS 45904.
26 *Letters*, p. 666.
27 Lawrence to Marson 23 April 1929: Bodleian Tss.
28 Lawrence to Trenchard 14 September 1929: Trenchard Papers.
29 Smith, pp. 49–53.
30 *id*, p. 48.
31 Trenchard to Lawrence 16 September 1929, *Letters*, p. 673.
32 Liddell Hart. *Memoirs*, I, p. 344.

33 *Letters*, p. 677.
34 Lawrence to Trenchard 18 December 1929: Trenchard Papers.
35 *Letters* p. 683, Lawrence to Charlotte Shaw 29 August 1929; 5 October, 14 October 1930: Add MSS 45904.
36 Smith, p. 102 *et seq.*
37 Lawrence to Charlotte Shaw 6 February 1931: Add MSS 45904.
38 A. W. Lawrence. *Letters to T. E. Lawrence*, p. 180.
39 Lawrence to Charlotte Shaw 16 February 1931: Add MSS 45904.
40 Smith, p. 106.
41 *Letters*, pp. 713–14.
42 Lawrence to Charlotte Shaw 8 March 1931: Add MSS 45904.
43 *Letters*, p. 715.
44 *id*, p. 718.
45 Smith, p. 110.
46 *Letters*, p. 725.
47 *id*, p. 760.
48 Lawrence to Charlotte Shaw 15 February 1932: Add MSS 45904.
49 *id*, 18 September 1931: Add MSS 45904.
50 *id*, 17 April 1928: Add MSS 45904.
51 *id*, December 1934: Add MSS 45904.
52 See *The Trial of Roger Casement* (1960 and 1964) edited by H. Montgomery Hyde, *passim.*
53 Lawrence to Bernard Shaw 19 July 1928: Add MSS 45904. The remainder of this letter with the exception of one word (Savage) has been published in *Letters*, pp. 615–18.
54 Lawrence to Charlotte Shaw 11 December 1934: Add MSS 45904.
55 *Letters*, p. 788.
56 Lawrence to Marson 25 June 1930: Bodleian Tss.
57 *id*, 25 November 1932: Bodleian Tss.
58 *Letters*, p. 760.
59 Lawrence to Charlotte Shaw 16 May 1932: Add MSS 45904.
60 A.W. Lawrence. *Letters to T. E. Lawrence*, p. 213.
61 *Letters*, p. 744.
62 Lawrence to Charlotte Shaw, 18 September 1931: Add MSS 45904.
63 Smith, p. 211.
64 Lawrence to Charlotte Shaw 14 October 1931: Add MSS 45904.
65 Lawrence to Trenchard n.d.: Trenchard Papers.
66 Smith, p. 147.
67 *id*, p. 149.
68 Trenchard to Lawrence 17 March 1933: Trenchard Papers.
69 Lawrence to Trenchard 20 March 1933: Trenchard Papers.

70 *Letters*, p. 764.
71 Note by Bullock in Trenchard Papers.
72 Smith, p. 164.
73 Smith, p. 172.
74 *Home Letters*, p. 384.
75 Liddell Hart. *T. E. Lawrence*, p. 433.
76 Lawrence to Marson 22 June 1933: Bodleian Tss.
77 Lawrence to Charlotte Shaw 23 August 1933.
78 *Home Letters*, pp. 385–6.
79 Martin Gilbert. *Winston S. Churchill*, V, p. 707 (where the visit is misdated 1935).
80 Lawrence to Marson 21 December 1933: Bodleian Tss.
81 *id*, 23 November 1934.
82 LHB II, p. 215. *Letters*, p. 802.
83 *id*, p. 221.
84 Lawrence to Charlotte Shaw 2 February 1934: Add MSS 45904.

Chapter 7   *L'Envoi*

1 *Friends*, p. 545.
2 *id*, p. 547.
3 AHB: Interview with Air Commodore F. J. Manning 20 November 1975.
4 Ronald Storrs. *Orientations*, p. 452.
5 *Letters*, p. 834.
6 Shaw-Ede, p. 58.
7 *Friends*, p. 549.
8 *id*, pp. 550–1.
9 *id*, p. 559.
10 *id*, p. 546.
11 Lawrence to Trenchard 13 December 1934: Trenchard Papers.
12 Trenchard to Lawrence 14 December 1934: Trenchard Papers.
13 Lawrence to Trenchard 6 February 1935: Trenchard to Lawrence 7 February 1935: Trenchard Papers.
14 Smith, p. 178.
15 *Letters*, pp. 844–5.
16 Lawrence to Charlotte Shaw 26 January 1935: Add MSS 45904.
17 LHB I, p. 181.
18 Blanche Patch. *Thirty Years with GBS*, p. 84.
19 Lawrence to Charlotte Shaw 31 January 1935: Add MSS 45904.
20 AHB: Manning interview.

21 *Letters*, p. 853; LHB I, p. 183.

22 *id*, p. 849.

23 The transcription of this tape-recorded interview, which runs to 22 pages, is preserved in the Air Historical Branch of the Ministry of Defence.

24 *Letters*, p. 854.

25 *id*, p. 858. AHB: Lawrence's personal files.

26 *Letters*, p. 859.

27 *id*, p. 860.

28 *id*, p. 863.

29 On this prosecution brought by the police, see Norman St John Stevas. *Obscenity and the Law* (1956), p. 107; also Alex Craig. *The Banned Books of England* (1962) p. 94.

30 *Letters*, p. 864.

31 *id*, p. 87.

32 Lawrence to Marson 6 April 1935: Bodleian Tss.

33 *id*, 18 April 1935: Bodleian Tss.

34 *Friends*, pp. 570–2.

35 *Letters*, p. 870.

36 Bodleian MSS, cited Mack, p. 408.

37 Imperial War Museum: Lawrence Papers.

38 *Letters*, p. 872.

39 Henry Williamson. *Genius of Friendship 'T. E. Lawrence'*, p. 75. There is no truth in the suggestion implicit in Desmond Stewart's recent biography that Lawrence had some affinity with Mosley's Fascist movement. In a talk with Liddell Hart in June 1934, according to Hart, Lawrence said the Fascists had been after him; he jokingly added that 'he wouldn't help them to power, but if they gained it, he would agree to become "dictator of the press" – for a fortnight. That would suffice, to settle the press and him': LHB, II, p. 222. In fact, he never met Mosley nor did he ever have any direct personal communication with him, in spite of later rumours to the contrary, a fact confirmed by Mosley himself in his autobiography: see Sir Oswald Mosley. *My Life* (1968), p. 226. Lawrence's admission to Liddell Hart is confirmed by two letters from Lawrence to a Mosley aide dated 12 May and 17 May 1934 from Southampton in which Lawrence categorically asked the aide not to make him 'any part of your Club'. These letters, currently in the possession of Mr Robert Payne of New York, are to be deposited in the Berg Collection of the New York Public Library. (Information communicated by Professor A. W. Lawrence.)

40 *Letters*, p. 872.

41 *Friends*, p. 565.

42 *Secret Lives*, p. 270 *et seq*. The material on which Knightley and Simpson based their account was subsequently deposited by the *Sunday Times* in the Imperial War Museum in six boxes 69/48/1–6.

43 Storrs. *Orientations*, pp. 453–4.

44 In a sworn statement dated 6 June 1968 before a commissioner for oaths Bruce gave details of eleven floggings administered by him to Lawrence between 1923 and 1934. Imperial War Museum: Lawrence Papers 69/48/3. Knightley and Simpson. *Secret Lives* p. 276.

45 It has been suggested that Frampton was the 'Old Man' of Lawrences' flagellation fantasies.

46 *Secret Lives*, p. 276.

47 Trenchard Papers II/27/108/2.

48 Clare Sydney Smith to Charlotte Shaw 20 May 1935: Add MSS 45922.

49 Lawrence to Charlotte Shaw 27 May 1927: Add MSS 45903.

50 Churchill. *Great Contemporaries*, p. 50. See also City of Oxford High School for Boys. *Proceedings at the unveiling of the Memorial to Lawrence of Arabia* (Oxford, 1937).

51 *Home Letters*, p. 12.

Select Bibliography

A. MANUSCRIPT SOURCES

The MS of *The Seven Pillars of Wisdom*, which was extensively revised while Lawrence was serving in the Royal Air Force and the Royal Tank Corps, was subsequently presented to the Bodleian Library, Oxford, where it is now preserved, as also is the MS of *Minorities*. A holograph fair copy of the third draft of *The Mint* in Lawrence's hand, given by Lawrence to Edward Garnett, is now in the Houghton Library of Harvard University. This is the only MS of the complete work known to be in existence. About two hundred holograph letters from Lawrence to various correspondents including Robert Graves and Bruce Rogers are also in the Houghton Library.

The original third draft of *The Mint*, typed by Lawrence on the office typewriter in Karachi with MS additions in Lawrence's hand, from which the MS fair copy at Harvard was made, and which Lawrence seems to have regarded as his working copy, was given by him in batches to Charlotte Shaw. It is now in the British Library (Add MSS 45916): see above, p. 154 *et seq.* Garnett also had a typescript made of the MS and this was also given to Charlotte Shaw (Add MSS 45917). It was used as the text for a few copies printed after Lawrence's death by Doubleday, Doran & Co of New York in 1935 to secure American copyright. A typescript copy of this version, recopied from Garnett's TS, was revised by Lawrence towards the end of his life with copious holograph annotations in pencil and ink. This TS, or a copy of it, is now in the Bodleian, and it was from this version that the limited and general editions of *The Mint* were published by Cape in London and Doubleday in New York in 1955.

Lawrence also gave a TS of *The Mint* to Lady Astor. Tom Driberg (Lord Bradwell) in his autobiography *Ruling Passions* (1977) recalls (at p. 154) that he was invited by Lady Astor to lunch at Cliveden during the last war and that Lady Astor produced the TS from an unlocked drawer and showed it to him.

A proof copy of *The Seven Pillars of Wisdom* with Lawrence's holograph annotations was presented by him to the library of the Royal Air Force College at Cranwell where it is now preserved.

Lawrence's personal files in the R.A.F. containing letters from Hugh Trenchard, the Chief of the Air Staff, and Oliver Swann, Director of Personnel at the Air Ministry, and much other material about Lawrence's service record, are in the Air Historical Branch of the Ministry of Defence, but this material is at present under restriction.

The correspondence between Lawrence and Trenchard not retained by the Defence Ministry is in the possession of Trenchard's son, the present Viscount Trenchard, together with other papers about Lawrence, particularly when he was in India.

The largest collection of Lawrence's letters, over five hundred, is probably in Texas University. The correspondents include Eric Kennington (90), Edward Garnett (77), Mrs Thomas Hardy, Maurice Baring, B. H. Liddell Hart, T. B. Marson, W. E. G. Beauforte-Greenwood, and many others.

Lawrence's letters to Mr and Mrs Bernard Shaw between 1922 and 1935, running to more than 400 holograph pages, are in the British Library to which they were left by Bernard Shaw (Add MSS 45903, 45904). He also left the library a small collection of his wife's letters to Lawrence (Add MSS 45922), but it has been surmised that at her request Lawrence destroyed many of the letters she wrote to him.

Lawrence's letters to Lionel Curtis are in the Codrington Library of All Souls College, Oxford. His letters to Robin Buxton are in the library of Jesus College, Oxford.

Besides a few original letters from Lawrence in the Bodleian, the library possesses a considerable number of transcripts of his letters and other material which have been placed under restriction until the year 2000 and at present can only be seen with the permission of the Lawrence trustees, of whom the principal trustee is Professor A. W. Lawrence.

A monograph which Lawrence wrote on 'School', i.e. the educational classes at Uxbridge, may have been intended to supplement chapter 9 of Part Two of *The Mint*. It consists of two folio sheets in Lawrence's handwriting, which have been framed and now hang in the entrance hall to the main administrative building at the Uxbridge Depot as a memorial to Aircraftman Ross and his time there. The MS has not been published.

The material assembled by staff members of the London *Sunday Times*, and used by Philip Knightley and Colin Simpson in writing their book *The Secret Lives of Lawrence of Arabia* (1969), is preserved in six boxes in the Imperial War Museum (69/48/1–6) and is no longer subject to restriction.

B. PRINTED SOURCES

ALDINGTON, RICHARD. *Lawrence of Arabia.* London: Collins 1955. *A Passionate Prodigality. Letters to Alan Bird from Richard Aldington 1949–1962.* Edited with an Introduction by Miriam J. Benkovitz. New York: The New York Public Library, Astor, Lenox and Tilden Foundations, 1975.

AMERY, L. S. *My Political Life.* Vol. 2. London: Hutchinson, 1953.

ARMITAGE, FLORA. *The Desert and the Stars. A Portrait of T. E. Lawrence.* London: Faber, 1956.

BARKER, RALPH. *The Schneider Trophy Race.* London: Chatto & Windus, 1971.

BOYLE, ANDREW. *Trenchard.* London: Collins, 1962.

BRENT, PETER. *T. E. Lawrence.* London: Wiedenfeld & Nicolson, 1975.

BROUGHTON, HARRY. *Lawrence of Arabia. The Facts without the Fiction.* Wareham: Anglebury Press, 1969.

BUCHAN, JOHN. *Memory Hold-the-Door.* London: Hodder & Stoughton 1940.

CHURCHILL, WINSTON S. *Great Contemporaries.* London: Thornton Butterworth, 1927.

CLEMENTS, FRANK. *T. E. Lawrence: a reader's guide.* Newton Abbot: David & Charles, 1972.

DAVIES, PETER. *Colonel Lawrence and others on 'Her Privates We' by Private 19022.* London: Davies, 1930.

DISBURY, DAVID G. *T. E. Lawrence of Arabia. A Collector's Book-list.* Privately printed, 1972.

DUNBAR, JANET. *Mrs G.B.S.* London: Harrap, 1963.

EDMONDS, CHARLES (C. E. Carrington). *T. E. Lawrence.* London, Davies, 1935.

FORSTER, E. M. *Abinger Harvest.* London: Edward Arnold, 1936.

GILBERT, MARTIN. *Winston S. Churchill* Vols. IV and V. London: Heinemann, 1975–6.

GRAVES, RICHARD PERCEVAL. *Lawrence of Arabia and his World.* London: Thames & Hudson, 1976.

GRAVES, ROBERT. *Lawrence and the Arabs.* London: Cape, 1927.

HARDY, FLORENCE E. *The Later Years of Thomas Hardy.* London: Macmillan, 1930.

HART, B. H. LIDDELL. *'T. E. Lawrence'. In Arabia and After.* London: Cape, 1934.
Memoirs. 2 vols. London: Cassell, 1965.

HOWARD, MICHAEL S. *Jonathan Cape Publishers*. London: Cape, 1971.

HYDE, H. MONTGOMERY. *British Air Policy Between the Wars 1918–1939*. London: Heinemann, 1976.

KNIGHTLEY, PHILIP and SIMPSON, COLIN. *The Secret Lives of Lawrence of Arabia*. London: Nelson, 1969.

LAWRENCE, A. W. (Ed.) *T. E. Lawrence By His Friends*. London: Cape, 1937.

Letters to T. E. Lawrence. London: Cape, 1962.

LAWRENCE, T. E. *The Seven Pillars of Wisdom*. London: Cape, 1935.

The Odyssey of Homer Translated by T. E. Shaw. London: Oxford University Press, 1935.

The Letters of T. E. Lawrence. Edited by David Garnett. London: Cape, 1938.

Letters from T. E. Shaw to Bruce Rogers. Privately printed, 1933.

More Letters from T. E. Shaw to Bruce Rogers. Privately printed, 1936.

Oriental Assembly. Edited by A. W. Lawrence. London: Williams & Norgate, 1939.

Shaw-Ede. T. E. Lawrence's Letters to H. S. Ede 1927–1935. London: The Golden Cockerel Press, 1942.

The Home Letters of T. E. Lawrence and His Brothers. Edited by M. R. Lawrence. Oxford: Blackwell, 1953.

T. E. Lawrence. Fifty Letters 1920–35. An Exhibition. Austin: Humanities Research Center, University of Texas, 1962.

The Mint. London: Cape, 1955 and 1973.

T. E. Lawrence To His Biographers Robert Graves and Liddell Hart. Two vols. in one. London: Cassell, 1965.

Minorities. Edited by J. M. Wilson. London: Cape, 1971.

MACK, JOHN E. *A Prince of Our Disorder. The Life of T. E. Lawrence*. London: Weidenfeld & Nicolson, 1976.

MACKENZIE, COMPTON. *My Life and Times*. Octaves Five and Six. London: Chatto & Windus, 1966–7.

MACPHAIL, SIR ANDREW. *Three Persons*. London: Murray, 1929.

MARRIOTT, PAUL J. *The Young Lawrence of Arabia 1888–1910*. Oxford: Privately printed, 1977.

NAMIER, L. B. *In The Margin of History*. London: Macmillan, 1939.

NATIONAL TRUST, THE. *Clouds Hill*. London: The National Trust, 1974.

NUTTING, ANTHONY. *Lawrence of Arabia. The Man and the Motive*. London: Hollis & Carter, 1961.

OCAMPO, VICTORIA. *338171 T. E. (Lawrence of Arabia).* Translated by David Garnett from the French. London: Gollancz, 1963.

PATCH, BLANCHE. *Thirty Years with G.B.S.* London: Gollancz, 1951.

RICHARDS, VYVYAN. *Portrait of T. E. Lawrence. The Lawrence of the Seven Pillars of Wisdom.* London: Cape, 1936.

ROBINSON, EDWARD. *Lawrence the Rebel.* London: Lincolns-Prager, 1946.

SMITH, CLARE SYDNEY. *The Golden Reign. The Story of my Friendship with Lawrence of Arabia.* London: Cassell, 1940 and 1949.

STEWART, DESMOND. *T. E. Lawrence.* London: Hamish Hamilton, 1977.

STORRS, RONALD. *Orientations.* London: Nicholson & Watson, 1945.

SYKES, CHRISTOPHER. *Nancy: The Life of Lady Astor.* London: Collins, 1972.

TEMPLEWOOD, VISCOUNT (SIR SAMUEL HOARE). *Empire of the Air.* London: Collins, 1957.

THOMAS, LOWELL. *With Lawrence in Arabia.* London: Hutchinson, 1925.

WEINTRAUB, STANLEY. *Private Shaw and Public Shaw.* London: Cape, 1963.

WEINTRAUB, STANLEY and WEINTRAUB, RODELLE. *Lawrence of Arabia. The Literary Impulse.* Baton Rouge: Louisiana State University Press, 1975.

WILLIAMSON, HENRY. *Genius of Friendship 'T. E. Lawrence'.* London: Faber, 1941.

WILSON, J. M. (Ed.) *T. E. Lawrence Studies.* Vol. 1 No 1 Spring 1976. London: Privately printed, 1976.

WINTERTON, EARL. *Fifty Tumultuous Years.* London: Hutchinson, 1955.

Index